# The Ultimate
# **BITCOIN**
# Business Guide

### For Entrepreneurs and
### Business Advisors

## KIRK PHILLIPS, CPA, CMA, CFE

# The Ultimate BITCOIN Business Guide

## For Entrepreneurs & Business Advisors

### KIRK PHILLIPS, CPA, CMA, CFE, CBP

### © 2015 Graben Enterprises, Inc. All rights reserved.

The information in this book is not intended to be a substitute for or construed as legal, tax, audit, accounting, investment advisory, financial planning, consulting or other professional advice. I'm a CPA but I'm not your CPA; therefore, please consult with an attorney, CPA, or other financial professional for guidance on your unique, individual and business situations before taking action regarding any of the matters discussed in this book. Bitcoin is a new concept that will be continuously monitored within the regulatory landscape so it's important to consult a professional when navigating unchartered waters. We have also provided a number of resources that you should investigate with proper due diligence and fiduciary responsibility consistent with the risk management theme woven throughout the book. There is a risk of loss with every endeavor and the same degree of caution should be applied to bitcoin.

Disclosure: I have put a significant amount of time into the creation of this material out of a passion to learn and inspire more than anything else. This came at the cost of foregoing other business opportunities; however, in full disclosure I have various affiliate relationships with many of the platforms outlined in this book to generate additional revenue in support of the project and to continue to provide value to businesses through bitcoin education and training. I maintained CPA integrity, independence and objectivity to the best of my ability presenting material beneficial to the reader regardless of any affiliation. I appreciate your support and understanding.

**Circular 230**

ISBN-13: 978-1517567293
ISBN-10: 1517567297
First edition 2015

Published by:
Graben Enterprises, Inc. 2015
2970 Market Street
BOX 37635 #32507
Philadelphia, PA 19101-0635


For bulk purchases contact TheBitcoinCPA@gmail.com

# TABLE OF CONTENTS

# Foreword

Dear Reader,

If you are searching for a guide to the Bitcoin universe, look no further.

Kirk Phillips has in the pages of this book captured a comprehensive look at everything Bitcoin related, from the history of its invention and major milestones in its development to practical advice on how to accept bitcoin and gain from its benefits.

As an early venture capitalist in the Bitcoin space, I've had the opportunity to see the evolution of Bitcoin from a small experiment a few years ago to its explosion into the public consciousness. This experiment has grown into a multi-billion dollar industry in a few short years and still has much further to go. That's why I can't emphasize enough how important it is for anyone involved in commerce of any kind to become knowledgeable on this topic as soon as possible.

Kirk makes a strong case that Bitcoin the payment network, and bitcoin the currency, are on a trajectory to disrupt existing financial systems, much as we have seen the Internet do in the fields of publishing and newspapers. Those on the right side of this shift will gain greatly while those using the legacy systems of yesterday should be aware of their risks as the world moves into this next phase.

It's as if you have been teleported through time to 1994 and an early adopter of the Internet is offering you a guide to how this new invention will change everything you know. A wise person would take him up on the offer and be ahead of this trend as it plays out around the world in the coming years.

I've known Kirk Phillips both from his work in the Bitcoin space and from meeting him in person at the Bitcoin conferences. It has been my pleasure to see his passion for teaching others about Bitcoin expand into the form of this book, into which he has poured a great amount of time, intelligence, and knowledge. Condensed here are literally thousands of hours of research, hundreds of in-person discussions, and expertise from every sector of the bitcoin industry.

The great thing about Kirk's writing style in this book is that he has removed many of the geeky terms and much of the industry lingo from his explanation and by doing so he has managed to capture the important lessons about Bitcoin without the reader needing to be a programmer or tech-savvy developer.

Reading through this guide you will see that rather than being dominated by Kirk's personal opinions or a particular ideology on the subject, the content is pulled from a variety of sources, including quotes from regulators, views from old-school bankers, voices from established venture capitalists, leaders from the Bitcoin industry itself, and investors evaluating the space.

One of the useful things I've seen in other book forewords is a list of specific things I will learn from the book by diving deeper. So here are the top takeaways you'll find in this book.

## 10 Things You Will Learn by Reading This Book

1.  How existing financial systems (banks and credit cards) came to be what they are today
2.  The history of Bitcoin's development, major milestones, and context for the industry
3.  Why the technology that powers Bitcoin (the blockchain) is superior to existing systems

4. How to value the bitcoin currency using different methods of valuation

5. Bitcoin myths dispelled and how to gain from the lessons of bitcoin scams

6. How to accept bitcoin the right way, manage the risks, and pick a merchant service

7. Best practices that are emerging around exchanges, transparency, and proof of reserves

8. How to manage your bitcoin security, passwords, and your digital identity

9. Advanced things you can use bitcoin for, including micro-transactions and social media

10. What the current rules are around Bitcoin taxes, accounting, and regulation and Bitcoin's impact on reducing fraud.

I think this quote from Roger Ver sums up how fundamentally important it is to have a working knowledge of bitcoin in the 21st century:

*"Bitcoiners are playing with real money, while the rest of the world is just using play money."*

I hope you enjoy reading this book as much as I did and that it leads you down the bitcoin rabbit hole yourself.

In Liberty,

David A. Johnston
Johnston's Law "Everything that can be decentralized, will be decentralized"

Twitter: @DJohnstonEC
Website: www.DavidAJohnston.me
Bitcoin: wallet.djohnston.bit

# Introduction & Intention

What's faster than a speeding bullet, more powerful than a locomotive and able to leap tall buildings in a single bound? We all know the answer is Superman. Now, what's 1,000 times faster and 1,000 times less expensive than a $1,000 credit card transaction? Well bitcoin of course, our modern-day financial superhero, come to save the day by helping you eliminate headaches, reduce expenses and have peace of mind around your business all at the same time.

As of 2014, Bitcoin—the new digital currency—is in the pre-Netscape era of the Internet we knew in 1994. Over the next two decades it has the possibility of radically transforming the way we use money and how business gets done. Those willing to learn will seize the opportunity and those who don't will be watching from the sidelines once again. Overstock.com, Dell, Expedia, Dish Network and Microsoft have all adopted bitcoin. Your business can't afford to wait another day to get on the bitcoin highway.

To put this in greater perspective, the United States Federal Reserve System celebrated its 100th birthday at the end of 2013 less than two weeks before bitcoin blew out the candles on its fifth. When someone turns 100 we usually think they've lived a good long life and when a child turns five we think they hold the promise of the future. Bitcoin holds the promise for the future of money. The biggest transformations in recent history are happening in 20-year cycles starting with the personal computer in the 1970s, the Internet in the 1990s and now Bitcoin in the 2010s.

Walter Wriston, former Citigroup Chairman and CEO, once said, "Information about money has become almost more important than money itself." I've applied that same thinking here and assert that information about bitcoin is indeed more valuable than bitcoin itself. The intention of this book is to provide that information with an eye on transparency, risk management and integrity. It's a road map of sorts, dispelling myths while adding vision and clarity from the reference point of a trusted advisor.

If you enjoy challenging the status quo and questioning your own way of thinking, no matter how long you've been thinking that way, then you're in for an incredible journey that requires an intellectual leap of faith. The paradigm-shattering potential of this new technology within a whole range of industries and occupations will make many people feel uneasy. You have to temporarily shelve "what you know" and start with a clean slate to absorb this new material and walk away with value. As Upton Sinclair wrote in *The Jungle*, "It's difficult to get a man to understand something when his salary depends on him not understanding it." The amount of money invested in bitcoin, the movers and shakers involved, the variety of start-ups and the records it has already set, speaks volumes.

If you're an entrepreneur, online business, retail biz, CEO or business advisor such as a CPA, financial advisor or attorney who is ready and willing to learn the benefits of bitcoin and why you should embrace it, then keep reading this book. It will give you the golden nuggets of bitcoin for business so you can get the maximum benefit with the least amount of risk.

And so your business can proudly say, "bitcoin accepted here."

# Why This Book Was Written

*If you would not be forgotten, as soon as you are dead and rotten, Either write things worth the reading or do things worth the writing." – Benjamin Franklin*

Franklin's quote inspired me to write a practical business guide worth the reading, to promote understanding and implementation of bitcoin with a corresponding educational and informational site. I am committed to helping entrepreneurs, business advisors and microbusinesses as well as big business get up to speed quickly on this exciting new technology. Those who have done things worth the writing, many of whom are included in this book, also inspired me and contributed to this project.

In lieu of the standard book dedication and acknowledgements, I dedicate this book to the passion and creativity of everyone in the bitcoin space and applaud your continued innovation that makes me want to get up every day and come back for more. With that said, I'd like to give a special thanks to my wife, Kennerly Clay, for tirelessly editing the book, to David Johnston for writing the forward, to Stephanie Murphy for producing the audiobook and to Patrick Byrne whose stand for "Truth Above Self" inspired me to write several important chapters in this book.

*The Ultimate Bitcoin Business Guide* is about understanding some of the following questions. How did we get here? Why do we have what we have? How does our current system work? How does Bitcoin work? What are regulators saying about it? What does Wall Street say about it? Why is the venture capital sector so interested? How can Bitcoin transform money? Why would consumers adopt it? Why should businesses adopt it? How can your business benefit? And finally, where are we going from here?

As Stephen Covey wrote in *The 7 Habits of Highly Effective People*, "To understand something is to understand its opposite." We'll use this as the starting point for our journey. Since Bitcoin is at the opposite end of the spectrum from our current money system, understanding where we are now will help us envision and create the future picture. The early chapters explore and expose the old financial model before transitioning into bitcoin for the rest of the book. My intention is that you finish the book feeling knowledgeable, inspired and empowered to implement Bitcoin to benefit your business, your customers, your vendors and other stakeholders.

*Let's get started.*

# Bitcoin Little Footnotes

The following terms may be used interchangeably throughout the book. My intention is to use the terms in a way that makes the material easy to understand within the context of a particular topic and in a way that's consistent with their use on various platforms, in articles or in the bitcoin space, even if the usage is not technically accurate. Every attempt had been made to distinguish the difference between common use and technical accuracy at relevant points throughout the book.

- bitcoin vs. Bitcoin: Bitcoin (capitalized) referring to the technology, protocol or network, and bitcoin (lower case) when referring to the currency unit itself
- Wallets, public key, public address, wallet address, user accounts, accounts
- Account holder, wallet holder, user, owner
- Private key, digital signature, authorization
- Passphrase, mnemonic seed, secret key
- Sending money, sending bitcoin, spending bitcoin, transfers
- Merchant, business, company
- Personal, individual, consumer
- Fiat, cash, fiat money, fiat currency, dollars, funds, money
- Digital currency, cryptocurrency, altcoins, bitcoin, virtual currency
- Cold wallets, cold storage, vaults
- Exchange, site, platform
- Bitcoin 2.0, metacoins, colored coins, appcoins
- Public ledger, blockchain, the technology, the protocol, the system
- Payment service providers, payment processors

# Bitcoin Sound Bites

The following bitcoin quotes give a flavor of what bitcoin is about, why people are engaged and how it will transform the world. They reveal insights from notable entrepreneurs, technologists, regulators, influencers and others.

*"Everybody hates banks, even I hate banks. [bitcoin] will force traditional institutions to adapt or die."*
- David Andolfatto, Vice President of the St. Louis Federal Reserve Bank

*"In 1995, the U.S. House of Representatives held hearing on 'the future of money' at which early versions of virtual currencies and other innovations were discussed. Vice Chairman Alan Blinder's testimony at that time made the key point that while these types of innovations may pose risks related to law enforcement and supervisory matters, there are also areas in which they may hold long-term promise, particularly if the innovations promote a faster, more secure and more efficient payment system."* - Ben Bernanke, former Federal Reserve Chairman, in a letter to the Committee of Homeland Security

*"Bitcoin is a payment innovation that's taking place outside the banking industry. To the best of my knowledge there's no intersection at all, in any way, between Bitcoin and banks that the Federal Reserve has the ability to supervise and regulate. So the Fed doesn't have authority to supervise or regulate Bitcoin in anyway."* - Janet Yellen, Federal Reserve Chairman

*"While my parents were in Turkey, I could get out my iPhone and videoconference them for free, but try to send them $100 and there's a lot of friction. The existing payment structure is decades old and there is a chance for real breakthroughs."* - Raj Date, former deputy director of the Consumer Financial Protection Bureau

*"I do think Bitcoin is the first [encrypted money] that has the potential to do something like change the world."* - Peter Thiel, co-founder of PayPal

*"Well technically speaking, the bitcoins aren't lost just yet just temporarily unavailable."* - Mark Karpeles, former Mt. Gox CEO, in the case of the missing bitcoins

*"Bitcoin will happen with or without China."* - Gil Lauria, Managing Director of Equity Research, Wedbush Securities, in response to China banning financial institutions from transacting with bitcoin

*"Instant transactions, no waiting for checks to clear, no chargebacks (merchants will like this), no account freezes (look out PayPal), no international wire transfer fee, no fees of any kind, no minimum balance, no maximum balance, worldwide access, always open, no waiting for business hours to make transactions, no waiting for an account to be approved before*

*transacting, open an account in a few seconds, as easy as email, no bank account needed, extremely poor people can use it, extremely wealthy people can use it, no printing press, no hyper-inflation, no debt limit votes, no bank bailouts, completely voluntary. This sounds like the best payment system in the world!"* - Trace Mayer, entrepreneur, investor, journalist, and monetary expert

*"Economists and journalists often get caught up in this question: Why does Bitcoin have value? And the answer is very easy. Because it is useful and scarce."* - Eric Voorhees, Founder of Coinapult

*"Credit card companies have had a monopoly that's lasted far too long."* - Steve Beauregard, Founder of GoCoin.com

*"In contrast to real currency, 'virtual' currency is a medium of exchange that operates like a currency in some environments, but does not have all the attributes of real currency. In particular, virtual currency does not have legal tender status in any jurisdiction. This guidance addresses "convertible" virtual currency. This type of virtual currency either has an equivalent value in real currency, or acts as a substitute for real currency."* - From FinCEN's March 2013 guidance on virtual currencies

*"With e-currency based on cryptographic proof, without the need to trust a third-party middleman, money can be secure and transactions effortless."* - Satoshi Nakamoto, Inventor of Bitcoin

*"What do we have here? A stroke of genius I think."* - David Andolfatto, Vice President of the St. Louis Federal Reserve Bank

*"If crypto is the answer, what's the question? What system respects the consent of its participants while undermining the centralized institutions we have come to distrust?"* - Patrick Byrne, Overstock CEO

*"We have elected to put our money and faith in a mathematical framework free of politics or human error."* - Tyler Winklevoss, Winklevoss Capital

*"We believe Bitcoin can become a major means of payment for e-commerce and may emerge as a serious competitor to traditional money transfer providers. As a medium of exchange, Bitcoin has clear potential for growth, in our view."* - David Woo, Head of Global Rates & Currency Research, Bank of America

*"They clearly don't understand bitcoin is far more than a currency/store of value/financial instrument; it is a protocol that will revolutionize dozens of industries. It's like the next layer of the Internet. This is a massive undervaluation."* - bitcointalk user Matt608 in response to Woo's already positive report

*"There are three eras of currency, commodity-based, politically-based and now math-based."* - Chris Dixon, technology investor

*"Bitcoin is a technological tour de force."* - Bill Gates

*"I think bitcoin is rat poison."* - Charlie Munger

*"I think either Charlie or Bill is right."* - Warren Buffett

*Later, Buffett blasts bitcoin on NCBC Squawk Box saying, "Stay away from it. It's a mirage, basically. It's a method of transmitting money. It's a very effective way of transmitting money and you can do it anonymously and all that. A check is a way of transmitting money, too. Are checks worth a whole lot of money just because they can transmit money? Are money orders? You can transmit money by money orders. People do it. I hope bitcoin becomes a better way of doing it, but you can replicate it a bunch of different ways and it will be. The idea that it has some huge intrinsic value is just a joke in my view. It's a very fast money order."* – Warren Buffett, Chairman and CEO, Berkshire Hathaway

*"Mr. Buffett, did you read the Credit Card Chaos, Money Transfer Madness and Banking Burnout Bonanza chapters?"* - Kirk Phillips, author of The Ultimate Bitcoin Business Guide

*"Warren has gone out of his way for decades to avoid understanding new technology. Not a surprising result."* - Marc Andreessen @ pmarca tweet in response to Warren Buffett

*"This may be the purest form of democracy the world has ever known, and I for one, am thrilled to be here to watch it unfold."* - Paco Ahlgren, financial analyst, Wi-Fi Alliance

*"Bitcoin is in the 1994 pre-Netscape era of the Internet. I believe there are multiple billion dollar companies that are going to be built in bitcoin."* - Jeremy Allaire, founder of Circle Internet Financial

*"Everything that can be decentralized will be decentralized."* - David Johnston, Founder of Decentralized Applications Fund and BitAngels

*"Bitcoin will do to banks what email did to the postal industry."* - Rick Falkvinge, IT entrepreneur

*"There may be as many reasons to support Bitcoin as there are Bitcoin supporters. But we believe Bitcoin holds out a number of powerfully beneficial social and economic outcomes, including global financial inclusion, enhanced personal liberty and dignity,*

*improved financial privacy, and a stable money supply for people in countries where monetary instability may threaten prosperity and even peace."* - Patrick Murck, general counsel of the Bitcoin Foundation

*"You can't stop things like Bitcoin. It will be everywhere and the world will have to readjust. World governments will have to readjust."* - John McAfee, Founder of McAfee

*"Bitcoin is the beginning of something great: a currency without a government, something necessary and imperative."* - Nassim Taleb, author and scholar

*"All I know is this money is more secure than the money that is in my investment bank."* - Tim Draper, managing director of VC firm Draper, Fisher, Jurvetson and winner of 30,000 bitcoins from the U.S. Marshalls' auction

*"At the end of the day, we've never seen anything like this before."* - David Woo, Head of Global Rates & Currency Research, Bank of America

*"The right to invest and innovate is in the grips of the few with the resources. They force us to ask them permission to innovate and deny our freedom to participate. This is ostensibly to 'protect' us from our lack of intelligence. Ironically, these same 'protectors'*

*would not mind if we gamble our meager savings at casinos or on the lottery, lest we accidentally do something of value and climb a step on the economic ladder."* - Manifesto from Swarmcorp.com crowd funding platform

*"What I would love to see is a financial services industry that's a fraction of the size it is today. People are going to realize one day looking backwards that the whole world of digital money was every bit as important as the world of digital information and the Internet. The Internet unleashed this ability to get unbelievable amounts of information about anything and the world of digital money which is now coming is going to unleash a similar set of benefits."* - Halsey Minor, Founder and CEO of Bitreserve

*"We're seeing millennials trust a currency that is created in the ether, more than they trust fiat currency by government. I think that trend, whether it's a restaurant review or a taxicab or the way you exchange value, is something they believe in and we want to be on top of it because I think it's going to impact you and I."* - Jeffrey Sprecher, NYSE Chairman

*"The average user should pick up bitcoin. To experience the future of money. To gain a glimpse into an exciting technology. To learn about how money could be in the future and also become aware of how limited money and banks are today."* - Andreas Antonopoulos, Bitcoin evangelist and author of Mastering Bitcoin

# Currency Chameleons

You may ask yourself, well, how did we get here? Let's answer this question by reviewing the history of exchange, the evolution of payment methods, the development of banking and currency in the United States and the birth of the Federal Reserve System.

## Payments and Trade

Payment for goods and services started with the trading one thing for another. The vegetable grower needs baskets to carry vegetables so she trades vegetables for baskets. This barter system is so simple and effective it's still used today. A problem arises when the vegetable grower needs baskets but the basket weaver doesn't need vegetables because he grows his own. Common currency solves this problem when a group of people use something as an agreed upon medium of exchange to trade for anything else. Once upon a time, commodities like salt had a high value for preserving meat and preventing spoilage, therefore people mutually agreed that salt was a valuable currency for buying things. Shells, spices, salt, furs, and many other resources have been used throughout history to get business done.

Elaborate clay pieces were used as a form of coin in early Mesopotamia from 8000 BC in conjunction with accounting systems that led to the development of writing.[1,2] The idea of using something as a common currency for payments has lasted thousands of years. Only the thing that represents the common currency has changed over the centuries. The evolution of payments looks like this:

⇨ Barter
⇨ Coins (gold, silver and other)
⇨ Paper money (fiat currency)
⇨ Plastic (credit cards)
⇨ PCs (online payments)

⇨ Mobile (payments by phone)
⇨ Private digital (airline miles or cell phone minutes)
⇨ Bitcoin

Each new form of payment failed to replace the one before it and every payment method listed above is still used today.[3] As technology continues to advance in developing nations by providing easy access to Internet services and smart phones, a shift from paper money to mobile will create the fastest adoption of new payment methods in history in the same way mobile phones leapfrogged landlines.

## That Much Paper?

People in developed nations might assume that 85% of transactions are made with plastic because it's so widely used. Yet after hundreds of years 85% of the world's retail transactions still take place with paper money, which is third on the payment evolution list above. Bartering, too, is as alive and well today as it was thousands of years ago, whether it happens between neighbors or through an online portal such as Itex.com, a platform that allows anyone to trade goods or services. Plastic, PCs, mobile and private digital payment methods are very recent innovations relative to the time scale of currencies and payments over the past few thousand years. These methods will be discussed in a later chapter on understanding credit cards and banking as a basis for understanding Bitcoin.

## Revolutionary Roll Forward and Dual Central Banking Failures

Let's look at the development of currency in the United States from the American Revolution to the beginning of the Federal Reserve System. We're simply focusing on the United States because the U.S. dollar has been the world reserve currency and effectively paints a picture about banks, government-issued currency and corresponding regulations. Similarities can also be made to the development of currency and central banking in other countries.

The Continental Congress printed the nation's first paper money known as "continentals," which eventually became worthless by the end of the Revolutionary War. Alexander Hamilton, Treasury Secretary and central banking system advocate, led the formation of the First Bank of the United States located in Philadelphia in 1791. Thomas Jefferson and like-minded agrarians opposed the idea of a powerful centralized bank and Congress failed to renew its charter in 1811. Thomas Jefferson eloquently suggested in a letter to John Taylor, "And I sincerely believe, with you, that banking establishments are more dangerous than standing armies; and that the principle of spending money to be paid by posterity, under the name of funding, is but swindling futurity on a large scale." [4]

The Second Bank of the United States failed for similar reasons in 1836 fueled by Andrew Jackson's disdain of centralized, banker-controlled power. Jackson wrote:

"Congress has established a mint to coin money and passed laws to regulate the value thereof. The money so coined, with its value so regulated, and such foreign coins as Congress may adopt are the only currency known to the Constitution. But if they have other power to regulate the currency, it was conferred to be exercised by themselves, and not to be transferred to a corporation. If the bank be established for that purpose, with a charter unalterable without its consent, Congress have parted with their power for a term of years, during which the Constitution is a dead letter. It is neither necessary nor proper to transfer its legislative power to such a bank, and therefore unconstitutional." [5,6]

A pair of Presidential Roosevelts echoed the sentiment. First Theodore Roosevelt, 26th U.S. President, observed, "Behind the ostensible government sits enthroned an invisible government owing no allegiance and acknowledging no responsibility to the people," [7] followed by Franklin D. Roosevelt, 32nd President of the

U.S., who declared, "The real truth of the matter is that a financial element has owned the government since the days of Andrew Jackson." [8]

## Paper Notes and a Pair of Panics

There were 8,000 state-chartered banks by 1860, each one issuing its own paper notes in the Free Banking Era of no federal regulation that also witnessed five financial panics including the Panic of 1893 and the Panic of 1907. The National Banking Act of 1863 created nationally chartered banks and the first uniform currency even though state banks continued to flourish.[9] The Philadelphia and Reading Railroad went bankrupt, which precipitated the Financial Panic of 1893 including hundreds of bank failures, railroad company failures, stock market declines, high unemployment, business failures and bank runs all leading to the country's worst depression to date. [10, 11]

The next United States major banking crisis began in October 1907 starting with a run on and eventual demise of the Knickerbocker Trust caused by rumors around the bank president's involvement in the copper market scandal. The National Bank of Commerce announced it would no longer accept Knickerbocker checks, which resulted in widespread withdraws that produced a cascading collapse of other banks due to an overall lack of faith in the financial system.

These perceptions of financial insecurity unraveled the system by causing otherwise solvent banks to become insolvent, thus making the system unreliable while creating disdain for the banking industry and The New York Stock Exchange. J.P. Morgan stepped in with his own money and persuaded other bankers to do the same in an effort to save the New York Stock Exchange from collapse. Morgan was initially considered a hero for saving America's financial system but was soon demonized for being the leader of the "king bankers" of the money trusts, thereby controlling all things in banking and industry. Congressional hearings on the financial crisis placed Morgan front and center while Congressman

Charles A. Lindbergh, an outspoken Federal Reserve critic, and two other journalists used Morgan's testimony against him to paint a picture of an elite, self-serving, banking class. [12, 13]

## Birth of the Fed

The chaos that ensued from the 1907 crisis and the Congressional hearings eventually led to proposals for a United Reserve Bank, first by prominent banker, Paul M. Warburg, and later by Senator Nelson W. Aldrich who proposed the "Aldrich Bill" essentially adopting the framework of Warburg's plan. Warburg stated, "Nothing short of a central bank will effect a solution of the currency problem," while realizing that without a national education campaign a high level of public mistrust would defeat any central banking bill. Morgan even hosted a notorious bankers' meeting at Jekyll Island, Aldrich and Warburg included, replacing the normal staff among other acts to maintain secrecy. Warburg then proposed an education and propaganda campaign, which eventually morphed into The National Citizens' League. The league was established to create the illusion of a non-banker-influenced organization that was "by the people and for the people" and to educate the public on the sound principles of central banking reform. Warburg wrote, "It is unfortunate that the general attitude of the country towards New York and Wall Street is such that any measure proposed from here would be doomed from the start." [14]

The Aldrich Bill was quickly defeated in 1912, but the strength of the central banking movement eventually resulted in the Federal Reserve Act passed on December 23, 1913, and signed by President Woodrow Wilson. This was not a grand agreement celebrated by everyone but one with as many critics as there were supporters, a battle that ultimately ended with the Federal Reserve banking system we now have. [15]

Congressman Lindbergh angrily declared:

"This Act establishes the most gigantic trust on earth... When the President signs this Act, the invisible government by the Money Power, proven to exist by the Money Trust Investigation, will be legalized...The money power overawes the legislative and executive forces of the Nation and of the States. I have seen these forces exerted during the different stages of this bill..."

"The new law will create inflation whenever the trusts want inflation. From now on depressions will be scientifically created." [16]

## Turning 100

The Federal Reserve turned 100 years old on December 23, 2013, in spite of continued criticism for a lack of transparency and other financial breakdowns.

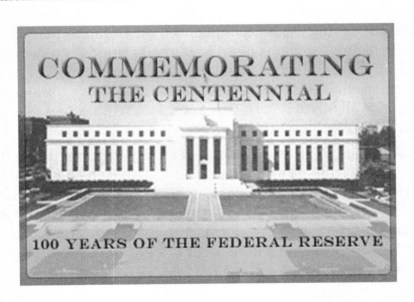

Image courtesy of The Federal Reserve

The following pictograph shows the relationship between the Federal Reserve Bank, the Board of Governors, the Federal Open Market Committee and the 12 U.S. Federal Reserve Banks, and of course the private banking system. We should also consider the United States Treasury, which is the equivalent of an individual or business account holder at a bank, which in this case is the Federal Reserve Bank. The U.S. Treasury is in the business of collecting taxes from its customers who are the U.S. taxpayers. This is an extremely complicated system with a host of powerful parties.

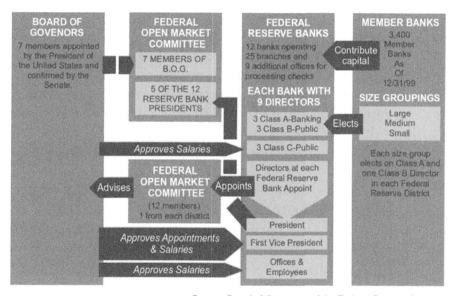

*Source: Board of Governors of the Federal Reserve System*

Image courtesy of The Federal Reserve

## The Fed's Four Functions

The Fed serves four functions all of which are generally similar to the operation of central banks as follows:

1. Maintain stability in the financial markets by regulating monetary policy including controlling the supply of money with related interest rates and other tools. The Federal Reserve through the Federal Open Market Committee arbitrarily controls the flow of money by buying and selling U.S. Treasuries or United States Bonds.

2. The Federal Reserve System provides support to the private banking system by holding reserve money deposits on its behalf to facilitate lending of money between private banks. Customers deposit money in bank accounts, the bank lends the money to other people and the bank is only required to keep a little bit of cash on hand. This is known as the "fractional reserve system" (FRS). Therefore, when banks are short on cash the Federal Reserve will lend them some.

3. The Federal Reserve is a lender of last resort as demonstrated recently during the great recession of 2008. This is where the phrase "too big to fail" comes from. A large financial institution on the verge of bankruptcy will be saved by the white knight Federal Reserve System through almost any financial aid necessary to ensure the United States and worldwide financial systems don't implode.

4. The Fed is responsible for overseeing the nation's payment systems as well as protecting the rights of consumers. The Fed is woven into the fabric of the private banking system.[17]

## Transparent or Translucent?

The Federal Reserve System states on its website it is extensively audited with 425,000 hours devoted to auditing a long list of actions, an indicator that it is the most audited organization in government. The Government Accountability Office (GAO), congressional appearances, voluntary disclosure, press conferences, statement releases and weekly balance sheet releases are listed among the many ways the Fed is transparent.

However, Title 31 Section 714 of the United States Code states that some actions of the Fed are exempt from audit as follows:

1. Transactions for or with a foreign central bank
2. Deliberations, decisions, or actions on monetary policy matters
3. Transactions made under the direction of the Federal Open Market Committee
4. Discussion or communication among or between members of the Board [18, 19]

But some, like retired congressman Ron Paul, take issue with these exemptions. Congressman Paul introduced bill H.R. 1207, The Federal Reserve Transparency Act, on February 26, 2009, with the following speech to Congress:

"Madame Speaker, I rise to introduce the Federal Reserve Transparency Act. Throughout its nearly 100-year history, the Federal Reserve has presided over the near-complete destruction of the United States dollar. Since 1913 the dollar has lost over 95% of its purchasing power, aided and abetted by the Federal Reserve's loose monetary policy. How long will we as a Congress stand idly by while hard-working Americans see their savings eaten away by inflation? Only big-spending politicians and politically favored bankers benefit from inflation..."

"...Since its inception, the Federal Reserve has always operated in the shadows, without sufficient scrutiny or oversight of its operations. The Federal Reserve can enter into agreements with foreign central banks and foreign governments, and the GAO is prohibited from auditing or even seeing these agreements. The Federal Reserve Transparency Act would eliminate restrictions on GAO audits of the Federal Reserve and open Fed operations to enhanced scrutiny." [20]

Paul's transparency act would essentially remove the exemptions claimed by the Fed. [21] Congressman Ron Paul introduced the Federal Reserve Transparency Act several times before passing the torch to his son, Senator Rand Paul, who pushed the 2013 version of the bill.

## A Flaw and the Great American Meltdown

The Fed's central banking paradigm was stress tested in the midst of the 2008 Great Recession of the United States and the rest of the world. The $700 billion U.S. Troubled Assets Relief Fund (TARP)[22] prevented a total financial unraveling yet everyone wanted answers, especially from the regulators tasked with responsibility for overseeing various markets. Where did the regulation fail? Who was responsible? Why did this happen in the first place? And how long had this been going on?

The answers to these questions and more would be extracted from multiple U.S Congressional hearings with regulators and big business. A classic C-SPAN excerpt near the end of 2008 between Rep. Henry Waxman, a democrat from California and chair of the Financial Market Regulators House Oversight and Government Reform Committee, and Alan Greenspan, famed Federal Reserve Board Chairman from 1987 to 2006, follows. The ongoing battle over the equilibrium point between regulation and free markets has exposed a flaw in regulatory thinking. More explanations abound in the chapter on Regulatory Zigzagging.

Federal Regulation of Financial Markets, C-SPAN excerpt:

**Waxman**: "Dr. Greenspan I want to start with you, my question for you is simple. Were you wrong?"
**Greenspan**: "Partially, but let's separate this problem into its component parts."

**Waxman**: "Dr. Greenspan, you had an ideology, you had a belief that free competitive markets are by far the unrivaled way to organize economies. 'We've tried regulation. It's not meaningfully worked.' That's what you said, that's your quote. Do you feel that your ideology pushed you to make decisions that you wish you had not made?"

**Greenspan**: "Well, remember that what an ideology is, is a conceptual framework with the way people deal with reality. Everyone has it. We have to. To exist you need an ideology. The question is whether it is accurate or not. And what I'm saying to you is yes, I've found a flaw. I don't know how significant or permanent it is, but I've been very distressed by that fact. A flaw in the model that I perceived is the critical functioning structure that defines how the world works so to speak."

**Waxman**: "Dr. Greenspan, your view of the world, your ideology was not right, it was not working."

**Greenspan**: "Precisely, that's the reason I was shocked because I've been going for 40 years or more with very considerable evidence that it was working exceptionally well."

**Waxman**: "Where do you think you made a mistake?"

**Greenspan**: "I made a mistake in presuming that the self-interest of banks and others were such that they were best capable of protecting their own firms." [23]


A few noteworthy influencers further expressed their feelings about 2008 in the award-winning movie, The Flaw:


*"This crisis is a total failure of markets."* - Joseph Stiglitz, Nobel Prize-winning economist and Columbia University professor

*"It's a debt crisis but it's also a crisis of economic theory."*
- George Cooper, Fund Manager, Blue Crest Capital

*"This is horrifying. All the people that we've trusted have turned out to be completely untrustworthy."* - Nell Minow, Corporate Watchdog, The Corporate Library

The United States had its first debt downgrade in 2011 while Alan Greenspan provided this vote of confidence, "The United States can pay any debt it has because we can always print money to do that so there is zero probability of default." [24]

Did Dr. Greenspan forget about his own "flawed thinking" congressional testimony? Simon Dixon, former investment banker and founder of Bank to the Future, provides some insight. "The problem right now," he says, "is that capitalism is built on an unsustainable banking system where the petrol, the fuel of capitalism, is money, and money is built upon a process whereby in order for it to be created it has to be created as debt and that completely skews where money is allocated and who can access capital...I believe we have a banking problem and that leads to a corporation problem...The only way you will ever get the government to change is a complete meltdown. They have no appetite to change prior to any kind of meltdown. They chose the exact cause of the problem as the solution to the problem and I believe they will do that forever." [25]

## Currency Chameleons Takeaway

The transparency, fractional reserve, central banking tug-o-war has fueled conspiracy theorists and Fed opponents for decades. Some of the founding fathers and early leaders opposed federal centralized banking while free banking, bank failures, multiple depressions and shaky consumer confidence eventually gave way to the birth of the Federal Reserve System. It has continued to evolve over the past 100 years, navigating the Great Depression, two world wars and the Great Recession of 2008. Many other world central banks have failed while some of the brightest economists believe central banking is paramount to financial stability. Big banks have been dubbed too big to fail, but can a nation be too big to fail? Will the central banking model work for the next century for the United States and other countries? Are we hanging in the balance or are we safe and secure with the current system? Will it take an epic meltdown to fundamentally change the basis of global banking and money? What would it take to create a new model with all of the good and none of the bad, something celebrated with a grand consensus on a global level and one that benefits all worldwide stakeholders from developing nations and the wretched poor to the power elite while dissolving fraud, greed and corruption? Let's continue the journey and discover some possibilities for another way.

# Credit Card Chaos

## From Checks to Credit Cards

Checks were used in the United States even before 1853 when the New York Clearinghouse Association was established to process the huge volume of check transactions. Checks are still alive and well today over 150 years later.

Merchants started to issue merchant charge cards in the 1950s extending credit to customers for purchases only at their respective stores. Some of these still exist today such as the Sunoco card or the Macy's card. Smaller banks in California then tried to create a unified credit card that was available to use at any participating retailer, but the banks could not get enough momentum for widespread acceptance.

## Disruptive Drop

Innovators disrupted the system by creating a plastic card that could be used to buy anything from any store that accepted it. In 1958 Bank of America launched BankAmericard, the brainchild of Joseph P. Williams and B of A's in-house think tank. They carefully studied the failures and successes of merchant cards like Sears in rolling out their successful campaign. They reached the tipping point through a massive credit card drop in California where hundreds of thousands and then millions of live working credit cards were distributed to customers.

Unsolicited credit cards just showed up in mailboxes with ready to use credit limits. This is not to be confused with the credit card offers that show up today with a fake plastic card gimmick requiring an application for approval. The credit card drop got traction when everyone took advantage of what seemed like free cash. Fast adoption was not without problems, like a default rate that was four to five times higher than projected, in addition to massive amounts of credit card fraud, both of which were not anticipated.

## Today's Twins

The original BankAmericard has morphed into the Visa cards we know today dominating the credit and debit card market. MasterCard Interbank card was created when a consortium of banks got together to create a credit card competitor to the Visa card. [26, 27]

Visa and MasterCard have a notorious track record for antitrust and class-action lawsuits from consumers as well as competitors like American Express and Discover. They've also set records for the highest dollar class action settlements in history. "Visa and MasterCard are the ringleaders, organizers, and enforcers of a conspiracy among U.S. banks to fix the price of ATM access fees in order to keep the competition at bay," said Jonathan Rubin of Rubin PLLC, one of the plaintiffs' lawyers in the class action suit. [28]

## The Life of a Credit Card Purchase

Jill goes to the shop online or in person using a credit card for payment. She swipes her credit card or clicks the submit button which transmits the data via a point-of-sale (POS) terminal or payment gateway, which then sends the transaction to the "issuing" bank for Jill's credit card. The issuing bank clears the payment with the merchant's "acquiring" bank while the credit card association (e.g., Visa) authorizes the sale over the payment network. Basically, the banks and the payment network confirm there is money in Jill's account, says the transaction is good and makes the payment on Jill's behalf. All this happens in a few seconds and Jill happily walks away with her new product or service.

## Convoluted Fees

The merchant who sold to Jill currently pays 3 to 4% of sales in credit card processing fees or $3,000 to $4,000 for every $100,000 in sales, which is mainly comprised of an interchange fee or swipe fee. Jill's issuing bank happily collects the interchange fee and the merchant's acquiring bank gets a smaller processing fee, both of which are part of the collective "MDR" or merchant discount rate.[29,30]

## Laundry List of Fees & Factors

There is a laundry list of different types of fees, rules and rates which when blended together make up this 3 to 4% cost.[31] This system is so convoluted and difficult to understand that business owners feel frustrated and overwhelmed by it all.

Here are some of the factors that *affect the cost of accepting credit cards:* [32]

- Is the card present or not present? Charges with cards not present cost more.
- Is it a debit card or a credit card? Credit cards cost more.
- The size and type of business you're in? If you're in an industry with more chargebacks then the cost is higher. This is an "insult to injury" cost.
- Average ticket size or sale amount? Smaller average sales usually cost more.
- Card brand, country of issue, regions and jurisdictions, and business card vs. personal card are other factors affecting cost.

And here are some example costs associated with accepting credit cards:

- Monthly minimum fee averaging $25 per month regardless of a credit card sale.
- Monthly statement fee averaging $10 per month also paid regardless of a sale.
- Interchange (swipe fees) ranging approximately 1-4% plus a fixed per transaction fee averaging $.10 to $.30.
- Gateway monthly payments ranging from $5 to $15 per month for online or e-commerce businesses.

- POS credit card terminal lease or purchase. For example, a lease may be $40 per month for 36 to 48 months or a purchase may be $495.
- Rolls of card terminal receipt paper averaging $30 per roll.
- PayPal and similar services have simplified some of these issues by offering a flat 2.9% + $.30 per transaction.

## Hoops, Fees and Headaches

Cross-border credit card sales give merchants the privilege of paying an ISA (international service assessment) on top of interchange fees. Every time merchants jump through hoops they get to pay another fee. Depending on the product or industry, credit cards may also hold a hefty cash reserve to cover fraud and charge backs. Essentially, hair-trigger fraud controls designed to detect and prevent fraudulent transactions are blocking otherwise legitimate transactions, which is creating more hidden costs in lost sales, loss of customer goodwill and all-around frustration.

Online merchants are the benefactors of an additional "card not present" fee up to 1% more than when a card is physically present at a retailer. The 1% premium can quickly turn into a 100% nightmare because online merchants are responsible for all fraud-related chargebacks. Bitnet.io CEO and payments industry veteran, John McDonnell, describes the pain like this, "So when we add up the total cost of acceptance it's not the 2-4% it's really 8 to 10 to 12% depending on the industry. So if you are a retailer accepting credit cards that's really what you are paying. The fully loaded cost of accepting cards online is in the neighborhood of 10%; which is an incredibly corrosive cost to the margins in some thin-margin businesses." [33]

## What does MasterCard say about interchange fees?

MasterCard states, "If interchange rates are set too high, such that they lead to disproportionately high MDRs, merchants' desire and demand for MasterCard acceptance will drop. If interchange rates are set too low, card issuers' willingness to issue and promote MasterCard cards will drop, as will consumer demand for such cards.

In response to these competitive forces, we strive to maximize the value of the MasterCard system by setting default interchange rates at levels that balance the benefits and costs to both cardholders and merchants."[34] On this topic, Steve Beauregard, founder of Gocoin. com, said, "Credit card companies have a monopoly that's lasted far too long." [35]

The following diagram depicts the true nature of Credit Card Chaos. Don't strain to hard trying to understand the flow or you might get a headache. The visual nature provides a glimpse into the complicated nature of a credit card purchase.

## Credit Card Chaos

Ecommerce CC Purchase Path High Level Steps

Image courtesy of Ashok Misra, Alina Consultants

Credit Card Chaos ensues in the following 14 steps: [36]

1. Consumer presents card for purchase to merchant.
2. Merchant sends authorization for amount to payment gateway.
3. Payment gateway routes the transaction to the correct brand network.
4. Brand network routes authorization to consumer's issuing bank.
5. Issuing bank replies with authorization response (approved or declined) to the brand network.
6. Brand network directs response to payment gateway.
7. Payment gateway submits response to merchant.
8. Merchant communicates response to consumer at browser.
9. Merchant sends settlement message to gateway at end of day in batch for final settlement amount.
10. Gateway sends settlement file to brand network.
11. Brand network sends settlement to issuing bank.
12. Issuing bank sends settlement amount to brand network.
13. Issuing bank debits consumer credit card account for the amount.
14. Merchant acquiring bank receives funds and credits merchant account.

Now, just take a deep breath. I promise it will be okay!

## Seconds to Sell and Days to Collect

The merchant's bank receives the payment from Jill's bank but the money doesn't clear and become usable to the merchant for several days even though the verification of available funds allowed the merchandise to be sold in a few seconds.

For example, if a credit card swipe takes one to three seconds to verify and two to five days for merchants to receive their money, then it takes 57,600 to 432,000 times longer to receive money than it does to make the sale! Let's call this "the usable money to approval ratio" and don't forget banking holidays when you make the calculation. It's outrageous and unacceptable to wait that long for money, yet everyone's become comfortably numb to the status quo of Credit Card Chaos. Relative to countries like Argentina, it's a welcome choice compared to a 30-day wait for credit card payouts coupled with soaring inflation—a true example of insult to injury. I'd be scared to calculate the usable money to approval ratio on this one.

## A Merchant's Bonus: The Hidden Costs

If the fees and waiting time weren't enough, merchants get the added reward of headaches for their patience.

- Merchants may have to go through an underwriting process to accept credit cards depending on the sales of the merchant and the types of customers just like being underwritten for a loan. For example, one application for a service provider asks for detailed personal information, two years of income statements and corresponding balance sheets.
- The underwriting process may result in multiple inquiries on your personal credit report with a potentially negative impact.
- Cross-border or international transactions with different currencies are so complex they come with a 600-page manual. Who has time to understand that in any size company?
- Businesses may be required to have a reserve or post a bank guarantee to offset chargebacks. In addition to waiting five days for your money, the bank graciously keeps some of your money so you can't use it.
- Every business that accepts credit cards must be payment card industry (PCI) security standard-compliant. Fortunately, small merchants can sign a self-assessment questionnaire (SAQ), while Tier 1 merchants with more

than $6MM in card transactions have a huge PCI audit expense to stay in compliance.

- Someone in the business has to stop what they're doing and deal with chargebacks which could take at least an hour to research, assemble documentation and submit to the acquiring bank or merchant services provider. The amount of time employees or owners spend dealing with chargebacks is a significant hidden cost.

## Credit Card Chaos Takeaway

This section was not designed to be a complete analysis of credit card processing nor for anyone to remember all the moving parts. It's an exercise in asking, why does it take so long to get paid? Why is it so complicated and difficult to understand? Why are there so many hidden costs? Why is the simple act of getting paid by customers not so simple? This is a wheel-spinning exercise that takes away from business owners being able to focus on what's going to make their business grow.

For the last 60 years we have been using the same payment system for goods and services. While MasterCard and Visa and other credit and debit cards are convenient for consumers, they carry a unique set of frustrations and are a perpetual thorn in the side of merchants because of all the fees and headaches. This stale system is simply setting the stage for the next disruptive drop, a necessary precursor to transformation of the tired old credit card model.

The cost of fraud and the cost of maintaining and securing personal information, the PCI compliance mentioned earlier, accounts for the substantial cost of maintaining the current system. The credit card hacking of tens of millions of Target customer accounts in 2013 and Home Depot accounts in 2014, among others, begs the question, is it possible to keep large amounts of private data secure? The best and brightest companies with unlimited resources can't keep your information secure and their vulnerabilities are juicy pickings for hackers. Expending resources to safeguard vast amounts of duplicated personal data is an exercise in futility. Consumers have to endure long and painful fraud monitoring on their credit profiles as a result of hacking while merchants' reputations are damaged and millions more are spent to perpetuate the same cycle in a race to outsmart the hackers.

We'll soon see how bitcoin can transform the convoluted nature of Credit Card Chaos.

# Money Transfer Madness

Money transfers can refer to a number of different payment systems, including electronic funds transfers, bank wires, the Hawala system, money orders and remittances. This section focuses on remittances in the context of transferring money internationally, usually by a foreign worker sending money to someone in their home country. The World Bank estimates that global remittances are growing at 5% reaching $581 billion in 2014 with a majority going to developing countries. Remittances are lifelines to the poor coupled with an average global cost of 8.4%. Therefore, an average $100 money transfer costs $8.40 while the total global annual cost to consumers is an estimated $33.6 billion. The International Money Fund, IMF, estimates informal, unrecorded cross-border money flows could be 50% larger than recorded money flows, making a staggering total of worldwide remittances.

Earlier on I referenced Raj Date, former deputy director of the Consumer Financial Protection Bureau, who relayed the story of how it was easier to send an iPhone video to his parents in Turkey than it was to send $100. Let's look at this issue more closely with following example:

Let's say Gregorio lives in the U.S. and needs to send $100 to his brother, Jose, in Guatemala. He gets in his car and drives to the nearest Western Union, pays $100 cash plus a $15 transfer fee and sends the reference number to his brother. The $115 goes on a journey of its own before his brother can collect the $100. The $15 fee is split equally among the parties in the transfer process.

## Transfer Agent

The current money transfer process is very complicated and can require as many as 10 parties to complete an international money transfer. The sender usually bears the cost of the transfer fee. The person who wants to send cash goes to a money transfer agent like Western Union who collects the payment, and the receiver's information, then verifies the sender and deposits the payment. The sender receives a reference number from the agent so the receiver can get the money on the other end. The transfer agent gets a $5 cut of the total $15 fee paid by Billy.

## Money Transfer Provider

Next, the money transfer provider oversees the agent, provides compliance for the transfer process, and also provides technology network support. In addition the money transfer provider also settles with the agent and with the payment network. Each party in the process has a separate transaction between themselves that's part of the overall settlement process. For example the person sending the money and the agent have a separate transaction, the agent and the money transfer provider have a separate transaction for their part of the process and so on. The money transfer provider gladly takes a $5 cut at this point in the process.

## Payment Network

The payment network settles with the money transfer provider, makes any necessary currency conversions and manages the payout agents. The paying agent for the sender, the payout agent for the receiver, the money transfer provider and the payment network are usually not the same company if it's an international money transfer. In addition, each of the parties in this transaction has its own bank that the money is passing through while the information part of the transaction is being processed. The payment network takes the final $5 from Billy's transfer fee. [37]

## Payout Agent

Finally! Jose can go get his money. He goes to the nearest payout agent with the reference number and gets the cash. Depending on the payout agent Jose may have to pay another fee. The payout agent may be a different company than the transfer agent depending on the country-to-country transfer creating another level of complexity and cost in the process. It's an inconvenient, clunky, fee-hefty process just to send money from one person to another. Even a $75 Western Union transfer from one person to another in the same U.S city could strip another $8 from your pocket. [38]

# Money Transfer Madness

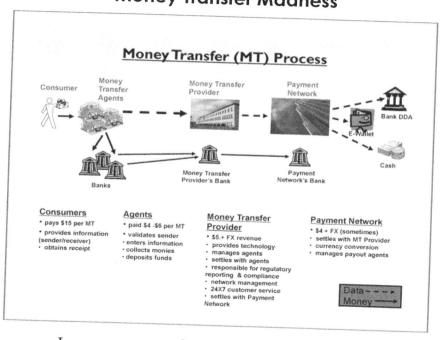

Image courtesy of Simon Nahnybida, ZipZap

A money transfer can have as many as 10 parties to complete the transaction:

1. Sender
2. Transfer agent
3. Transfer agent's bank
4. Money transfer provider
5. Money transfer provider's bank
6. Payment network
7. Payment network's bank
8. Payout agent
9. Payout agent's bank
10. Recipient

## The Irony

In some cases smaller money transfer operators acting as the payout agent may charge an additional fee to the beneficiary to cover possible exchange rate fluctuations. The banks and agents can also earn indirect fees in a classic game of float by investing funds before payouts to the beneficiary, especially in countries where the overnight interest rate is very high. Meanwhile, a World Bank study has provided insight that remittances significantly reduce poverty in many developing countries. Most of the people making remittances have made huge personal sacrifices, including being separated from family members, yet pay a huge fee to send a typical transfer of a few hundred dollars. The cost of fees for larger payments made for trade or investment in the course of business are much lower as a percentage of the amount transferred. More sophisticated people in an individual or business capacity have access to and knowledge of alternative methods such as foreign exchange brokers which have several low-cost products relative to services like Western Union, Money Gram, Euronet and other banks. [39]

# Money Transfer Madness Takeaway

Money transfers in the form of remittances represent a huge portion of worldwide money flows and a significant lifeline between foreign workers and their family members in many countries around the world. This type of money transaction is more valuable to the sender and recipient, based on their needs, than any transaction type in the world. Even the cost of credit card chaos pales in comparison to the cost of money transfers.

Why is the cost of buying goods or services so different than moving money from one place to another? Why is the cost of moving money so expensive when the cost of sending information in an email is free and instantaneous? If Gregorio had to hand-deliver cash to his brother by traveling from the U.S. to Guatemala the time and cost would outweigh the $15 fee. In this case, the fees charged by money transfer and remittance providers seem like a bargain; otherwise, a 10% tax for sending money hardly seems like a value-added service.

Let's keep moving forward and find out what bitcoin can do for this Stone Age process.

# Banking Burnout Bonanza

Let's review the finer points of banking, including additional ways to move money around, the corresponding fees and the supporting structures. This is another set of complicated money systems to go along with Credit Card Chaos and Money Transfer Madness. But don't be dismayed. The best part is just around the corner and your patience will be rewarded for wading through the old-rail money swamp.

## SWIFTly Speaking

The Society for Worldwide Interbank Financial Telecommunication (SWIFT) was formed in 1973 to create interoperability among the various national and regional banks and financial networks. It links more than 10,000 financial institutions in more than 200 countries using a standard protocol for securely communicating financial information. SWIFT does not hold accounts for it member banks, facilitate funds transfers or perform clearing or settlements. It merely transmits financial information called payment orders on behalf of banks that maintain and settle their own accounts. [40]

For example, Bank A places a payment order with the SWIFT system for transmittal to Bank B after authorization from Bank C. SWIFT formats the message and guarantees a secure reliable delivery to its final destination at Bank B. Banks A and B debit and credit customer accounts and settle the transaction with Bank C's authorization. SWIFT is a member-owned cooperative with three centralized data centers in the United States, Netherlands and Switzerland. It generates an average of 23,000,000 worldwide messages a day, as of June 2014. It contributes the following four things to the financial world:

1. A secure and reliable communications network for the exchange of financial information among banks otherwise

taking place in a patchwork of incompatible systems
2.  A standard communications protocol or syntax for sending financial information that can be understood by any other network whether or not SWIFTNet is used
3.  Products and services such as connection software allowing for financial communication, business intelligence and compliance tools
4.  A way for the financial community to come together to collaborate on defining standards and shaping practices

## The Automated Clearinghouse

There are multiple national and regional automated clearinghouses operating around the world. For example the European Automated Clearing House Association (EACHA) is an association of automated clearinghouses from 21 different countries covering most of Europe. A review of the United States ACH system provides a general overview of bank payment processing. The Automated Clearinghouse (ACH) system is a U.S. nationwide network used by depository institutions to send batches of electronic debit and credit transfers or payments and deposits to each other. The Federal Reserve and the Electronic Payments Network (EPN) are the only two ACH operators with each processing about 50% of ACH transactions. The EPN is owned and operated by The Clearing House Payments Company, a 160-year-old monopoly. They also provide electronic check clearing and wholesale funds transfer services.

ACH debits are withdrawals from an individual or business account for payments such as mortgages, utility bills and vendor payments. ACH credits are deposits into an individual or business account for things such as payroll, tax refunds and customer receipts. ACH payments can be used for recurring and one-time payments without having to incur credit card processing fees. The ACH network is governed by the self-regulatory Electronic Payments Association formerly NACHA. [41, 42, 43]

## An ACH in Action

The ORI Corp. has just contracted with a new vendor, REC Corp., which requires ACH payment for office equipment. ORI is the ACH originator and REC is the receiver.

1. An originator, whether an individual or a business, initiates an ACH direct deposit or direct payment usually through their online banking login instead of writing a check.
2. ORI's bank, called the Originating Depository Financial Institution (ODFI), batches ACH transactions from multiple customers and forwards them to the ACH operators at a predetermined interval.
3. The ACH operators, the Federal Reserve and the Clearing House, receive multiple ACH batches from multiple ODFI's. The transactions within the batches are sorted and sent to the Receiving Depository Financial Institution (RDFI), the bank on the other end of the transaction.
4. The receiver's bank account is debited or credited for payments or deposits by the RDFI while the ACH operator settles the transactions with the RDFI's settlement account.

ACH payments can be initiated by a bank or by third-party providers like paysimple.com and firstach.com. ACH payments take one to two business days to settle depending on weekends and holidays. If ORI Corp. makes an ACH payment on Friday of Labor Day Weekend, the payment may not settle until five days later on the following Wednesday. Fixed transaction fees are lower than credit cards but monthly subscription fees may apply when using third-party providers. Examples of fees may include:

1.   Per transaction fee of $.34 for an ACH Debit and $.49 for an ACH Credit or a fixed fee like $.55 for all ACH transactions.
2.   Monthly account fee ranging from $14.95 per month to $34.95 per month depending on the services offered on a platform.
3.   Discount fee or a surcharge for high-risk transactions over the per-transaction fee.

Chase business services charges $25 for 25 ACH transactions per month and $.15 for each additional transaction. Individual bank accounts on the other hand may offer free ACH bill payment services.

## Bank Transfers

The faster you want to transfer money the more expensive it is. Bank transfers to accounts at different banks owned by the same account holder come with a price. Bank of America's transfer fee menu, for example, has the following charges: [44]

- Same day wire $25
- Next business day $10
- Three business days $3

A three-day transfer sent on a Wednesday before Memorial Day won't arrive until six days later on Tuesday. If the payment has to be made by Friday then the premium for sending and receiving your own money triples from $3 to $10. Some banks give VIP treatment to customers who transfer money from one account to another at the same bank by rewarding them with a hold on their own money. In one moment you have access to your money and in the next moment you don't.

# Bank Wires

A bank wire is a money transfer that takes place directly between two banks without a third-party clearinghouse. The transaction is individually processed whereas ACH transactions are processed in batches. ORI Corp. would pay a wire fee of $25 and up to send a payment while the receiving bank may charge REC Corp. a similar wire fee if they required a wire instead of an ACH as in the previous example.

# ATM Fees

Some people think ATM stands for automatic teller machine but it really stands for automatically take money. Everyone dreads the moment when they're jammed up for cash and have to use a rinky dink ATM with a $3 fee while getting a bonus $2 fee from their own bank. A $20 withdrawal gets wacked with 25% in fees.

# Special Privileges

Business bank accounts enjoy special fees just for being a business account such as:

- Minimum monthly balance fees up to $30
- Online access fees up to $15
- Cash processing fees for cash deposits
- Minimum balance limits required to avoid a fee

Individuals and businesses both get the honor of incurring these types of fees: [45]

- NSF check fees up to $35 (a check you bounced or authorized transaction that hit your account when it had insufficient funds)
- Returned deposit fees up to $20 (a check you received that bounced)
- Paper checks up to $50 or more per order
- Debit card replacement $5

- Human teller fees
- Cashier's check $10

## Paper Checks

Federal Reserve Banks provide check collection services for depository institutions or banks. A bank processes checks drawn on or written from the customer of another bank by either forwarding them directly to the paying bank, sending batches of checks to a check clearinghouse service or by using the services of the Federal Reserve. The bank that received checks is the collecting bank while the bank that pays the checks is the paying bank. Checks are now processed electronically thanks to Check 21, an Act that reduced federal paper check processing facilities from 45 to 1 as of 2010. Check writing is now a partially electronic yet declining Stone Age payment method still embraced by the check-writing generation. The cost of a check can be $4 to $20 considering the total lifecycle from check writing to reconciliation.

There are many more banking complexities not even covered in this section. By now, however, you should be able to better understand bitcoin's opposite and the three major symptoms of banking burnout: [46]

1. Paying a laundry list of different fees to use your own money
2. Waiting a long time to use your own money
3. Frustration and headaches of using your own money

*Same as it ever was.*

## Banking Burnout Bonanza Takeaway

Credit Card Chaos and Money Transfer Madness are as complicated as the Banking Burnout Bonanza. Our complex worldwide banking system is made up of hundreds of components including central banks, self-regulatory organizations, government agencies, private banks, third-party service providers, proprietary networks, middlemen, foreign currencies, standard protocols and different payment methods each with a different set of rules magnified by all the countries of the world. All of these things have been bolted on top of one another over the decades without fundamentally improving the system. In the old model the information about a transaction and the money in the transaction essentially take separate paths, which doubles the complexity.

It's time for an overhaul and thanks to bitcoin that time has come. Bitcoin turns hundreds of components and hundreds of different currencies into one simple system with one simple currency. Bitcoin is a network, a currency, and a protocol all at the same time. Let's dive in and find out more about bitcoin the beautiful.

# Bitcoin Simplified

By now you understand the opposite, the old money systems of yesterday, and are ready to explore the bitcoin paradigm, the new money system of the future. The old model is on one end and the new model is on the other end of the money possibility spectrum. You may experience some skepticism and wariness along the way. It's okay. Every bitcoin proponent went through some stage of skepticism because there is really no comparison and no reference point for bitcoin. But keep seeking to understand. The reward will be worth it.

## The Genesis

Satoshi Nakamoto, the mysterious person or group persona who created Bitcoin, authored a whitepaper on October 31, 2008, entitled, "Bitcoin: A Peer-to-Peer Electronic Cash System," which gave birth to bitcoin and led to release of the code. The first bitcoins were mined on January 3, 2009, and a few days later long-time crypto enthusiast, Hal Finney, became the first person to receive a bitcoin transaction from Satoshi. [47] Bitcoin is a peer-to-peer network; therefore, Satoshi and Hal were the first two peers, or nodes in the network. They both used their own computers to install the first version of the bitcoin code making it decentralized and distributed. In other words, no company was created to invest big money in a centralized network with servers, a chief technology officer, or proprietary technology and software code that would need to be updated by company employees and considered intellectual property.

More and more people got jazzed about the idea and installed the free code on their computers thus becoming the next peers, or nodes, in the network. Any of the peers are free to update the open source code, fix bugs or make improvements without permission; however, code changes are only accepted and implemented by majority agreement. The peers who contribute accepted code modifications are core developers.

## Currency & Cryptography

Bitcoin is a digital currency supported by software code based on cryptography, the math of infeasible, hard-to-break algorithms. Bitcoin, capitalized, refers to the technology that supports the digital currency and bitcoin, lowercase, refers to the digital currency itself. No one owns the Bitcoin code or network, but anyone can own bitcoin, the digital currency. There are also hundreds of other digital currencies besides bitcoin.

Bitcoin is the culmination of creative thinkers and cryptographers over the past couple decades who said, let's create new money and a new financial system from scratch using cryptography and thus eliminate the need for trust and centralization of power. There were several pre-bitcoin attempts to materialize the concept until bitcoin solved some of the previous challenges and gained traction. It's also easier to understand Bitcoin as a technology whose first use case happened to be a digital currency project called bitcoin. [48]

## No Printing or Minting

Bitcoin is completely digital because there are no bitcoin bills printed nor metal bitcoins minted. Many bitcoin icons and images depict bitcoin in the form of a metal coin; however, this is only for representational, marketing and other purposes. Various metal novelty bitcoins with zero value are available for those who like buying and collecting physical coins but there is no connection between novelty bitcoins and the real digital bitcoins. Casascius. com created physical, collectible coins embedded with bitcoins, but they're only available now as a novelty coin while some original Casascius coins are resold on eBay. Tgbex.com, The Global Bitcoin Exchange, makes limited edition physical coins in various metals including pure silver embedded with bitcoins ranging from .5 BTC to 20BTC. TGBEX is able to offer these coins because they are based in the bitcoin regulation-friendly, Isle of Man.

# Casascius Novelty Bitcoins

Image courtesy of Casascius Coins (www.casascius.com)

## Code, Nodes and Miners

Bitcoin code is open source software that has been continually improved by developers since its creation. Anyone can install the software for free but it's not necessary to buy bitcoin or make purchases in bitcoin. The people who install the code become a "node" in a peer-to-peer distributed network just like any Internet user is part of the Internet. The rules of the bitcoin game are woven into the code, essentially shifting from "In God We Trust" to "In Math We Trust."

An individual or business who sets up a node can also be a bitcoin miner who voluntarily supplies computing power via their own computers to support the network. Every miner is a node in the bitcoin network but not every node is a miner. Miners validate transactions, group them into blocks and add them to a public ledger called the blockchain. The first transaction between Satoshi and Finney became the genesis block. The blocks are like chain links added to an ever-growing unbreakable transaction chain. Their transaction-validating, security-providing, value-added computing power is rewarded by the mathematical release of bitcoins thus returning value back to the contributors.

## Example of a peer-to-peer computer network

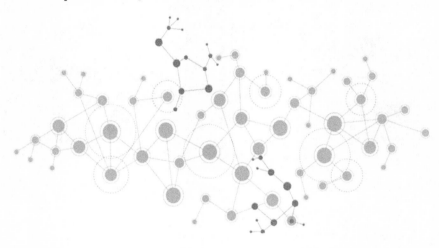

Image credit Thinkstock Photo (Rach 27)

## Contribution & Reward

The early node-installing hobbyists were essentially all bitcoin miners because anyone could participate by downloading the software and running it on an average personal computer. Bitcoin exchanges didn't exist and the only way to get bitcoin was to install the software, support the system and get rewarded with bitcoins. Miners use one-way hashing algorithms to calculate a winning number for a block of transactions, which is known as "solving the block," and thus earn the bitcoin block reward. The bitcoin reward started at 50 bitcoins per block and halves every four years. The miners are like students solving a math problem and the first one to solve the problem gets a bitcoin reward.

The solution to the problem includes a hash, a number that can't be reverse engineered, thus creating the unbreakable nature of the blockchain. A given block contains its own hash and the hash of the previous block, thereby linking the blocks together via interconnected hashes. For example, block number 52 includes the hash of block 52 and the hash of block 51. Block number 51 includes the hash of block 51 and the hash of block 50, and so on, forming the blockchain all the way back to the genesis block. The winning miner's solution is called a "proof of work" because all the losing miners can recalculate the winning solution, thus proving the work was done by the winner.

## Blockchain example with transaction blocks linked together with proof of work

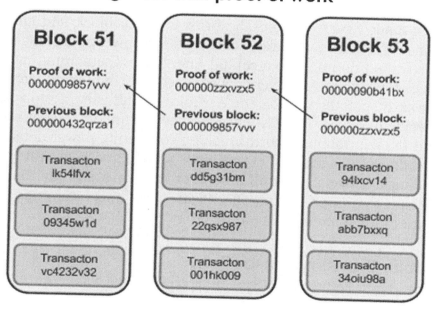

Image courtesy of a bitcoiner

Peter Van Valkenburgh, Coin Center Director of Research, sums up the miner's math competition as follows, "To prevent miners from fraudulently corrupting the blockchain, the Bitcoin protocol makes miners compete...The solution is to ask for a string that will be difficult to generate quickly, a specific sort of output string, one that starts with a certain number of zeros...That long line of zeros at the start of the hash is statistically improbable, like flipping a coin and getting heads thirteen times in a row...Nonetheless, there is a particular combination of hash inputs that will result in a hash output that starts with all those zeros...Eventually, one miner will happen upon an input that will give them a hash with the requested number of zeros at the start." [49]

Because miners are kept in the check by the competition, they are able to keep people and their transactions in check by making sure transactions have a valid signature and bitcoins are not counterfeit (e.g., previously spent) by cross-referencing the blockchain. This is the magical part of the technology that can be applied to multiple financial and non-financial applications.

Since first place gets the prize for each block and all other miners get nothing, the race for computing power or hashing power has turned mining into a capital-intensive, supercomputing arms race of big business server farms investing in, and manufacturing, the latest, greatest equipment. A whole new industry in application-specific hardware (ASICs) has emerged to support bitcoin mining and the continuous record-breaking computing power demanded by miners. The concept of mining is simple and beautiful yet the technical aspects could fill a book of their own and are therefore beyond the scope of this one. Please visit bitcoinmining.com to learn more about bitcoin mining. [50, 51]

## Public Domain Transactions

Blockchain transactions can be easily viewed via block explorer platforms such as blockchain.info, which also provides free bitcoin wallets. Transactions can be traced from a given day all the way back to the genesis block depending on how far back you want to search related transactions. Simply copy a bitcoin address and paste it in the search field of the block explorer. The transactions are in the public domain but generally the parties to the transactions are anonymous, thus creating pseudonymity where part of the transaction is transparent and part of the transaction is private. This combines the best of both worlds into one. The blockchain adds transparency value into the equation, which hasn't existed before in the course of human history. Bitcoins and the blockchain are identical because the transaction, the ownership of bitcoins, and the record of the transaction are one in the same. "What's the advantage of an online ledger transparent to anyone?" poses Jeffrey Carter, angel investor and trader. "Because in the real world, it's terrifically hard to trust anyone. Hard to even trust the words of a supposedly reputable business. Individuals and companies don't live up to their word. The blockchain would keep them in line." [52]

## Full Faith of Fiat

Bitcoin is on the opposite end of the spectrum from traditional fiat money, or money issued by governments, so it's difficult to look for direct ways to compare it. The end user experience of buying things and making payments online with credit cards and without using any physical bills or coins is the closest similarity to use of digital currency. In every other aspect, however, bitcoin is completely different. Bitcoin is digital cash and should be managed and treated with the respect of cold hard cash.

Bitcoin is a voluntary currency system and more importantly a choice for everyone around the world because it's not issued by a government or central banking authority. Fiat money is only backed by the full faith and credit of the issuing government therefore it has value because people are willing to trust their government and willing to accept it in exchange for goods and services. Fiat is Latin for "it shall be" or said another way "because I said so" and in this case the "I" is the government. Bitcoin is backed by the full faith of math which strips out backdoor manipulation and control in the hands of a few. On day one bitcoin had value as a complete off-the-shelf package including a network, a digital currency and a protocol woven together as one. Users equate bitcoin value to its security, simplicity, ease of use, almost no fee, frictionless, trustless, store of value and medium of exchange benefits. [53]

## Bitcoin Ecosystem

The entire bitcoin ecosystem is simply a network of users, exchanges, merchants, core developers, miners and other supporting services. Users simply buy or sell bitcoin or buy and sell goods and services with bitcoin. Exchanges are websites that allow users to buy and sell bitcoin and other cryptocurrencies using their own fiat currency. Merchants sell goods and services by accepting bitcoin as a form of payment. Developers contribute to the core bitcoin code by fixing bugs, adding features and improving efficiency and capacity. Bitcoin miners support the operation of the system by validating transactions and securing the bitcoin network. See the chapter on the bitcoin ecosystem for a more in-depth analysis.

## Buy Bitcoin, Sell Stuff

Miners started accumulating bitcoins but there weren't a whole lot of places to spend it. The challenge was getting merchants to adopt it and providing consumers an easy way to buy and spend it. Multiple bitcoin exchange sites have created an easy way to exchange bitcoin for fiat money and vice versa without having to become a node in the network. Meanwhile, payment service providers created tools for online and retail merchants to easily accept bitcoin.

## Push vs. Pull

Every customer, business or other user needs a bitcoin wallet to send and receive bitcoins. A wallet has a minimum of one bitcoin address and it can be a collection of multiple addresses roughly similar to a physical leather wallet containing multiple credit and debit cards. A bitcoin address is a public "send to" address for receiving bitcoins from other users or customers. In other words a customer would send bitcoin from their wallet to the public address of the business they're buying from. A public bitcoin address can be handed out to anyone without the fear of fraud akin to handing out a deposit-only account number. In addition, a bitcoin payment push is permanent and non-reversible.

A bitcoin wallet also has a corresponding private key, which is used as a digital signature that's needed to send bitcoin from an address, but they are not needed to receive bitcoin. Private keys are like a special digital pen used to sign and authorize bitcoin payments. A customer "pushes" bitcoin payments from their wallet to a business. Conversely, credit card payments and checks are permissions for banks to "pull" payments from an account, which also allows anyone who gets a bank account or credit card number to make fraudulent withdraws in a number of ways. Richard Gendal Brown, IBM banking innovation architect, gets straight to the point, stating, "It's easy to understand why the system was built the way: what else would you have done with 1960s technology? The pull model employed by the card processors is a wonder of the world. But it's also an artifact of its time. Would you design it that way if you were starting from scratch today?" 54

## An Oversimplified Example of How Bitcoin Works

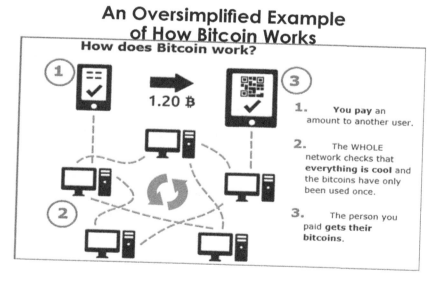

Image courtesy of bitcoin.org

Notice how the diagram is visually simpler than the one's for Credit Card Chaos and Money Transfer Madness, which feel confusing, cluttered and chaotic.

## UPS Tracking Analogy

You can also think about sending bitcoins as similar to shipping a package via United Parcel Service. Each block of transactions in the blockchain has a UPS-like tracking number called a hash. New transactions are grouped together in blocks of several hundred transactions where each block is like a UPS box filled with packaging peanuts labeled with a tracking number and loaded on a truck. The delivery is complete when the customer receives the scanned package. A bitcoin transaction is complete when its added to a transaction block and confirmed into the blockchain by miners' consensus with a hash that references the previous block all the way back to the first transaction. The status of a UPS package can be traced with its tracking number like a bitcoin transaction can be traced with its hash.

## Bitcoin Simplified Takeaway

Financial transactions in our current system are considered sacred personal information. Now imagine if you could log in and see every bank transaction for all Bank of America customers at the same time. This mind-blowing new paradigm means you can verify the amount of bitcoin in a bitcoin address and verify specific transactions in a publicly viewable ledger. You can see the transactions but you generally don't know whom they belong to. It demonstrates just how different the systems are.

When someone makes a bitcoin purchase, the transaction becomes part of a unified ledger called the blockchain. If the same purchase is made with a credit card, there could be seven or more parties involved, each one recording the transaction in their own books and records. The merchant records the sale, the customer records a purchase, the acquiring bank records interchange fees, the issuing bank records discount fees, and so on. This duplication of efforts demonstrates an extremely inefficient use of technology and human resources compared to a transaction in a single ledger. Bitcoin makes it as easy to pay someone halfway around the world as it is to pay your next-door neighbor. All the in-between third parties in bank, credit card and money transfer processes are reduced to simple peer-to-peer transactions.

Traditional bank account holders have to verify themselves via phone before asking a question or accessing their own information, usually in the process of solving some kind of account issue. Credit cards, debit cards and bank accounts are susceptible to fraud and everyone knows it's only a matter of time before their finances are hacked.

Bitcoin holders, on the other hand, call on themselves since they are 100% responsible for managing and safekeeping their bitcoin. The responsibility trade-off is a result of risk being shifted to each end user vs. handing over responsibility and control to a third-party. Fraud, too, is reduced to an unprofitable game in the bitcoin model where attacks would have to be made on millions of users instead of a few data silos of large corporations. Bitcoin reduces overall risk with a cost benefit proposition that solves the Credit Card Chaos, Money Transfer Madness and Banking Burnout Bonanza headaches. Banking holidays, banking hours, sudden rule changes, mystery fees and waiting for money are a thing of the past. Welcome to the new paradigm.

# Bitcoin Milestones

Bitcoin has some impressive milestones in just a few short years. A review of the some of these key milestones creates a context for understanding the momentum, VC investment, platform innovations and overall enthusiasm for this technology.

## Bitcoin Birthday

The mysterious Satoshi Nakamoto drafted the bitcoin concept in a whitepaper on October 31, 2008. Nakamoto mined block zero, the genesis block, on January 3, 2009, thus sending the first bitcoin transaction shortly thereafter. Bitcoin turned six years old in 2015.

## River of Capital

Venture capital investment was over $90 million in 2013 with about three-quarters of it coming from the United States. This doesn't include any capital invested from startup founders or other parties. VC investment in cryptocurrency startups through the end of 2014 topped $432 million, more than quadruple that of 2013, while outpacing early stage Internet investment from 1995. The projected 2015 investment run rate is $916 million. [55, 56, 57, 58]

Some notable VC investments include:

**March 13, 2014**

Xapo, a Palo Alto startup, offering ultra secure bitcoin cold storage vault services for bitcoin and digital currencies, raises $20 million. On July 8, 2014, Xapo raises another $20 million, setting a new record at the time for the most capital raised by a bitcoin startup. [59, 60]

**March 26, 2014**

Circle Internet Financial's consumer-facing, bitcoin-buying and spending platform raises $17 million, thus bringing its total venture capital investment to $26 million. [61]

**May 13, 2014**
BitPay, the leader in bitcoin payment processing services, raises $30 million in the largest investment round to date in the digital currency industry. [62]

**May 30, 2014**
BitFury raises $20 million, strengthening its lead as producer of ASIC mining hardware, hosted mining solutions and bitcoin mining operations. [63]

**June 16, 2014**
BitGo's enterprise-level, patent-pending, multi-signature wallet technology solves storage and security concerns for institutional investors and businesses catching investors' attention resulting in a $12 million funding round. [64]

**June 27, 2014**
Venture capitalist Tim Draper and his investment firm are the single winning bidder of almost 30,000 bitcoins in the U.S. Marshalls auction of the famed Silk Road bitcoin seizure. The value is around $19 million based on current rates at auction time. [65]

**October 7, 2014**
Bitcoin wallet and bitcoin charts provider, Blockchain.info, raises $30 million in its first round of outside financing. [66]

**January 20, 2015**
Universal bitcoin platform, Coinbase, sets another record with a $75 million funding round, grabbing attention with surprise investors including the New York Stock Exchange, USAA and BBVA, a large bank based in Spain.[67]

**March 10, 2015**
21, Inc., a stealth mode bitcoin startup, announces a $116 million all-star funding round shattering all previous funding rounds by bitcoin startups. 21 doesn't reveal its product offering or strategic plans with the announcement, leaving that open to speculation. [68]

## Miners Millions

In 2013, bitcoin miners invested $200 million in computer equipment and generated $300 million worth of revenue passing $1 million mined per day in November of that year. Eight mining pools account for over 80% of all the hashing or computing power while daily mining revenue averages more than $2 million per day through mid-2014, a doubling of 2013 revenue. Ghash.io launched in July 2013 and quickly became the largest mining pool reaching almost $250 million in mining revenue in one year. [69, 70, 71]

## Record Breaker

The bitcoin price rose 56 times in 2013 from a modest $13 at the beginning of the year making it the highest asset appreciation in history. The 2011 to 2013 compound annual growth rate racks up to 84,066%.

### October 5, 2009
First exchange rate established. 1 U.S.D. is worth 1,392.33 BTC, according to the New Liberty Standard.

### November 6, 2010
Bitcoin capitalization hits $1 million and bitcoins reach $.50 on the Mt. Gox exchange.

### March 28, 2013
Bitcoin breaks $1 billion and keeps on going throughout 2013.

### November 29, 2013
Bitcoin hits all-time high of $1,242 on Mt. Gox, representing a market capitalization of approximately $13 billion and surpassing Western Union, number one in the money transfer category, while landing in the fourth slot behind payment processors Visa and MasterCard. On the same day, one bitcoin is worth more than the spot price for an ounce of gold. [72, 73, 74]

# Roller Coaster

Bitcoin's rollercoaster ride demonstrates its continued resilience.

**June 8, 2011**
First bubble. Bitcoin prices crash after reaching a high of $31. By November, they're worth about $2 each.
**April 10, 2013**
Second bubble. Bitcoin reaches $266 on Mt. Gox then crashes on the back of hack attacks and exchange downtime.
**December 18, 2013**
Third bubble. China clamps down on Bitcoin, which sends prices downward to a low of nearly $300 after reaching a high of over $1,200. [75]

## Ready Regulators

Singapore shows its leadership and pro-business stance once again by quickly providing tax guidance for bitcoin transactions on January 8, 2014. Other countries are scratching their heads, trying to figure out how to tax bitcoin, while Singapore's IRAS steps up and writes clear, easy to understand rules. [76]

FinCEN, the U.S. Financial Crimes Enforcement Network, issues a statement on March 18, 2013, defining convertible virtual currency as a medium that can transfer value from one place to another or between persons with the ability to be exchanged for and valued in fiat currency. Bitcoin and virtual currencies fall under this definition. In addition, exchangers and administrators of convertible digital currencies have to register as an MSB, or money service business. [77]

## China Clampdown

The Central Bank of China orders all banks to shut down the accounts of all bitcoin exchange operators by April 15, 2014, threatening to punish banks that do not comply. This comes on the heels of China banning financial institutions from trading it a few months prior. Bitcoins could still be purchased with cash, however. [78]

## A National Law

Canada passes the first national bitcoin anti-money laundering law on June 19, 2014, requiring MSBs to register with FINTRAC. Foreign businesses providing services to Canadians or conducting business in Canada must also comply, creating another layer of navigational complexity. Banks are not allowed to open accounts for unregistered businesses. [79]

## Congressional Lovefest

The U.S. Senate Committee on Homeland Security & Governmental Affairs held the first congressional hearing on bitcoin on November 18, 2013. Senior Obama officials, the Director of FinCEN and officials from the Justice Department and the Secret Service recognized its potential with a sentiment towards avoiding stifling regulation. The hearing was generally considered a positive session for bitcoin while one article in The *Washington Post* called it a "bitcoin lovefest." [80]

## Hands Off Japan

The leading Liberal Democratic Party in Japan issues a statement on June 19, 2014, saying it will not regulate bitcoin for the time being even though a final decision is forthcoming. This was surprising news considering the infamous Mt. Gox implosion and bankruptcy happened in Japan. [81]

## Okay in the U.K.

The United Kingdom's HM Treasury issued a largely positive report on digital currencies in March 2015, a first attempt to consider regulatory and consumer issues. The report includes a framework for voluntary standards of consumer protection while intending to avoid an extreme regulatory burden. HM Treasury would also work closely with financial services regulator, the Financial Conduct Authority, to develop a "regulatory sandbox" within which bitcoin startups could experiment with ideas. The U.K is already a significant worldwide financial hub largely considered friendly towards digital currency companies. [82]

# New York BitLicense

New York becomes the first U.S. state to propose specially tailored digital currency regulations on July 17, 2014. Bitcoiners are outraged by the overreaching regulatory burden not to mention the short, 45-day response period. As Brad Delong points out, "If you borrow short and lend long, you're a bank, and if you don't, you're not a bank. Bitcoin businesses can't lend money like traditional banking but would effectively be subject to even more regulation. Much of the proposal mirrors existing federal and state regulations heading towards the full expense of getting a New York State banking license." [83]

Final New York Department of Financial Services BitLicense regulations are issued on June 3, 2015, creating a regulatory faction in the bitcoin community. The reaction was swift as digital currency exchange, ShapeShift.io, halted services to New York customers within days. ShapeShift CEO Eric Voorhees responded by saying, "Since New York has mandated unethical and dangerous data collection of users, we have no choice but to suspend service to that territory...We hope other jurisdictions will be less reckless with the private information of their residents. Finally digital commerce can be safe—if only regulators would let it happen." [84]

Meanwhile other well-funded bitcoin startups are moving full steam ahead for licensure. BitLicense chief architect, Ben Lawsky, announces the final rule, "We have a responsibility to regulate new financial products in order to help protect consumers and root out illicit activity. That is the bread and butter job of a financial regulator. However, by the same token, we should not react so harshly that we doom promising new technologies before they get out of the cradle. Getting that balance right is hard, but it is key." [85]

Public policy advocate, Coin Center, had this reaction, "The final version of the BitLicense is out and it has failed to address our two top concerns: an overbroad definition of virtual currency business activity and an unprecedented and discriminatory state-level, anti-money laundering regime. Our consolation today is that the future's looking bright on the other coastline. The current draft of California's equivalent legislation, AB 1326, is much better than the BitLicense." [86]

## Now Lawful and Not Like Lawsky

California, which previously prohibited anything but lawful money of the United States, passes a law effectively lifting the ban on bitcoin and other digital currencies. Roger Dickenson, the bill's author, states that community currencies are important payment systems between businesses and customers. [87] California's proposed digital currency regulations are more straightforward requiring licensure for any business maintaining full custody and control or combination of exchange services involving fiat and digital currencies while leaving AML (anti-money laundering) policies to the federal government, consistent with state money transmission laws. Coin Center concludes, "California is winning."

## First Sovereign Crypto

The first cryptocurrency of a sovereign nation is adopted by the traditional Lakota Nation from South Dakota, United States, as their national currency on February 23, 2014. They hope it will set the precedent for other countries to abandon their fiat currency. Altcoins have created the possibility for micro-nations to easily adopt a digital currency where they couldn't otherwise afford to produce their own fiat currency. [88] This is a classic technology breakthrough from something that couldn't be done before.

## Merry Merchants

Beginning in 2013 only a couple thousand merchants accepted bitcoin, but that number spiked to over 80,000 at the end of 2014, mostly comprised of Coinbase and BitPay customers. Some of the top Internet sites by Alexa ranking to accept bitcoin include wordpress.org, reddit.com, okcupid.com and namecheap.com. [89]

The following merchant milestones are part of the growing merchant adoption.

**January 7, 2014:** Overstock commits to becoming the first major retailer to accept bitcoin, recognizing its 2% margins have a lot to gain by eliminating its 2% cost of credit card fees.

**January 23, 2014:** Tiger Direct, the leading online electronics retailer, announces it will accept bitcoin through its online stores.

May 29, 2014: Satellite TV provider, Dish, with $13.9B in revenue, will start accepting bitcoin in July 2014.

**June 9, 2014:** i-Pmart, Malaysian e-commerce giant, announces it will accept bitcoin and hold 100% of the bitcoin it receives without converting it to fiat currency.

**June 12, 2014:** Expedia, one of the largest online travel services, accepts bitcoin for hotel bookings on its U.S. site. Its global VP says Expedia is in a unique position to solve travel booking by accepting bitcoin.

**June 16, 2014:** Digital River, a $30B online payment service provider, announces adding bitcoin as a payment option to its small- and medium-sized business service solution in the U.S.

**July 18, 2014:** Dell becomes the world's largest e-commerce business to accept bitcoin with revenue nearly four times that of DISH Network.

December 11, 2014: Microsoft becomes the largest company in the world to accept bitcoin with $86 billion in revenue and $172 billion in total assets.

## Bitcoin Conferences

One of the first official bitcoin conferences was held in San Jose, CA, on May 17, 2013. Now there are dozens of major conferences held around the world in 2015 and beyond hosted by different organizers focused on specific areas such as finance, banking and venture capital to more general themes.

## Wild Wallets

Blockchain.info, the most popular bitcoin site, had its 1,000,000th bitcoin wallet download on January 6, 2014, up from only 100,000 at the start of 2013. It finished out 2014 with 2.8 million wallet downloads. There were almost 8 million total wallet downloads through the end of 2014. [90, 91]

## That's Fast

Transaction blocks are solved based on a target difficulty level and the more difficult the target the more computing power it takes to solve. The hash rate in gigahashes per second is used to describe the combined computing power of the bitcoin network rising from about 12,500,000 GH/s to 325,000,000 GH/s over a one-year period in 2014. Likewise, the difficulty level for solving a block rose from about 825,000,000 to about 45,000,000,000 over the same period. One gigahash is a billion hashes per second; therefore, bitcoin mining equipment, ASICs, essentially guess the answer to the difficult target number billions of times per second. The hashing power of ASICs and the combined power of the network are scaling to calculate in terahashes or trillions of hashes per second, petahashes or quadrillions of hashes per second and beyond. This explains the incredible investment in and innovation race for specialty-designed ASIC mining hardware. [92]

## Bitcoin Dominance

Coinmarketcap.com lists 490 cryptocurrencies with a total marketization of $3,619,431,069 in mid-January 2015. Bitcoin claims over 80% of the total market even after several days of significant price declines during the same period.

# The Top 10 Cryptocurrencies

| # | Name | Symbol | Market Cap | Price | Available Supply | Volume (24h) |
|---|------|--------|-----------|-------|-----------------|-------------|
| 1 | Bitcoin | BTC | $ 2,871,902,786 | $ 209.17 | 13,730,125 | $ 59,049,700 |
| 2 | Ripple | XRP | $ 519,359,822 | $ 0.016765 | 30,978,075,200 * | $ 2,164,340 |
| 3 | Litecoin | LTC | $ 49,731,793 | $ 1.40 | 35,625,004 | $ 3,203,690 |
| 4 | PayCoin | XPY | $ 46,774,807 | $ 3.79 | 12,344,602 ** | $ 167,332 |
| 5 | BitShares | BTS | $ 26,680,608 | $ 0.010681 | 2,497,973,773 * | $ 250,433 |
| 6 | Stellar | STR | $ 16,608,205 | $ 0.004654 | 3,568,947,600 * | $ 140,691 |
| 7 | MaidSafeCoin | MAID | $ 14,877,163 | $ 0.032874 | 452,552,412 * | $ 6,670 |
| 8 | Dogecoin | DOGE | $ 13,448,109 | $ 0.000138 | 97,536,999,100 | $ 629,408 |
| 9 | Nxt | NXT | $ 12,410,564 | $ 0.012411 | 999,997,096 * | $ 39,036 |
| 10 | Peercoin | PPC | $ 7,117,022 | $ 0.323294 | 22,014,087 | $ 105,808 |

Image courtesy of coinmarketcap.com,
Crypto-Currency Market Capitalizations, 1-16-15

## Through No Fault of Bitcoin

In October 2013 the Feds shut down the Silk Road website and arrest 29-year-old Ross Ulbricht for alleged narcotics trafficking, computer-related fraud, and money laundering. The U.S. Marshals later sell at auction the bitcoins seized in the bust. Bitcoins had nothing to do with the seizure. They were just in the wrong place at the wrong time.

## Final Goxxing

All trading was halted on Mt. Gox, the original bitcoin exchange, on February 25, 2014, ultimately resulting in a $450 million bankruptcy filing in a case of the missing bitcoins. Disgruntled customers greeted founder Mark Karpeles in front of the corporate office with signs like, "Mt Gox, are you solvent?" and "Mt. Gox, where is our money?" This prompted the government of Japan to hold hearings on the regulation of bitcoin.

## Bitcoins & Bloomberg

After getting hundreds of requests from customers, Bloomberg lists bitcoin prices for the first time on April 30, 2014, for its 320,000 subscribers. Hedge funds, banks, institutional investors and professional investors all use Bloomberg terminals, so the listing gave bitcoin a major stamp of approval while becoming a true bitcoin milestone.

## Bitcoin Rank

According to Coinometrics, which specializes in institutional-level bitcoin data and research, bitcoin is the 79th most valuable currency out of 191 countries as of June 30, 2014, based on a market cap of under $9 billion. Basically the value of a given fiat currency in circulation is determined by an M1 analysis to determine its total value for purposes of this ranking. [93]

## The Wrong Face of Bitcoin

Newsweek publishes an article in March 2014 titled, "Bitcoin's Face: The Mystery Man Behind the Crypto-Currency," claiming Dorian Satoshi Nakamoto, living modestly in California, was the real Satoshi Nakamoto. Many bitcoin enthusiasts thought the article was overreaching in its attempt to revive the magazine. Andreas Antonopoulos organized a bitcoin fundraising drive to support Dorian for being wrongly identified as bitcoin's creator.

## Bitcoin ATM

On October 29, 2013, Robocoin installed the first bitcoin ATM in Waves Coffee House in Vancouver, Canada, with over $10,000 in transactions on the first day. This is the start of a worldwide explosion of ATM installations. [94]

## O-"bit"-uaries

Somehow Bitcoin keeps dying over and over again according to nearly 75 headlines posted in blogs and articles reading: "Why Bitcoin Will Fail As A Currency," "So, That's the End of Bitcoin Then" and "Why Bitcoin is doomed to fail," as noted on bitcoinobituaries. com in June 2015. [95]

## Bitcoin Milestones Takeaway

Milestones are a great way to see something from a different viewpoint and bitcoin milestones are no different. Regulation is a significant and ongoing topic that will be addressed in other chapters such as Regulatory Zigzagging. New milestones will be achieved as Bitcoin technology is adopted and applied across multiple disciplines.

There have been some amazing records in investments, price appreciation, wallet downloads, market cap, hashing, mining revenue and merchant adoption. These records will be broken or have already been broken and provide a forecast of Bitcoin's trajectory and future picture. What milestone will you and your business add to the list?

# Bitcoin Ecosystem

Just like any ecosystem the bitcoin ecosystem is comprised of many complex components some of which are analogous to components in the traditional financial system. It's easier to understand the whole bitcoin ecosystem by reviewing a summary of the various pieces. Much of this ecosystem will be highlighted in more detail while other parts are beyond the scope of this book.

**Bitcoin miners** are like computer farms that provide transaction confirmation, validation and network security by voluntarily supplying computing power. They are now mainly comprised of syndicates or groups who pool mining power and make significant investment in computer equipment. The first miner to solve a block of transactions is rewarded bitcoins for adding it to the blockchain ledger as the entire network confirms it. Solving transaction blocks is a method for securing the decentralized network by using computers to calculate a very difficult target number established by the bitcoin protocol. Computers guess the target number billions of times per second in a process called mining.

**Bitcoin nodes** are computers running the bitcoin core client, the software, including a complete download of the Bitcoin blockchain. All the nodes collectively form the bitcoin network and propagate transactions across the network after performing various validity checks. Miners group the transactions and start solving blocks as described above. Every miner is a node but not every node is a miner.

**Bitcoin mining hardware suppliers** manufacture specialized computer equipment with the main purpose of solving transaction blocks as fast as possible. ASICs, or Application Specific Integrated Circuits, are the latest evolution in bitcoin supercomputing. They're likely to evolve into the next generation of specialized equipment the same way ASICs evolved from simple CPU mining. Some manufacturers are also bitcoin miners while cloud-based mining services allow anyone to participate in bitcoin mining.

**Bitcoin exchanges** provide a service that allows individuals and businesses to buy and sell bitcoin with their respective fiat currency. Hundreds of altcoins can also be traded depending on the platform in a digital currency to digital currency transaction without any fiat. Bitcoin is usually required to start buying altcoins although multiple trading pairs exist for the various altcoins. The exchanges also provide a price discovery mechanism and market liquidity ranging from simple trading to complex trading tools and analysis for institutional investors.

**Bitcoin payment service providers** are web-based platforms allowing retail and online merchants to accept bitcoin and other cryptocurrencies as payment for goods and services. They have shopping cart plug-ins, dashboards to manage payments, payment terminals and other tools including simple email invoicing. This is roughly similar to PayPal and other credit card processors.

**Bitcoin wallet services** allow users to send and receive bitcoin or buy and sell things with bitcoin. A wallet is simply software, a web-based or mobile application with a collection of bitcoin addresses. Wallets may be provided as part of an exchange service or payment service provider. There are many different types of wallets and reasons for using them, including whether or not you are a business or consumer, frequency of use and amount of bitcoins stored. Wallets are covered in extensive detail in another chapter.

**Security, compliance and technology services** companies provide the technology and the implementation services for bitcoin exchanges, wallet providers and other specialized services required by bitcoin businesses. In some cases the service may be a white label technology platform. Other services specialize in the security aspect of bitcoin-related services. Verification and AML/KYC compliance services deliver customer verification services for exchanges and compliance programs required by KYC (know your customer) and AML (anti-money laundering) regulations. These services are also known as infrastructure services.

**Bitcoin directory and social networking sites** provide directories for business listings and/or individual profiles, which may include a Facebook-like social networking component. The directories may include numerous other features beyond the listing service. Some bitcoin-related social sites are designed specifically for the bitcoin community.

**Bitcoin core developers** contribute to the ongoing development and improvement of the bitcoin protocol. Generally, anyone who submits a GitHub pull request for a proposed improvement later adopted into the code is considered a core developer. There are just a few people who are considered the main core developers.

**Alternative protocol developers** create new open source platforms or APIs generally published on GitHub or their respective websites freely available to anyone. Entrepreneurs can use these tools to create new business models or to interface with existing systems. A new protocol may be a new alternative to bitcoin or an altcoin.

**Altcoins and other cryptocurrencies** are alternatives to bitcoin with several hundred different types that may vary by their intentions, use and protocol. These altcoins can be traded on certain exchanges for fiat currency or other altcoins as well as used for payments for goods and services depending on the coin.

**Supporting services** are platforms developed to support bitcoin consumers and businesses such as tax reporting tools, analytics, price feeds and a multitude of other apps.

**News sites** are 100% focused on reporting the best news and information happening in the bitcoin universe. In addition, blogs and forums provide a platform for anyone in the bitcoin community to interact, ask questions or make comments.

**Global conferences** host a gathering of the best and brightest minds in bitcoin to speak on emerging topics, new startups and the latest trends to share ideas and, most importantly, create a networking environment. They also include vendors in many of the categories listed here who may also be speakers in the conference. The conferences may also be geared toward a specific angle or be more general in nature.

**Venture capital and startup incubators** supply the capital and mentoring necessary for startups to get from a minimum viable product or concept phase to a commercially viable product or service. Many bitcoin-only-focused venture capital groups have recently emerged.

**Hybrid or universal services** combine many of the above components into a single platform making it challenging to categorize or group them into a single category. For example, some platforms have combinations of components such as a payment service provider, an exchange, a wallet and analytics while others continue to add components to gain a competitive advantage.

## Bitcoin Ecosystem Takeaway

The Bitcoin ecosystem is continuing to evolve with the emergence of universal platforms due to competition and scale while grabbing a disproportionate share of venture capital investment in 2015. Infrastructure platforms are also evolving into infrastructure as a service, including white-label platforms. Bitcoin's growth will accelerate from wider application of the technology in the financial sector and an increased appetite for blockchain data analytics. Wallet services will evolve into storage of multiple digital currencies and digital assets interoperable with multiple platforms, especially mobile apps, while melding our financial lives into a seamless user experience.

# Bitcoin Tipping Point

## Gladwell Tipping

In his book *The Tipping Point*, Malcolm Gladwell examines the factors that lead to exponential growth for many different products and trends. The three key points that result in the tip to widespread popularity and adoption are The Law of the Few, Stickiness, and the Power of Context. [96] Bitcoin has a strong case for all three.

What things will influence the bitcoin tipping point? When will the tipping point happen? Has the tipping point already happened? A review of the chapter on bitcoin milestones makes it look like the tipping point has arrived. The more likely case is that we're on the cusp of the tipping point in 2015 with lots of opportunity for existing as well as new and emerging businesses to create new business models that thrive in the bitcoin universe.

## The Few

The Law of the Few says that a few key influential people must champion an idea to move it toward the tipping point. There are clearly many key people who are championing Bitcoin from the CEOs of startups to the venture capitalists investing in them. All you have to do is review the speaker profiles for an event like Inside Bitcoins to conclude that champions are leading the way at light speed. [97]

## Sticky

Stickiness is the factor that gets people to pay very close attention to a product, trend or TV show. Often the unconventional nature of something contrary to the norm creates the stickiness necessary for the tip. Bitcoin is without a doubt an unconventional system combined with a whole new paradigm for the way we use, spend and keep money. Bitcoin could be called "stickycoin" for its disruptive potential as a medium of exchange and the broader application of the blockchain for transforming both financial and non-financial models.

## Context

The power of context relates to the environment where the product or trend is introduced. If the timing or environment is not right then the tipping point can't be attained. Consumers and businesses share frustrations with payment processors, government control of money, difficulty of transferring money and traditional banks. Credit cards and personal identifiable information security breaches have become exorbitantly costly. This old rail, gigantic silo information model has proven ineffective. Now is the perfect timing between bitcoin and breaches.

## Recipe for Tipping

The bitcoin tipping point recipe is a mixture of regulation, consumers, businesses, technology, ease-of-use, perceived benefit, frustration with current systems, investment, problem solving and many other factors. In some cases Bitcoin benefits for one group are detriments to another such as the benefit of no sales chargebacks to merchants may be a perceived detriment to the consumer because they can't dispute charges as they're able to do with credit cards.

## Adoption Life Cycle

The technology adoption life cycle is based on a widely accepted concept called "the diffusion process" published in 1957 by Joe M. Bohlen, George M. Beal and Everett M. Rogers. The authors explain technology adoption based on the demographic and psychological profiles of different groups of adopters, and how new ideas spread through communication channels and social systems over a period of time.

## The Diffusion Process

A normal distribution bell curve mirrors the adoption process moving from "innovators" to "early adopters" then to "early majority," "late majority," and finally, "laggards." Normal distributions have predictable percentages for each of the stages; therefore, the percentage of a population can be calculated for a given stage. For example, the innovators represent 2.5% of the total population while the early adopters represent 13.5%. A worldwide population of seven billion people rounded to the nearest whole number, times 2.5%, equals 150 million people who will eventually represent the innovators. Statistics reveal that 150 million people are not using bitcoin in 2015, but as the innovators continue to come on board, the "majority" will certainly follow.

## The Diffusion of Innovations

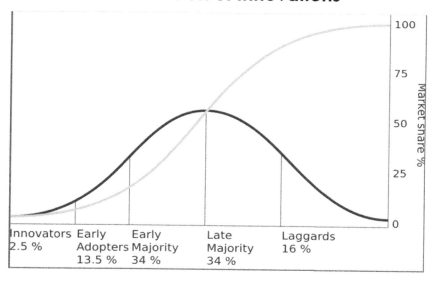

Image courtesy of Everett Rogers in the public domain

With successive groups of consumers adopting the new technology (shown in blue), its market share (yellow) will eventually reach the saturation level. [98]

## 1/10% Adoption

Reddit posts and various articles attempt to estimate the number of bitcoin users including bitcoin client software downloads, the number of wallet downloads, registered forum users, and site popularity. If we round the number of bitcoin users to 7,000,000 at the end of 2014, then the percentage calculates to a 1/10% adoption rate of the world population of 7,000,000,000 which puts bitcoin at the very beginning of the innovators stage. To put this into greater perspective, the Internet is celebrating its 20th birthday in 2014 with a worldwide adoption of less than 50%, which lands it at the top of the technology adoption life cycle. Jeremy Allaire, founder of Circle, said, "Bitcoin is in the 1994 pre-Netscape era of the Internet" and that mainstream adoption would likely happen in 2024.[99] By that time, bitcoin will be in the early majority stage, consistent with the adoption and progression of the Internet we've seen over the last two decades. Given the magnitude of the Internet, we should not underestimate the social influence of bitcoin innovators and early adopters.

## The Only Thing Comparable

Adam Ettinger, managing partner of Strategic Council Corp. and a specialist in technology law, helped numerous clients navigate the pioneering days of the early Internet. He recently pondered the question, is bitcoin past the tipping point? After contemplating multiple paradigm shifts and disruptive technologies, he concluded, "The only thing to which I can compare bitcoin digital currencies with any justice is the commercialization of the Internet itself from 1994 to 1996."

Ettinger's four tipping point indicators are:

1. Technology is not just an improvement but a fundamental change in how people do things and how they can make money. From what has already been outlined it's clear that bitcoin is a fundamental change in how people use and spend money.

2. Courts find it difficult to apply the law and legal experts agree that the laws must change before technology can make significant advances. If the laws don't change, it would otherwise stifle technology adoption. The regulation

debate is one the biggest ongoing topics in bitcoin right now.

3. The investment community funds every area of an entire ecosystem. Venture capital has invested in just about every area of the bitcoin ecosystem. The bitcoin ecosystem chapter lays out the diversity of the system while the bitcoin milestones pages highlight the astonishing investment being made in the cryptocurrency model.

4. The public is captivated by new technology even if they don't know how to use it. It's probably safe to say that captivation is way ahead of widespread use.

Ettinger concludes, "The Internet fundamentally overhauled how everyone would do nearly everything just as bitcoin will enable the same scope of change, and we are past tipping point." [100]

## Network Effect

Metcalfe's Law, also known as the "network effect," was a term originally used to describe the Ethernet and networks of communication devices. [101] It has since evolved and gained even more relevance as the Web has evolved and we've seen a proliferation of connectivity via social media, for example. The network effect explains the value of a network as roughly the square of the number of connected users. If the number of users is N, then the value of the network is N squared, therefore a network with 1000 users has an approximate value of 1,000,000 and so on as illustrated in the diagram below. [102] As 2014 worldwide smart phone adoption passes 25%, the network infrastructure already exists for a massive bitcoin network effect considering the many bitcoin apps available today. Smart phone adoption will continue to accelerate in developing countries as 2.5 billion "unbanked" people with Internet access can instantly become their own bank and transfer value anywhere in the world with bitcoin apps including some that allow users to send bitcoin via text messages.

# The network effect shown by the possible connections of a telephone network

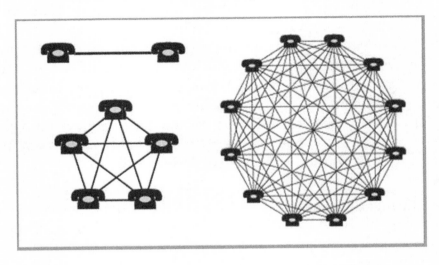

Image courtesy of Derrick Coetzee in the public domain

## Bitcoin Tipping Point Takeaway

Has bitcoin reached the tipping point? It appears there is no right or wrong answer to this since an analysis of different theories results in different conclusions. Your response will be based on your own point of view and definition of tipping point. An analysis of the diffusion of innovations and technology adoption lifecycle may lead some to think bitcoin is just ramping up while others may draw a different conclusion or give more weight to different set of metrics. Regardless of where bitcoin is in the adoption cycle, it is clear that bitcoin has serious momentum given the millions in venture capital investment and a path correlating with Internet adoption and innovation. Stickiness, context, communication channels and social influence are powerful contributors to adoption while the regulatory lag could create a gravitational slowdown. The network effect may overcome all obstacles if the intrinsic value of the bitcoin network and blockchain live up to expectations.

Opportunity is always present and available in the beginning stages of anything. Congratulations on discovering bitcoin in the early opportunity stage with the scales "tipping" in your favor as it were. It's like discovering the Internet all over again in 1994 when there were just 2,700 websites! Now is the time to go out there and seize the opportunity while we're on the verge of what could be the greatest "network effect" we've ever seen.

# Bitcoin Billions

## What's the fair value of bitcoin?

Does the price of bitcoin on a given day reflect its true value? If the market price doesn't reflect value, how can we figure out what the value is? This is an oft-heated debate among economists, cynics, bitcoiners, venture capitalists, research analysts and others. There's a valuation model and a market for every type of asset and bitcoin already has a price index so we just need a valuation model to reel in the debate and put a stake in the ground.

Gil Luria, managing director of equity research for Wedbush Securities, summed up the challenge in September 2014, stating, "Bitcoin is unlike any financial instrument that existed before it, which makes it so much more difficult to value. The range of potential outcomes is so great (in my mind between $0 and $1 million) that it is much harder to value than stocks and small changes to its potential change its value dramatically." [103]

Following is an array of different approaches to weave in and help you relate the new bitcoin paradigm to existing frameworks.

## Intrinsic Inspiration

ALFAquote.com has created a model to calculate the fair value of bitcoin relative to the market price of bitcoin inspired by the principles of Benjamin Graham's value investing model for determining the intrinsic value of an asset. Denis Hertz, ALFAquote product manager, says, "Venture capitalists assign 'beyond the clouds' figures of $100,000. Financiers, who are far away from technology, say bitcoin has no intrinsic value. We decided to do the job of a fair price measurement that will help investors assess the attractiveness of bitcoin." The model, however, is more closely tied to metrics for valuing gold, which already draws a range of conclusions from analysts.

In this case the ALFAquote model uses a bitcoin mining-based formula by considering the dance among the change in the cost of mining equipment, mining equipment performance or hashing power, and factors of production like electricity costs. For example, a review of the ALFAquote chart shows the difference between bitcoin fair value of $466 and bitcoin market price of $251 on March 25, 2015, as the bitcoin price potential of $215 or 85.6%. Said another way bitcoin is undervalued by $215 based on this formula. [104]

## $10,000 bitcoins

Tim Draper, partner at venture capital firm Draper Fisher Jurvetson, whose firm purchased all 30,000 Silk Road bitcoins in the infamous U.S. Marshall's auction in June 2014, is bullish on bitcoin. Of bitcoin's potential value, Draper proclaims, "I guess the markets aren't seeing what I'm seeing. An entire economy is being rebuilt. I have a price target of $10,000 in three years. Even that may be pessimistic." This September 2014 statement is worth paying attention to given Draper's long and successful track record for capitalizing on emerging opportunities. Even though he doesn't give a hard and fast formula, he goes on to back his claim with this assertion, "It's a new way of storing capital, and a new way of moving capital. Faster money means a better economy." [105]

## Outperform

Gil Luria and Aaron Turner, equity research analysts at Wedbush Securities, assessed the fair price of bitcoin by analyzing the price target of the Bitcoin Investment Trust (GBTC), the first over-the-counter NASDAQ-listed bitcoin investment fund, launched in 2015. "We see BTC as a financial instrument the likes of which has not previously existed, which requires a new valuation approach," say Luria and Turner, who describe bitcoin as more like equity in a payment network. They go on to say, "However, since BTC does not generate cash flow like an equity, we use a commodity-like valuation approach that values each BTC as a 'packet' in limited supply that fuels the bitcoin network."

## Superior Alternative

The demand for bitcoin will come from payment applications, which are significantly better than the alternatives. Three applications for potential worldwide bitcoin disruption include cross-border online payments, remittances and micropayments resulting in a 10%, 20% and 20% penetration, respectively, by 2025. Additional use cases and factors accelerating bitcoin adoption include the following:

- Bitcoin as a banking alternative in distressed economies such as Greece
- Machine-to-machine transactions, aka "The Internet of Things"
- Anchor for other blockchain applications in various industries
- Third-party trust-based services accounting for 20% of U.S. GDP and being ripe for disruption
- Well-known incumbents embracing bitcoin and incorporating it into their business models

## Global Working Capital

The present value of the price of bitcoin of $409 is necessary to support the expected level of economic activity in 2025 compared to the current price of BTC of $270 on July 7, 2015, as used in the report. The economic activity is mainly comprised of penetration of the three payment applications described above. This also equates to a $40 price target for GBTC, which serves as a proxy to the bitcoin price at a ratio of 1/10. The analysis distinguishes between bitcoin held for investment and bitcoin held for working capital (i.e., store of value vs. medium of exchange) starting at 26% and 74%, respectively, in 2015. Interestingly, the amount of bitcoin held for investment is estimated to decline by 2% per year to 4% in 2025 with a corresponding 96% held as working capital. The amount of working capital bitcoins becomes the amount of bitcoins available for transactions used as a substitute for alternative payment methods.

## The Expected Value

The analysts provided an alternative view including the weighted average of potential outcomes, which is a classic expected value calculation with a price spread ranging from zero to $1,000,000. In the worst case, with a 50% probability, bitcoin is taken over by a superior altcoin, or, an unforeseen Achilles heel leads to its demise. In the best case, with a .02% probability, it becomes the global working capital of trade. The middle outcome, dubbed the "PayPal Outcome," has a 49.98% probability of being the alternate payment method of choice. The expected value of the three possibilities is shown in the chart below at $400, including comparable valuations of payment providers.

## Bitcoin Valuation Framework

**Figure 2: Bitcoin Valuation Framework**

| | Outcome | $/BTC | Probability | Probability Weighed |
|---|---|---|---|---|
| "Napster" Outcome | - Overtaken by another coin<br>- Fatal flaw uncovered<br>- Broadly made illegal with strict enforcement | $0 | 50.00% | $0 |
| "PayPal" Outcome | - Specific use cases take hold (e.g. remittance, micro transactions, machine-to-machine, etc.) | $400 | 49.98% | $200 |
| "Internet" Outcome | - Bitcoin becomes global working capital of trade ($20 trillion monetary base) | $1,000,000 | 0.02% | $200 |
| | | | Probability-weighted outcome | $400 |

*Source: Wedbush Securities, Inc.*

**Figure 3: Comparable Valuations ($M)**

| | Ticker | Market cap | P/E 2015 | 2016 |
|---|---|---|---|---|
| Visa | V | $132,655 | 25.9x | 22.4x |
| Mastercard | MA | 104,792 | 26.8x | 22.6x |
| American Express | AXP | 78,775 | 14.0x | 13.4x |
| PayPal | PYPL | 44,340 | | |
| Discover Financial | DFS | 25,816 | 10.9x | 10.0x |
| Western Union | WU | 9,862 | 11.6x | 11.1x |
| Square | | 6,000 | | |
| Stripe | | 5,000 | | |
| Bitcoin | BTC | 3,807 | | |
| Blackhawk Network | HAWK | 2,273 | 18.9x | 16.7x |
| Green Dot | GDOT | 988 | 13.7x | 12.4x |
| MoneyGram | MGI | 459 | 11.9x | 8.8x |

*Source: Company data, Wedbush Securities, Inc.*

Image courtesy of Wedbush Securities, Inc.

The huge differences in the range of outcomes means that a tiny change in perception could result in a giant swing in price. Luria and Turner say it like this: "If market perception of the likelihood of the best case outcome changes by .01%, that could drive a $100 change in current valuation, or >30% in today's prices." [106]

## The Monetary Base and Demand Angle

Ryan Selkis, Director of Investments at Digital Currency Group, takes the following approach in an Investopedia article called "An Easy Way to Measure Bitcoin's Fair Market Value." The total market value of a currency known as its monetary base is a combination of its transactional and reservation demand. Transactional demand is the amount of currency used for everyday purchases for goods and services while reservation demand is the amount of currency stored for long-term savings. The amount of currency needed to satisfy transactional demand is similar to the M1 money supply, an economic term for cash and deposits, and when combined with the amount of currency needed to satisfy reservation demand, both are similar to the M2 money supply, an economic term for savings and money market accounts plus M1.

Selkis says, "Theoretically, the fair market value of one bitcoin should simply be the dividend of its predicted future monetary base and bitcoin in circulation, discounted by a 'hurdle rate' an investor would require in order to invest in the speculative currency."

## Present Value

If bitcoin's monetary base grows to a conservative $1 trillion dollars in 10 years with a known amount of bitcoins in circulation of 21,000,000 then a bitcoin would be worth $50,000 in 2024. A present value calculation brings bitcoin to a value of $455 in 2014, considering an investor's 12% required rate of return grossed up to 60% for being five times more risky or volatile than growth stocks. The 2014 present value closely matches actual bitcoin prices, but swings in the assumptions create a wide range of possible values. Selkis goes on to explain that a fair value for bitcoin would be $7,250 if you double the monetary base and halve the rate of return. The present value calculation of a future estimated monetary base is a simple yet important calculation because the number of bitcoins in circulation is known with 100% certainty. Conversely, no one knows how much fiat currency will be circulating in 10 years and a similar calculation applied to a given fiat results in a wide range of values and a much lower statistical confidence level.

## Fair Value of a Transaction Mechanism

Eric Gravengaard, an equity derivatives portfolio manager, compared existing payment systems with bitcoin to determine a possible bitcoin fair value in a whitepaper titled, "What is a Bitcoin Worth as a Transaction Mechanism?" Visa, Western Union and PayPal transmitted $7 trillion, $400 billion and $179 billion through their respective payment channels in 2013. Gravengaard's hypothesis states, "We now present a valuation model that uses demand for transactions with comparable payment technologies as a method of establishing a price target for the value of Bitcoin. We assume that if the demand for on-chain Bitcoin transactions increases, the price of Bitcoin will rise keeping the velocity of Bitcoin constant." [107]

## Thin Velocity

At the time of publication of the whitepaper in February 2014, about 100,000 bitcoins or $52 million USD were moved from one wallet to another, representing a velocity of 1% out of a total bitcoin supply of about 12,000,000. The value of a bitcoin necessary for the Bitcoin network to match the transactional volume of Visa, PayPal and Western Union would be $958,000, $56,000 and $25,000 USD, respectively. While the underlying calculations are not clearly defined, essentially the velocity or the amount of bitcoins transacted would hover between 1-2% forcing the price of bitcoin to skyrocket if bitcoin replaced one of the existing payment models. The predictable supply of bitcoins is again the key factor in the assumption because the number of bitcoins in circulation can be calculated at any time in the past present or future. When the currency supply is fixed and determinable, as in the case of bitcoin, the direct relationship between price and transaction volume means that when one goes up the other has to go up. [108]

## Bitcoin Bubble

David Woo, an FX and rates strategist at Bank of America and one of the most respected researchers on Wall Street, set out with his team to find a fair value for bitcoin. Their analysis helps answer the question, "Is Bitcoin a Bubble?" in light of its almost 100-fold increase in 11 months during 2013.

## The Three Attributes

Money has three attributes: 1) A unit of account, 2) a medium of exchange, and 3) a store of value. The unit of account attribute allows the value of anything to be expressed consistently. For example, the value of computers, cars and tables stated in yen can be easily understood relative to one another.

According to Woo, bitcoin has many benefits as a medium of exchange but comes up short as a unit of account and a store of value. Bitcoin's volatility undermines its contribution as a store of value, which is closely tied to its value as a unit of account. Using the previous example, a new car and a new computer could end up on the books as 10 BTC because the computer was purchased when the price of bitcoin was higher while the car was purchased when the price of bitcoin was much lower, even though everyone knows that cars cost more than computers. [109]

## The 3 Milestones

Bitcoin's value as a medium of exchange and a store of value are more closely examined to figure out a possible intrinsic value for bitcoin. Woo identified three things that need to happen to support the implied fair value of bitcoin at a maximum market value of $15 billion or 1 BTC equaling $1,300 USD.

1. Bitcoin needs to account for 10% of all global e-commerce, business-to-consumer (B2C) transactions.
2. Bitcoin has to become one of the top three players in the money transfer industry.
3. Bitcoin's value as a store of value has to equal the price of silver. [110]

Determining bitcoin's intrinsic value as a medium of exchange requires evaluating both 1 and 2 above while a determination of bitcoin's intrinsic store of value is looked at separately.

## 10% of Global B2C

Woo looked at household checking and cash deposits relative to total U.S. consumer spending, or B2C, in 2012, determining that the average American holds 4% of their annual household purchases in cash. For example, a family that spends $30,000 on all of their household expenses has 4% or $1,200 in the bank or in cash at any given time. People spend a certain amount of money and hold a much smaller portion of that at any point in time, regardless of whether it's fiat currency or bitcoin.

U.S. e-commerce reached $244 billion in 2012 so that means that 4% or $10 billion was held in bank accounts and old-fashioned wallets. Assume 10% of the $10 billion, or $1 billion worth of bitcoin, is held for consumer spending. Since U.S. GDP is 20% of world GDP, $5 billion in bitcoin would be held for consumer spending worldwide with all other assumptions being equal. If bitcoin were used for 10% of global B2C spending, then its medium of exchange value would be $5 billion, simply by swapping dollars for bitcoin. [111]

## Money Transfer Madness

Remember this chapter? Money transfers are a medium of exchange where one party wants to send money to another contrasted with using money to buy things. This must be considered in determining a total medium of exchange value. The top three money transfer service providers in the world are Western Union, MoneyGram and Euronet, representing 20% of the total market with an average capitalization of $4.5 billion. If bitcoin joins this elite club, then its value for transferring money and its enterprise value would be $4.5 billion. Bitcoin has enterprise value considering it's a globally distributed network that anyone can use. The estimate for the total medium exchange value is $5 billion for e-commerce plus $4.5 billion for money transfers equaling $9.5 billion.

## The Value of the Store of Value

Bitcoin's store of value is closely related to precious metals. Gold is a cousin to bitcoin considering they are both scarce, pay no interest, and are more difficult to trace than other assets except cash. Gold has a very high store of value based on a successful 10,000-year track record, difficult for bitcoin to match as a 5-year-old. Bitcoin has also been five times more volatile and therefore five times more risky to own, which limits its valuation to 20% of gold's $1.3 trillion value. Gold is about 60 times more valuable than silver making it more likely for bitcoin to reach the reputation of silver in store of value. The bottom line with a few additional calculations is a $5 billion bitcoin store of value, which is close to the $8 billion worth of modern U.S. silver eagles.

## Total Tally

The estimated maximum market capitalization or total intrinsic value of bitcoin is rounded to $15 billion, which is the sum of e-commerce, money transfer and store of value estimates. There are approximately 12 million bitcoins dividing out to $1300 per 1 BTC. [112]

## Bitcoin Billions Takeaway

The different bitcoin fair value approaches result in a range of possibilities. However, the price appears to reflect its value, and if anything bitcoin has been consistently undervalued even with ALFAquote's more conservative valuation. The determinable money supply baked into the bitcoin protocol plays a huge part in the upside potential as demand for bitcoin scales from both a medium of exchange and store of value perspective.

Bitcoin's first use case as an alternative payment system creates a matchup with existing payment models and payment networks for purposes of figuring a fair price for bitcoin. Woo's analysis of the medium of exchange and store of value attributes of money gets to the heart of the matter for identifying how bitcoin has intrinsic value. His approach, therefore, was more sophisticated by describing how bitcoin has to achieve three things, including matching the value of silver, getting into third place for money transfer providers, and grabbing 10% of ecommerce transactions. The various approaches generally overlap each other when you consider remittances, payment networks, transactional demand

and stores of value. It's also apparent that small changes in some factors lead to big changes in possible fair values; thus, it's better to think of fair value as a range instead of an absolute number.

Many bitcoin enthusiasts argue that market analysts undervalue bitcoin because they're not considering the value of the additional benefits of bitcoin 2.0 projects. There's a whole range of possibilities where bitcoin can provide transformative value. These possibilities weren't considered because the research would be more subjective and speculative in nature and beyond the scope of the analysis. If these other scenarios could be objectively factored in, the range of bitcoin prices would be even more staggering. Bitcoin solves problems resulting in real world value.

The bottom line is those who take advantage of the unlimited benefits of bitcoin in their business will stand to gain the most in the long run. Hopefully by now you can see there is substance in the price of bitcoin. The intrinsic value of bitcoin is derived from the network, protocol and currency combination, which is something that's never existed with fiat currencies. So it's safe to say there hasn't been and there is no bitcoin bubble.

# Benefits of Bitcoin Breakdowns

Let's review business implosions in the bitcoin ecosystem to understand how valuable the impact and timing of these events is to the future of bitcoin and cryptocurrency. The media has greatly exaggerated bitcoin breakdowns, leaving much of the public misinformed and partially educated. As we all know, negative news sells so negative stories about bitcoin get easily picked up and distorted by mainstream media. For example, it is still widely believed in the general public that bitcoin was a company that went bankrupt when Mt. Gox failed, when, in fact, Bitcoin the protocol is not a company and nobody owns it; a hard-to-digest concept compared to the inherited paradigm in which everything is owned by someone or some company.

## Goxxed

Mt. Gox was the original bitcoin exchange and rose to become the largest exchange before ultimately imploding and filing for bankruptcy on February 28, 2014. In the process, approximately 750,000 bitcoins went missing to the tune of $500,000,000. Mt. Gox initially blamed "transaction malleability," essentially a bug in the bitcoin core software, as the reason for the mysteriously missing bitcoin. Mt. Gox later blamed hackers for exploiting weaknesses in their own system. Research has subsequently proven that malleability was not the issue. [113, 114]

Mt. Gox CEO Mark Karpeles was a self-taught programmer, but neither a security nor a crypto expert, whom many believe was in over his head. Mt. Gox appears to have been a poorly designed platform and as of June 2014, researchers were still examining data to figure out the intricacies of the failure. This was not a bombshell bankruptcy but a series of red alerts warning users over the course of many months. The impact on customers is the same regardless of whether this is a case of massive fraud or gross incompetence. [115]

The CEOs of six industry-leading, bitcoin companies issued a joint statement in the wake of the Mt. Gox collapse. A partial excerpt follows:

"The purpose of this document is to summarize a joint statement to the Bitcoin community regarding Mt. Gox. This tragic violation of the trust of users of Mt. Gox was the result of one company's actions and does not reflect the resilience or value of bitcoin and the digital currency industry. There are hundreds of trustworthy and responsible companies involved in bitcoin. These companies will continue to build the future of money by making bitcoin more secure and easy to use for consumers and merchants. As with any new industry, there are certain bad actors that need to be weeded out, and that is what we are seeing today. Mt. Gox has confirmed its issues in private discussions with other members of the bitcoin community..." [116]

## Fly Away Deposits

A bitcoin-mining hardware manufacturing company called Butterfly Labs sprang up in June 2012. The company promised a breakthrough in mining technology by offering new, application-specific integrated circuits (ASICs) for sale. Butterfly didn't actually have the equipment available for purchase so the company took pre-orders from thousands of customers. With the promise of computing speeds one thousand times faster than existing technology, miners were more than willing to make significant deposits for equipment ranging from a few hundred dollars to as much as $30,000 for a single machine. Many orders were likely for hundreds of thousands of dollars. Then customers waited and waited for over a year while Butterfly Labs attributed the delay to "manufacturing complications." [117]

The U.S. Federal Trade Commission (FTC) received thousands of complaints about Butterfly from customers around the world.

On further investigation, the FTC reported that 20,000 customers had made deposits totaling between $20 million and $50 million while receiving nothing in return over a year after placing their orders. Even if the original orders were finally shipped after such a long time, all the ASICs would be obsolete and worthless because of the rapid pace of innovation in mining hardware. One company representative was quoted as saying the delayed machines were only "as useful as a room heater."

The FTC ultimately responded by shutting down the company pending a court case for fraudulent and deceptive practices. Jessica Rich, director of the FTC's Bureau of Consumer Protection said, "We're pleased the court granted our request to halt this operation, and we look forward to putting the company's ill-gotten gains back in the hands of consumers."

Butterfly Labs has since been called "the second most hated bitcoin company" behind Mt. Gox. [118]

## Bitcoin Ponzi

Trendon Shavers founded the Bitcoin Savings and Trust (BTCST) in 2012 and promised investors 7% weekly returns or approximately 3600% annualized returns. Through his extensive online marketing efforts, he eventually collected over 700,000 bitcoins from 100 investors between 2011 and 2012. The BTCST was never incorporated and therefore was not a real entity that could operate as an investment vehicle. The ridiculous 3600% returns were paid to existing investors via investments made by new investors—a classic element of a true Ponzi scheme—while Shavers also promised huge returns with no risk. [119]

Lori Schock, Director of the SEC's Office of Investor Education and Advocacy said, "Ponzi scheme operators often claim to have a tie to new and emerging technology as a lure to potential victims...Investors should understand that regardless of the type of investment, a promise of high returns with little or no risk is a classic warning sign of fraud."

The SEC charged Shavers with violating anti-fraud provisions of securities laws resulting in over $40MM of civil fines in September 2014. As of November 2014 Shavers was charged with securities fraud and wire fraud in the first-ever federal criminal securities fraud case involving a bitcoin-related Ponzi scheme. [120, 121]

Unfortunately, many investors were duped while bitcoin got some bad press for being associated with illegal behavior. Ponzi schemers have been around long before bitcoin and they will use any method necessary to extract cash from hard-working investors.

## Bitcoin Bee Sting

Danny Brewster, CEO of Neo & Bee, a Cypress-based bitcoin exchange, is yet another CEO "stung" by bad news. In a pre-Neo transaction, a pair of bitcoin foul-play-crying newbies supposedly handed over cash to buy bitcoins from Danny who essentially either didn't buy the bitcoins or inappropriately comingled the bitcoins. Amidst a swirl of allegations and a Cyprus police arrest warrant, Brewster fired back in self-defense on Reddit. Employees later came out and claimed there was a major lack of transparency inside the organization. The Neo & Bee case illustrates not wrongdoing so much as conflict in appearance versus conflict in fact. The courts will decide on a conflict in fact while the bitcoin community has already decided on a conflict in appearance.

## Creating Quicksand

The reason the Neo & Bee case is so problematic is that a customer buying bitcoin from you without a bitcoin wallet—which was the case with Brewster—is like the CEO of Bank of America accepting a cash payment from you and then putting it in a drawer without creating a bank account for you. If you create a conflict in appearance then you create your own "quicksand"; you'll sink, regardless of any actual wrongdoing. It appears that Brewster created his own quicksand and then stepped right in it. The cost of this breaking news and related charges was a near price plunge to zero, the search for a new CEO, an arrest warrant and disclosure of personal woes supposedly justifying the shenanigans.

There are many more bitcoin breakdowns, hacks and frauds too numerous to mention and enough material to fill a separate book on the subject. There are always lessons to be learned, mostly from outside observers, and of course from those who were burned directly. When these stories are studied closely, many clues can be identified in hindsight, extracted and used as nuggets for future due diligence. Even a reputable organization can be susceptible to hacking and fraud; therefore, it's also important to understand whether a business has the wherewithal to weather a storm should they have to sail through one. Read every news story on this subject you can because there is no better way to learn.

## Do Your Bitcoin Due Diligence

Here are some things to look for when researching a bitcoin company.

1. *Look for transparency.* A website should include profiles of the major partners, founders and investors in the organization, including profile photos, addresses and contact information. The site should also include comprehensive FAQ's and other information explaining the company's services and processes.

2. *Check validity.* Verify a company's legal entity registration and licensing. Also perform a whois.net domain lookup to verify public status and cross-reference with the legal entity. A transparent company shouldn't need to make its domain registration private.

3. *Audit.* Confirm the company's email and phone contact information by actually emailing and calling. Test the service to see if it actually works as claimed by the company. Bad actors are the root cause of shenanigans and they show up in every industry, everywhere in the world, including bitcoin. Reddit and other forums can also serve as a barometer for integrity and transparency because nothing is off limits in these discussion platforms. In addition, staying up to date with bitcoin news is another

way to keep your finger on the pulse.

## Benefits of Bitcoin Breakdowns Takeaway

These bitcoin breakdowns support the assertion that integrity always starts with Tone at the Top, the conclusion of the Committee of Sponsoring Organizations (COSO), which was formed to analyze fraudulent financial reporting in 1985, and the same conclusion from every commission that reported on a financial crisis thereafter. The integrity of an organization can never be greater than the integrity of the CEO. All the customers in the cases cited may have suffered unrecoverable losses so always do your due diligence, look for transparency and integrity to minimize risk, and make sure things pass the smell test before putting hard-earned resources at unnecessary risk.

These legendary bitcoin breakdowns intersected a wave of innovation at just the right time. The bitcoin community knows bitcoin's success is in its hands and Mt. Gox demonstrated what not to do, which was a gift in itself. Innovation is addressing the breakdowns at lighting speed with an invisible hand of more creative, secure, transparent platforms better and faster than any centralized regulatory institution could enact any meaningful change. Self-regulation is inherently embedded in the bitcoin technology and is more valuable than imposed regulation. Proof of solvency, voluntary security audits, financial disclosure and bug bounties are examples of the shift toward more transparency.

So thank you bitcoin breakdowns.

# First Things First:
# Digital Identity Management

## Strategy from the Start

There are multiple platforms in every area of the bitcoin ecosystem and all of them require some variation on account registration, including emails, passwords, passphrases, PINs and other personal or business-related information. Some platforms don't require traditional login credentials; however, users have to securely store and manage some piece of information. Every time you create a new account your online profile expands, which increases the risk of breach with one or all of your accounts. Setting up and experimenting with many platforms is the fastest way to find out which ones match up to your risk tolerance—with security and convenience in mind.

A business or individual could easily have accounts and corresponding bitcoin wallets at dozens of bitcoin or cryptocurrency exchanges in the normal course of business. Exchanges also serve different purposes and a good strategy employs multiple platforms, as highlighted in the exchange chapter. That being said, the list of platforms in the average bitcoin arsenal can be quite long.

## Digital Risk

Identity, credentials and access management (ICAM) is at the heart of bitcoin and cryptocurrency management. ICAM is like the outer force field for bitcoin security. The term is most notably used by the U.S. government to refer to implementation of a standard set of policies and procedures around security. The same concept applies to both individuals and businesses.

The new bitcoin paradigm allows anyone to become his or her own bank and that includes 100% responsibility for bitcoin custody. (The secure bitcoin storage side of the equation is covered in the bitcoin wallets chapter.) Management of ICAM and management of bitcoin wallets are closely woven together because carelessness in one area leads to loss of bitcoins in another. Managing login credentials and digital identities were already important aspects of information security before but have now become hypercritical in the age of bitcoin. Thus, a well-designed strategy must include a password management system. [123]

Digital identity management, or DIM, has varied definitions, including the total digital footprint of a person and his or her respective businesses, all things social media, every Internet-based platform and related account, private and public information, communications, physical and digital security, including computers as well as business policies. Everything is essentially woven together with an email, the golden thread, that risks unraveling without the proper time and attention.

Awareness of digital identity management risk is the first step to better control. Understanding, for example, that your risk increases every time a new Internet-based platform and its unique characteristics are added to the mix. And that DIM becomes one and the same for business owners and their respective businesses, which magnifies the risk into a larger, dual-inseparable footprint to manage, and ultimately, even more to lose. When teams manage digital identities the risk is even higher as more hands are in the pie.

## Login Twins

Access to any platform is based on the principles of authentication and authorization. Authentication answers the question, "How do I know you are who you say you are?" Authorization answers the question, "You are who you say you are, now what can you do?" Every platform verifies some combination of three authentication factors:

1. Something you are: biometric fingerprint
2. Something you know: password
3. Something you have: smartphone or other device

Two-factor authentication uses two of the three authentication factors, such as something you know with either something you are, or something you have. Once authentication is proven, access is granted and authorization is usually assumed. For example, after logging into a banking website, money can be transferred or bills can be paid without any further actions by the user. However, when the amount of money is over a certain threshold, additional authorization may be required such as another 2FA code. Some cryptocurrency exchanges require an authorization for every trade.

There can be a subtle distinction between authentication and authorization when the same things used to authenticate are the same things used to authorize the purchase of bitcoins. As discussed in the wallets chapter, multi-signature technology, called "multi-sig," solves the authorization challenge while most of the authentication information is concentrated in the "something you know" category (think about all the info you have to cough up in order to register on a website). You can see why there's such a need to manage digital identities with a password management system. Understanding this concentration of information can help you understand the concentration of risk and the need to use every strategy possible to thwart hackers and reduce external threats as well as the risk of theft from the enemy within an organization. You can also be a threat to yourself and your business if you do a poor job of managing bitcoins. [124, 125]

## Another Layer

Some bitcoin platforms have traditional login credentials combined with managing bitcoins via passwords, passphrases, PINs and private keys within the platform. Think of using login credentials to access a website like using your front door key to access your house or office. Next, you would access bitcoins within the website by way of a bitcoin exchange platform or a bitcoin web wallet just like you would use a special combination to access a safe within your home or office. If you happen to lose the key to your "office," you can still get access to it by way of traditional username and password recovery. However, losing your bitcoin wallet passphrase, such as "idiot edge answer hum stream sway spread sometimes cell dig childhood hurt" is like losing the key (or combination) to your safe, and therefore losing access to your bitcoins.

With traditional banking, if you forget an online password, it can always be recovered and the risk of theft and getting hacked is only a mild fear for most. In the bitcoin model, you're given instructions and tool sets to properly manage your bitcoin wallets, but if you can't produce a bitcoin passphrase your bitcoins can't be recovered. Essentially, you—or your employees responsible for managing bitcoins—are your greatest risk.

## Another Benefit

Managing bitcoin wallets requires use of multiple platforms such as payment service providers, exchanges and web wallets to move bitcoins around in order to reduce risk or make purchases. For this level of usage, it is imperative to have a password management system, which will give you superhero-like powers for logging into the websites with speed, security and ease. Consider that a typical work task requires multiple logins for working back and forth among platforms. Lightning fast logins, thanks to a password management system, will turn you into a bitcoin power user and make you feel like a superstar. Just think, the average person has 25 logins per day, so if you had one minute of fumbling per login, times 250 working days, equals 2.6 wasted weeks per year logging into websites. Password managers eliminate the fumbling so you can use that valuable time to learn more about bitcoin. [126]

Use the admin console to activate access controls and provide the biggest benefit for businesses, allowing you to easily add or remove employees or subcontractors. When someone gets hired, access is granted and when someone gets fired or finishes a contract the access is revoked. While hackers are the outside enemy, team members inside of an organization are sometimes the enemy within. The enemy within poses the greatest risk because trust is extended and expected in the employment capacity when access to sensitive login credentials is given. Unfortunately, an employee who shifts from a good actor to a bad actor already has the keys to the kingdom when it comes to bitcoin, but enterprise-level password managers can at least minimize this risk with a host of dashboard controls.

## Digital Legacies

Corralling digital legacies is a challenge when it comes to wills and estates. Wills are not a good place to list passwords; therefore, an executor or other trusted parties should know how to access various accounts. There are many stories of spouses scrambling to figure out the electronic life of their loved one, from navigating bank accounts to social media profiles and even electronic document storage. Getting access to a spouse's numerous online profiles is a giant headache when you can't retrieve what you don't know about. Wills and business policies should include some instruction for accessing password management systems upon death or someone becoming incapacitated. When bitcoin is added to the equation, no access means a permanent loss of bitcoins.

## Cautionary Tales and Lessons Learned

Most folks use the same email and the same or similar passwords for all their accounts, including social media, financial accounts and everything in-between. When hackers get your email they already have the key to the top lock while brute force is the key to the bottom lock for breaking easy to remember passwords. If you are still keeping personal and business login credentials in a text file, spreadsheet, on paper or in draft emails, then you are at high risk for an attack. While risk can never be eliminated completely, there is plenty you can do for peace of mind. The following cautionary tales are filled with valuable lessons that will hopefully prompt you to step up your game and set up your outer force field.

## Phancy Phishing

Paul Boyer, creator of the "Mad Money Machine" podcast on the Let's Talk Bitcoin network, learned a tough lesson in the case of missing bitcoin donations. Paul happily received donations totaling 3.3875 bitcoins, about $2,000, from loyal listeners until he discovered a zero balance in his wallet at the end of June 2014. He never entered a bitcoin payout address with his payment service provider, which resulted in the accumulation of bitcoins that are normally paid out on a daily basis. A creative BitPay look-alike phishing scheme cleverly disguised an email with a "View Invoice" link requesting the refund of a customer payment. Paul took the bait by clicking the link while unknowingly handing over his password to the hacker who added his own payout address and received the 3.3875 bitcoins the following day. [127, 128]

Two-factor authentication, or 2FA, would have been a stopgap, but it wasn't activated on Paul's account. Fortunately, 2FA is used on almost every bitcoin platform, thereby significantly reducing the risk of a login breach. After a standard username and password login, a two-factor box pops up asking for a code, which is regenerated every 20 seconds by a smartphone app such as Authy or Google Authenticator. If hackers got a hold of your login credentials, they couldn't log in without your smartphone and the code. Still, 2FA is not a foolproof solution.

## Identity Ransom

Long-time bitcoin evangelist, Roger Ver, was attending a conference when friends started messaging their suspicions of a Facebook imposter. Someone hacked into an old Hotmail account of his, using it like a master key to retrieve logins for other accounts including a domain registrar that could have led to a total online identity hijacking. The hacker posted Roger's Social Security Number while demanding a 37.6 bitcoin identity ransom worth $20,000 at the time. Roger turned the tables and offered up a 37.6 bitcoin reward via Facebook and Twitter for info leading to the hacker's arrest. The viral bounty was too much to bear and the hacker quickly bowed down, handed over the login credentials and disappeared. [129, 130]

Fortunately, no bitcoins were stolen and having alert friends helped limit the hijacking to a few hours. But this tale shows how a single email account can be an attack vector or weak point for exposing an entire online digital identity. When the same email is used for all accounts it effectively weaves your entire digital identity together with a single thread. In addition, the more well known someone is and the more perceived wealth someone has, the greater the risk for getting attacked.

## A Tale of Social Engineering

Sam Lee, CEO of Bitcoins Reserve, and his company were victims of a creative social engineering attack starting with the U.S. Marshals public email leak of the Silk Road bitcoin auction list. Hackers were licking their chops over a juicy list of high rollers handed to them with a white glove. During this time, Lee received an email asking for a media interview, nothing suspicious there, but when he opened a Google docs link containing the supposed interview questions, the link unleashed malware that sucked out all the usernames and passwords from his Chrome browser, which then gave the hacker control of all the company's email addresses. The hacker then sent an email from Lee's account to the CTO requesting a client withdraw of 100 bitcoins, worth about $65,000 at the time. In this case, the "client" was the hacker and the bitcoins evaporated. While the hackers were able to take over Lee's entire digital identity, they could not penetrate the company's securely stored bitcoins.

"This is a weakness in our internal processes and procedures," said Sam Lee, "It has nothing to do with weaknesses in bitcoin because frankly bitcoin so far has none." [131, 132]

It's hard to defend against a hacker falsely posing as a trusted party, one of the slickest tools in a hacker's toolbox, but in this case the hackers hit the bulls eye because of a simple blind carbon copy mistake by the U.S. Marshals, which lead to social engineering, password breach and theft of a considerable quantity of bitcoins.

## Key to the Kingdom

Androklis Polymenis aka "kLee," an early bitcoin adopter and NXT (cryptocurrency) stakeholder, discovered his $1,000,000 of bitcoin and NXT had vanished. The theft likely came from a hacker who found kLee's unencrypted, plain text password file sitting in Dropbox. KLee put out a 500-bitcoin bounty, worth nearly $300,000, for return of the stolen crypto and identification of the hacker who eventually returned 462 of 1170 bitcoins while keeping the rest in exchange for kLee calling off the hunt. In the meantime, the NXT community was able to rally together and retrieve some of the stolen NXT tokens. About two-thirds of the cryptocurrency was never recovered yet it could've easily been a total loss. The breach was inevitable; given that kLee's password—the key to the kingdom—was sitting there on his computer in an unencrypted plain text file.

These lessons are painful to witness but highlight the importance of safeguarding bitcoin and other cryptocurrencies. "Holding your own bitcoin is like harnessing fire," says Alan Reiner, a self-proclaimed, ultra-paranoid crypto-nerd and founder of Armory, a bitcoin wallet desktop application for securely stashing bitcoins in cold storage. "Sometimes the biggest threat to users is themselves." [133]

## Golden Tales

Take these tales as "gifts" and put the lessons learned to use to avoid ending up in your own cautionary tale. Best practices for digital identity management include a password management system such as LastPass.com or Secret Server by Thycotic.com. You are 100% responsible for managing your bitcoins so reducing the risk of online profile breach starts by managing one account at a time.

Take the following steps to remove all the unnecessary risk from a poorly managed digital identity.

1. ***Choose a password management system.*** Select a password management system, create an account and start adding websites and login credentials. Do not use browser-based password managers such as the ones built into Chrome and Safari, but don't confuse this advice with the browser plug-ins needed for password managers. Businesses should create an enterprise-level account that

has an admin console for managing users. Individual users should also consider this additional functionality even though free versions are available.

2.  ***Add sites or platforms.*** Once the password manager is set up, sites can be easily added by logging into an account as you normally would. Most systems will prompt the user to save the site with a simple click. Sites can also be added manually with the URL, site nickname, username and password. If you previously saved all your usernames and passwords in a spreadsheet, adjust the columns to the import format and upload. Visit BestBitcoinBookEver. com/bonus today for a free import ready file of all bitcoin platforms in this book. Easy tutorials are usually available for mastering the setup. It's also important to add the following traditional information in the notes section of the site or platform profile to eliminate future fumbling with admin-related issues.

- Account number
- Date the account was created
- Email address on file if not used as the login credential
- Username if not used as the login credential
- Credit card or debit card on file if applicable (e.g., name, Visa account #1234)
- PIN numbers such as call-in PINs
- Security questions
- Email address, phone number and address of the platform
- Details of a paid subscription plan, amount, billing frequency, etc.

# Example of a Last Pass coinkite.com site profile with important notes

*Notice how it references a separate secure note, which stores the secret mnemonic key for extra security. A corresponding secure note example follows later in the chapter.*

Image courtesy of Last Pass

3. ***Test click the sites.*** Always go back and test click the site from inside the password manager whether you saved your sites one by one or imported a list. Sometimes minor changes like the login URL or username need to be adjusted. When you create and simultaneously save new accounts, the URL automatically picked up by the system is often not the login URL. For example, sitename.com/signup vs. sitename.com/login. Testing and correcting helps to avoid frustration.

4. ***Delete the old list.*** After you've successfully transitioned from a traditional password list it's time to delete that old file. If you go through the whole process of setting up a password manager yet you've kept your old file, then you wasted your time without reducing any risk. Old habits are hard to break and most folks have a difficult time deleting the old go-to password file for fear of losing access, or wanting to keep it just in case. Get over the hump by copying and pasting the old password list into a secure note available in most password managers. Delete the old file and you'll be glad you did.

5. ***Create a unique email.*** Email is what I previously referred to as the "golden thread" that weaves your entire digital identity together because most people use one email for everything. You must first distinguish email used for communication and email used for account creation. You must separate these two roles by using at least two separate emails. The Golden Thread Rule dictates that the email used for communication should be different than the one used to log in to all of your accounts. If you're a one-email user, hackers already have the first key to your kingdom the moment they get your email address. Create a new, second email account without using your own name or a word that could be associated with you. For example, set up an email like (anyword)admin@(yourcompanyname). com or use the random password generator to create an email such as 3Xrxy5Hk4m76@gmail.com. Instead of using the personal or business email address you always use, use your new "stealth" email the next time you log in. And of course, save it in LastPass. Little by little, do this with all sites you use. It will be easier to change accounts one by one instead of turning it into a major project.

6. ***Change passwords.*** Easy to remember passwords are easy to break. Consider that a hacker who knows your email is practically granted free access to your personal information. Change all of your passwords to a

minimum 16-character, hard-to-break password using the random generator provided within the password management software such as C%7$Cz#LGiWY1&QK. Password resets should be done in conjunction with the new email resets described above. Once you've changed your email, test logging into the site with the new email. Once you're confident the email change has been accepted, go back and change the password and test login again with the new password. Do not change both at the same time because some platforms tend to get confused. The password generator can be used for setting up new accounts and the password length can be expanded well beyond 16 characters. If you can't remember the password then it's harder to break. If you use a password manager, you no longer have to remember passwords because the system keeps them encrypted on the client side and not on the platform's servers.

Random Password Generation Example: Using 36 random characters of all character types

Image courtesy of Last Pass

7. ***Set up user IDs.*** Many platforms use an email address as the default username or login ID and it makes sense to use a consistent username such as the TheBitcoinCPA or your company name for multiple social media platforms and branding purposes. However, when it comes to bitcoin wallets, bitcoin exchanges and financial accounts, a different username should be created. Once again the random password generator can be used to create a random username. If the same username is used for social media and bitcoin sites, then a username revealed or exposed in some way lets hackers know you're doing business with a particular platform. For example, one crypto exchange has a rolling ticker displaying recent purchases by username and "trollboxes" (for incendiary chat and commentary) also displaying usernames. There's no need to give this freebie to hackers so be sure to disguise usernames when appropriate.

8. ***Create false answers and security questions.*** Everyone's familiar with setting up a security question triple play like, What is your oldest sibling's middle name? What street did you grow up on? And, What was the name of your first pet? Facebook and social media do a good job of spreading personal information around the Internet making it easy for hackers to find answers to some of these questions. In addition bad actors can employ tools usually reserved for private investigators, fraud examiners and companies authorized for background checks to mine personal and public information. The best way to thwart this risk is by creating false answers to security questions. Simply keep track of the questions chosen and their corresponding false answers in the notes section of the site profile in your password manager. Alternatively, create a standard set of false answers to the commonly ask questions and keep those in a secure note within the password manager instead of creating new false answers for each site profile that requires it.

9. ***Activate security features.*** Only use a password management system with 2FA, two-factor authentication. If it doesn't have 2FA then don't use it. A password manager, the master key for all your login credentials, is more secure when reinforced by 2FA. It should also be activated on every bitcoin platform and any other service that offers it. 2FA is available as an app or a physical device like the YubiKey. The following additional features should also be considered when choosing a password manager and activated upon setup:

- Use timed logout feature (e.g., password manager logs out after 30 minutes of inactivity)
- Set up forbidden URLs on a global basis
- Activate password re-prompt for secure notes when appropriate
- Use shared folders for platforms used by multiple team members
- Check boxes to hide passwords for certain users
- Consider 2FA physical devices for additional security (i.e., YubiKey)

## Secure Bitcoin Wallets & Platforms

Bitcoin-related sites may require special attention beyond standard login credentials. Sometimes a passphrase, a group of random words, is required to access your bitcoin. If you lose the passphrase, you lose your bitcoins—period; therefore, your passphrase must be handled very carefully. Some sites don't have standard login credentials and only require a passphrase. In either case, the passphrase should be saved in the encrypted password field in the password manager. There's still a small risk of losing the passphrase so it should also be written down and kept in a physical safe.

The inner force field techniques highlighted in the bitcoin wallets chapter should be used in conjunction with the outer force field techniques discussed here. Bitcoin platforms have special considerations for saving critical information in the notes section of the site profile in addition to the ones outlined in Step 2. Depending on the platform, the following unique information should be added to the notes section or to a secure note that contains info but doesn't log into anything:

- Bitcoin wallet identifiers
- Bitcoin address, if static; some platforms produce new addresses for every transaction
- Passphrases or secret mnemonic key (see example in image below)
- Secondary passwords
- Security questions and answers
- Platform PIN
- Corresponding mobile app PIN if applicable
- Platform support email
- Account ID or user ID number
- Multisig information including other transaction signers
- Identification of wallet backups by method, location and date (e.g., thumb drive in safe on 12-31-14)
- Fiat funding source by name, account and type (e.g., ABC, Inc, Acct#1234, checking)
- Fiat funding methods and related platform funding information
- Any other valuable information on a case-by-case basis

## Secure note example to secure a Coinkite multisig setup

Image courtesy of Last Pass

A large bitcoin stash coupled with infrequent transactions requires a higher level of security, and therefore passphrases, the keys to a bitcoin wallet, should either by stored on paper or a USB thumb drive in a safe. Alternatively, the passphrase can be added to a secure note with the "require password re-prompt" feature activated. This feature requires the password of the password management system to get access to a secure note. If a password manager is left open on a computer for a short time, then a bad actor couldn't get into the secure note without the password.

Secure notes can also be used to manage other sensitive information. For example, Kryptokit only requires a simple password to send bitcoins from your browser, but it's better to stash in a secure note instead of in your head.

## Additional IT Security

Computer and network security can never be reviewed too many times. An in-depth analysis is beyond the scope of this book; however, it deserves mention along with identity, credentials and access management. Anti-virus and anti-malware software should be installed on all computers and all software and operating systems should have automatic updates enabled. A few additional IT security considerations include:

- Wireless security
- Protected sharing
- Firewalls
- Router/IP addressing
- Physical access
- Backups

Last Pass and Thycotic's Secret Server are examples of password management systems supporting individuals, small businesses and even large organizations. You can also do a Google search on password manager reviews to compare and contrast different features.

## Last Pass.com

There are many great password managers, but Last Pass has a free version available for individual users and an enterprise paid version for businesses, which includes multiple, two-factor authentication options. The paid version, only $24 per user per year, has an admin dashboard for multiple users and access controls. It even has a security scorecard showing the strength of your overall password profile. The free personal version can plug into a separate enterprise account for a seamless user experience. Several reviews rate Lass Pass #1 in its category while providing the best overall value for features and ease of use.

## Thycotic.com

This enterprise-level service called Secret Server allows large organizations to create, share and manage passwords. They support user groups in the tens of thousands, but they also have packages available for smaller businesses. Organizations with special compliance needs such as HIPAA or SOX mandates are well suited for this product. They also have self-serve group management, thereby eliminating the need for expensive help desks. Some additional features include permissions, audit trails and automatic password changing.

## Dancing Barcode

We would be remiss if we didn't mention Clef, a two-factor login solution for websites that doesn't store usernames and passwords in a database. The GetClef.com mobile app generates a unique digital signature every few seconds using RSA public key cryptography with essentially nothing for hackers to steal. Simply hold your mobile phone up to a computer screen and the app syncs with a dancing bar code called the wave. The login and the 2FA become one in the same without having to remember or use traditional login password combinations. When you use the app you'll experience the magical simplicity of site access.

Clef increases registration conversion by 30% while eliminating the forgotten password problem. In addition, only 15% of users set up traditional 2FA security like Authy or Google Authenticator, which leaves the other 85% exposed to greater hacking risk. Clef also eliminates this poor opt-in rate because the two-factor is essentially backed into the system.

When it comes to bitcoin platforms Clef solves the website login problem like any other site. However, bitcoin private keys, passphrases and related info still have to be secured, as covered in later chapters. Website platforms set up Clef and conversely, end users set up password managers. Therefore, Clef can only be used when implemented by the website itself. Clef and other innovations will continue to gain traction with superior security and ease of use. It is the username/password model that is flawed—not password managers, which are designed to provide best practices for managing the old model—but many years from now password managers will take on a different role, or cease to exist altogether.

## First Things First: Digital Identity Management Takeaway

The "silver bullet" for digital identity management is a combined strategy for maximizing security while reducing the risk of a breach to the lowest level possible. Good risk management requires having a keen eye on all the "little" things. The principles in this chapter are the key to creating a strong foundation as a bitcoin power user and moving forward with the rest of this book.

If you have a poorly managed profile, you can't afford to waste another day. If one account gets hacked, they can all get hacked. Applying best practices to multiple accounts takes time so start by making one change per day and the momentum will carry you to completion. Remember that your password manager contains the keys to your kingdom so create a good password with 2FA enabled. Email is the golden thread that weaves your entire digital identity together; therefore, you must use at least one email for communication and another email for user accounts and platforms. This might be the most valuable piece of information in the entire book and it can't be repeated enough.

Start securing your digital identity and your bitcoins today-- and take more vacations with all that newfound time and peace of mind.

# Bitcoin Merchant On-Ramp

## Payment Service Providers

Bitcoin payment service providers or payment processors have platforms so merchants can easily accept bitcoin for goods and services. They have shopping cart plug-ins, online dashboards, payment terminals, multiple invoicing, payment acceptance methods and other tools. Merchants can choose to cash out their bitcoin into fiat currency or split between the two. These platforms are the backbone for merchants who accept bitcoin. Some of the general features available from payment processors are:

- Keep 100% of bitcoins or split between fiat and bitcoin
- Charge $1 get $1 with next day cash-out to fiat currency
- Merchant dashboard
- Multiple shopping cart plug-ins and APIs
- Multiple, fully integrated SAAS-hosted solutions like Shopify.com
- Hosted checkout for merchants with three bitcoin payment methods:
    - Click to pay URI
    - Scan to pay QR code
    - Copy and paste bitcoin address
- Customer invoicing delivered by email or SMS
- Recurring invoicing, buying bitcoin or selling bitcoin
- Flat fee, monthly subscription model
- Free, entry-level service plans and free incentives [134, 135]

## Bitcoin the Opposite

In general, the benefits of accepting bitcoin are the opposite of the headaches outlined in Credit Card Chaos and Banking Burnout Bonanza. For every old model headache there's a brilliant bitcoin benefit. Merchant benefits include the following:

- Payment processing fees usually less than 1%
- Sign-up incentives
- Subscription-based processing fees with up to 90% savings
- Zero sign-up costs and no expensive POS equipment
- Low integration cost depending on the size of the business
- Chargebacks and fraud are a thing of the past
- No PCI compliance and related costs
- Long application forms and credit approvals don't exist
- No foreign currency conversions and special fees
- Almost instantly available bitcoin
- Instant fiat conversion eliminates unwanted price volatility
- No credit card database breaches
- Micro transactions are now feasible

These benefits alone are inspiring enough to put the book down and get moving with bitcoin. The question isn't, "Should our business adopt bitcoin?" but, "When will our business adopt bitcoin?" and "Will our competitors adopt it before we do?"

It's equally important to understand how the drivers of consumer adoption are intertwined and related to the drivers for merchant adoption. While not every consumer is a business owner, every business owner is a consumer. The two are opposite sides of the same coin. Consumer benefits include the following:

- Bitcoin is always available with a mobile phone or the Internet.
- There's no need to carry a wallet with credit cards or cash.
- Transfer bitcoin to anyone anywhere in the world at anytime.
- There are almost zero fees to transfer bitcoin to another person.
- Banks and PayPal can't freeze your funds.
- Foreign currency conversions are a thing of the past.
- Credit card-like information doesn't float around in cyberspace.

- Bitcoin transactions offer some anonymity and privacy.
- The unbanked public has instant access to a payment system.
- Unauthorized merchant withdraws don't exist.
- No banks are necessary.

Of merchant on ramping, Steve Beauregard, founder of GoCoin, said it best at Inside Bitcoins NYC: "Shoppers should be rewarded for being loyal customers instead of charged more to compensate for expensive chargebacks."

## A Look at Bitcoin Payment Processors

The leading bitcoin payment processors include the following:

**Bitpay.com** is a U.S.-based pure bitcoin payment processor. They are pioneers in payment processing with a focus on providing a great merchant interface and ease of use. A new bitcoin payroll API allows employers to pay an employee's net check in bitcoin. It's also integrated with Fulfillment by Amazon (FBA). BitPay also announced a free, unlimited, forever payment processing subscription plan for smaller businesses.

**Coinbase.com** is a U.S.-based payment processor known as a universal platform doubling as an exchange for buying and selling bitcoin. Both merchants and consumers can create accounts and get a bitcoin wallet although consumers wouldn't necessarily use the payment processing tools. Merchants can set up subscription billing for customers who also have a Coinbase account. The vault service allows more secure bitcoin storage with 48-hour retrieval using multiple parties for authorizing withdraws to another wallet. It's like a secure savings account of sorts. Coinbase accounts come with a USD wallet for holding U.S. dollars directly on the platform with an instant bitcoin buy and sell feature.

**GoCoin.com** allows merchants the ability to accept Bitcoin, Litecoin, Dogecoin and Tether, a USD pegged coin with the benefits of bitcoin but without the volatility. Their click-to-bill feature makes it easy to send invoices via email or SMS. Merchants are cross-promoted to customers in the GoCoin network. GoCoin also provides extensive merchant analytics tools and API documentation for merchant checkout customization. The analytics help merchants take a proactive approach to stimulate bitcoin adoption among their customers by identifying and adjusting to customer behavior. A myriad of popular shopping cart plug-ins are also available.

**Coinify.com** is a European universal platform based in Denmark. They provide merchant solutions, including mobile checkout, point of sale, hosted invoicing and web payments. The enterprise service extends the merchant solutions to other payment service providers who want to offer bitcoin as a payment method for their customers. Similar to Coinbase, they have a trading platform for buying and selling bitcoin with a linked bank account.

**Coinkite.com** is a Canadian-based web wallet, payment terminal and debit card service allowing consumers and merchants to buy, sell, accept and store bitcoins. They have one of the first bitcoin merchant terminals similar to credit card terminals. The terminals can be used in an ATM-like exchange mode to buy or sell Bitcoin or Litecoin, or switched to retail mode to accept bitcoin from customers.

## Coinkite Terminal and Debit Cards

Image Courtesy of Coinkite

Coinkite's unique feature set is especially great for retail merchants. Coinkite is fanatical about security, employing hardware security modules and a dead-man switch which allows customers to access bitcoins in the event of Coinkite's business failure. "We chose to be a bitcoin company in the bitcoin way," says Rodolfo Novak, CEO of Coinkite.

Some additional features include:

- Built-in audit feature to verify bitcoins
- Customer tipping
- Double receipts for yourself and the customer
- Paper wallet printing
- Exchange rate markups
- Coinkite debit cards

**Paystand.com**, the world's first all-inclusive payment solution, brings three payment rails together in a payments as a service (PaaS) subscription model, including credit cards, eCheck and bitcoin. Merchants have the option to upcharge for credit card swipe fees or to show the savings from the other options. For example, a $199 purchase using a credit card costs $5.51 more than bitcoin and $4.51 more than an eCheck, as shown in the payment method box. Customer choice and the related financial impact is clearly communicated in real dollars. This versatile service gives merchants the ability to accept payments from their customers in all places, including social media.

## Payment methods and related savings

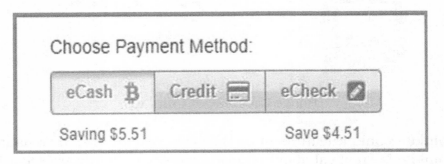

Image courtesy of PayStand

Some additional features include:

- Multiple web integrations
- Standard checkout includes credit card, eCheck and bitcoin
- Low credit card interchange fees
- Payment flexibility allows for passing on fees or absorbing them
- Monthly subscription model
- No payment redirect to another page

## Accepting Bitcoin and Multiple Altcoins
The world of altcoins is expanding rapidly so merchants should also consider accepting a range of cryptocurrencies to expand customer reach.

CoinPayments.net is like the BitPay for altcoins allowing customers to pay for goods or services using over 50 different cryptocurrencies. Payments can be converted to fiat currency or another altcoin with the option to automatically send coins to another wallet outside the platform. Several altcoins can be set up to auto convert to another coin. For example, Peercoin can be set to auto convert to bitcoin or another coin of your choice. A unique payout address can be set for each coin while fiat payouts can be set up using a linked Coinbase account for U.S. customers and similar platforms for residents of other countries. Merchants have the flexibility to accept any supported altcoin and customize the payout based on business strategy and risk management. CoinPayments states, "You can set your payout addresses to go directly to an exchange. We highly recommend Cryptsy.com since they (optionally) support automatically selling your coins when you deposit them, lessening your risks of exchange rate fluctuation."

Merchant tools include simple and advanced checkout options, email invoicing, multiple types of payment buttons and multiple shopping cart plug-ins, among others. These options make it easy to get set up whether or not you're tech savvy. The platform also features a public coin vote for getting new coins accepted and an in-store business directory.

## Customize Your Payments Platform

Cointopay.com is a customizable and versatile digital currency payment service provider. Merchants and consumers can choose among three service levels, Secure Cloud, Autonomy and White Label depending on the requirement of implementation, the number of coins accepted and desired control of your wallets. The Secure Cloud is a fully hosted wallet service, while Autonomy allows merchants to run their desktop and cloud wallets linked to the platform, whereas the White Label allows running your own payment provider service.

Merchants can accept dozens of different altcoins and either keep them or cash out to fiat. Cointopay specializes in merchant on-boarding and back-end integration support allowing merchants to accept, hold and cash out coins to match their customer service and business strategies. Cointopay founder, "Chris," explains, "With our service you can host any coin wallet daemon that you want to work with. Our design includes a customizable, full-service stack, wallet architecture with multiple options, a platform layer bolted on top and shopping cart plug-ins for WooCommerce, WordPress and Shopify."

The White Label service has developer, personal, business and enterprise licenses so merchants can be their own payment processor, while reducing centralized, third-party risk inherent with most bitcoin payment service providers. For example, a custom payments platform could be created for privacy-based coins, then re-branded and sold as a service to other businesses and consumers. The modular nature of Cointopay, aka the Coinpress. club release, allows multiple decentralized platforms to be woven together via the service exchange feature called Interconnect, one of the value propositions of the White Label and general platform services. Any type of payment architecture can be created, including any combination of wallets, for a diversified asset risk reduction strategy. Desktop wallets can be used to receive bitcoin while the Cointopay API can be set up to direct altcoins to individual Poloniex, Bittrex or Bleutrade exchange accounts.

This may seem counter-intuitive to the discussion on bitcoin exchange risk, but it demonstrates the power of being able to decentralize your assets in combination with the auto-sell features of those exchanges. Chris goes on to say, "We uphold the right to self-determination and transfer of value independent of third parties and pursue 'Decentralize Everything' as our main business mantra." Traditional bitcoin payment processors offer limited coins such as Bitcoin, Dogecoin and Litecoin. CoinPayments and ShapeShift expand the range of altcoins acceptance, yet have limited design flexibility and can't be customized to allow the "coin of choice" concept, while any coin can and will be accepted with Cointopay. Their mission is to support all coins in one single platform while continuing to expand the set of features.

## Dashboards & Funds Settlement

The BitPay admin panel allows an immediate cash out of bitcoin payments into several different fiat currencies while keeping some or all of the sale in bitcoin. For example, you can cash out 50% of the sale in U.S. dollars while the remaining 50% stays in Bitcoin. Fiat currency payouts are made on a daily basis. You get to choose whatever split works with your risk management strategy. If you don't want any price volatility then 100% of bitcoin sales can be cashed out as if the sales were made in your local currency. Customers don't know how much a business keeps in bitcoin or cashes out because it's all behind the scenes. The split feature is typical for most payment processors.

## BitPay's Funds Settlement Dashboard

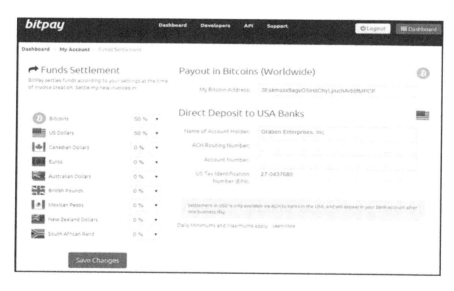

Image courtesy of BitPay

## Holding Bitcoin

Hopefully you choose to accept bitcoin, believe in the system and want to support it by keeping at least some of your sales in bitcoin to buy the stuff you already need. Your payout split should closely match the need to buy things in the same proportion of fiat and bitcoin. For example, if you use U.S. dollars on 60% of your purchases because your vendors don't accept bitcoin yet, then it makes sense to convert your bitcoin sales into a similar amount of U.S. dollars while potentially leaving the rest in bitcoin.

Bitcoin holdings come with purchasing power risk or volatility. The risk is that price downswings reduce bitcoin value and the amount of stuff you can buy with it. Conversely, an upswing increases purchasing power allowing you to buy more stuff.

## Plug-Ins

The payment service providers have dozens of plug-ins for the more popular shopping cart services like Shopify, Magento, WooCommerce, Ubercart, Zen Cart, and more. They also provide the API necessary for shopping carts that don't have a standard plug-in. Once the plug-in is installed, the shopping cart experience remains the same except that the payment choices now include a bitcoin pay button in addition to standard credit card buttons. Bitpay.com offers a great bitcoin payment button feature as an alternative to the shopping cart plug-in. The button is simply inserted directly on the product pages next to other payment options as desired.

## Merchant Hang-ups

Merchants naturally have concerns about using bitcoin, such as price volatility, liquidity, reputation risk, security, scalability, reliability, fraud risk, and implementation cost, which have all been addressed by continuous improvement of bitcoin payment-processing platforms. The fear of being left behind; unstable high inflation fiat currencies; payment friction; high transaction fees; long payment clearing times and competitor adoption are strong motivators for hanging up the hang-ups and adopting bitcoin.

# PCI Pain and Additional Drivers of Adoption

The major credit card networks are pushing expensive upgrades on companies to adopt the Europay, MasterCard, Visa (EMV) near-field communication (NFC) chip cards in the U.S. by October 2015. Companies that don't adopt the technology will be responsible for all fraud chargebacks shifting liability from credit card companies to merchants.

ACI Worldwide, which powers electronic payments and banking, states on its website, "The move to EMV gives financial institutions an opportunity to reinvent their business model for business lines which are facing reduced revenues." Bitcoin already solves all the things that EMV is attempting to solve without piling solutions on top of an old framework.

The PCI data security standard, one of the "gotchas" mentioned in Credit Card Chaos, strikes again. The EMV implementation is coupled with new PCI standards that take effect from time to time creating an ever-increasing, expensive maze of complexity. Consulting firms specialize in PCI compliance especially for larger companies. For example, a $500 million company could pay between $4 million and $40 million to set up PCI compliance with an additional $8-$12 million of ongoing compliance costs. Contrast this with a small business that has to choose from nine different self-assessment questionnaires and likely can't figure this out without paying for it. Therefore, most small businesses are not in compliance due to the negative cost benefit. Bitcoin simply vaporizes PCI because there is no sensitive financial information to store, nothing to breach, no PCI to comply with, no expensive consultants to hire and no mandated, expensive equipment upgrades. [136]

In the bitcoin world, PCI stands for "pretty cheap implementation." Only a bitcoin address is needed for bitcoin payments while credit card payments can require a page full of information including name, address and credit card info. Everyone has experienced the letdown of getting to a checkout page littered with input fields. In addition, foreign purchases on U.S. websites have a fraud rate in the 20-25% range making it difficult for many foreign credit card holders to make purchases on U.S. websites. Bitcoin extinguishes foreign payment friction completely.

## Bitcoin Billing Limitation

Bitcoin users push payments to merchants, not the other way around, so its design doesn't allow for recurring subscription payments pulled from bank accounts, which we're accustomed to in the old model.

This is a stark contrast to stored credit card information requiring PCI compliance, but it's a fair trade-off. We all know the hassle of trying to disentangle from an unsavory merchant that keeps billing for unwanted services. Plus many bitcoin payment processors offer rebilling or recurring invoices but the payments are not automatic. People who've experienced this may like the one-way, consumer-to-merchant-feature of bitcoin. On the other hand, consumers can't "set it and forget it" for utility bills and other monthly services.

## Business Subscription Challenge

This lack of subscription capability is a potential pitfall for a business whose customers sign on once for monthly auto-billing and usually forget about the monthly cost, especially if they're getting value from the product or service. If they are no longer getting a monthly charge, they might experience the inconvenience of "losing" the service because they've forgotten to "push" the monthly fee via bitcoin.

Merchants that use Coinbase as their bitcoin payment service provider can set up subscription billing, but only for customers who also have a Coinbase account. This is short-term limitation as innovation will eventually close the gap with a subscriptions solution.

## Limitations Equal Opportunities

Now is a great time to creatively seek loyal customers by understanding the lifetime value of a customer. Make special deals just for bitcoin customers and they will love you for it. Offer some type of lifetime membership that overcomes the limitations of subscription billing. In addition, give bitcoin customers bonuses that other customers don't get such as free reports, videos, webinars, podcasts, products or discounts on upsells. Also give them priority access, previews to upcoming products and services, or special membership rights. The possibilities are only limited by your imagination.

## Unique bitcoin payment Issues

A customer makes a bitcoin payment on a website then gets distracted and pays a second time just a few seconds later. The merchant ends up with a double payment or overpayment that has to be refunded. Some bitcoin payment processors offer an overpayment button. For example, BitPay's hosted solution platform automatically creates a customer overpayment notification with a Request Refund button.

Customers may also inadvertently underpay an invoice or make multiple payments from different bitcoin addresses. A notification will usually appear telling customers how much they need to pay to complete an order. For example, bitcoin merchant Tiger Direct gives customers 15 minutes to complete an order. If time expires before full payment is made, the customer has 24 hours to call customer service and finish the order. After the 24-hour timeline is blown, the customer has to contact the payment processor (BitPay in this case) to request a refund. [137]

## Support Desk & FAQs

These unique situations and customers' new experiences of using bitcoin will generate a whole new set of customer inquiries; therefore, merchants should be prepared to handle it. Larger businesses have the resources for dedicated bitcoin support, while smaller businesses may want to add bitcoin FAQs to their websites. In addition, the top two to three FAQs could be addressed with an automated phone tree response leading to a customer service option if their question doesn't get answered. For your own business' website, develop how-to diagrams with screenshots including bitcoin payments, underpayments, overpayments and expired orders. Follow the examples in the "bitcoin help" pages of the larger bitcoin-accepting retailers.

## Claim You're the First

It's often valuable to claim you're the first at something. Being the first to claim you accept bitcoin in your niche or industry is no different. Only 3000 merchants accepted bitcoin at the beginning of 2013 exploding to over 100,000 in 2015. BitPay and Coinbase, two notable merchant service providers, saw their customer bases triple in a few short months.

As an example, I founded invizibiz.biz, a virtual accounting and back office service geared to start-ups and small- and medium-sized businesses. We provide all-in-cloud, all-paperless, outsourced business process solutions. Bitcoin is a natural extension of our business philosophy so of course we eagerly embraced it. In the process of researching bitcoin business directories and social media platforms, my company became the first to get listed in many accounting and consulting categories. Although I may not have found every directory, I can proudly say invizibiz is listed as the first Certified Public Accountants, Certified Management Accountants and Certified Fraud Examiners to accept bitcoin.

You might also find these bitcoin-accepting firsts interesting:

- Sacramento Kings, the first U.S. based sport team to accept bitcoin
- airBaltic, the world's first airline to accept bitcoin
- CheapAir, the first major online travel site to accept bitcoin
- AMECO, the first medical products manufacturer business to accept bitcoin
- Bees Brothers Honey, the first honey producer to accept bitcoin and the world's youngest bitcoin entrepreneurs
- University of Nicosia, the world's first university to accept bitcoin
- Mathias Sundin, the first bitcoin-only political candidate

## Retail Merchant Adoption Tips

Both online and retail businesses have onboarding decisions for hardware, shopping carts, payment processors or point-of-sale systems. Retail brick and mortar businesses should consider staff training for a smooth bitcoin customer checkout experience. Setting up and accepting bitcoin is one thing while training staff is a whole separate exercise. Conversely, online businesses adopting bitcoin won't have the same staff training issues, but they may have more challenges with technology integration.

## It's in the Details

Restaurants or other businesses with on-the-floor customer interaction should use company-dedicated smart phones, if possible, to handle bitcoin sales. The small, seemingly trivial details are the important ones leading to a great customer experience. The bitcoin checkout experience should be as good as or better than existing methods. The better the staff is trained on these details the more likely a business will have a successful bitcoin adoption. "It shouldn't be hard to take people's money", says Paul Puey of AirBitz.co.

The following tips and best practices will help ensure taking people's money is easy.

- Use a smart phone with a home button.
- Increase or disable the screen lock time.
- Use a larger smart phone or small tablet
- Make sure the charger is easily accessible.
- Have at least two devices.
- The devices should be company-owned.
- Remove apps or place them in a subfolder.
- Place the bitcoin app in the docking station.
- Staff should know where the smart phones are at all times.
- Infrequently used devices can get lost in the shuffle.
- Train the staff on all the above.

When all the details are employed, staff is less likely to fumble around trying to accept a customer's bitcoin. The key thing is knowing where the device is and how to use it. Someone within the business should be tasked with taking the lead on implementing these tips and training the staff, including conducting practice runs with bitcoin payments.

## Counter Sales

Retail businesses with a counter-based checkout have some additional considerations for a great customer experience. The biggest bitcoin-accepting challenge is whether or not the current POS system integrates natively with bitcoin payment processors. SoftTouch is a POS example with native bitcoin integration. Any integrations requiring special programming come with additional costs that eventually won't be necessary when more standard integrations become available. Counter-based best practices should also include the following:

- Use a separate, dedicated tablet if POS integration isn't set up.
- Position the tablet next to the existing POS system.
- The tablet should be stationary or it won't be available when needed.
- A separate tablet avoids screen fumbling on the same device.
- Bookmark the bitcoin payment processor URL and make it the homepage.
- Put the application in the docking bar, if applicable.
- Train the staff on all the above.

There are three counter-based scenarios: 1) a POS system with bitcoin integration, 2) a POS system and a separate tablet used for bitcoin, or 3) a tablet used with both a Square swiper and a bitcoin payments processor. Tablet-using businesses with Square, PayPal or similar plug-and-swipe systems can easily add bitcoin with no setup costs and without being tied to legacy POS systems. The dual POS tablet setup allows ringing of sales on the POS while bitcoin payments are accepted on the tablet. A fully integrated POS setup is easier for staff, but may come with more initial cost and time to setup.

## Online Onboarding Challenges

Online businesses have to set up bitcoin acceptance on their websites, but don't have the staff training challenges of a retail business. Integrating bitcoin with existing shopping cart and payment platforms is the biggest challenge for online businesses. For example, if a well-established website has hundreds of products set up in a platform that doesn't easily integrate with bitcoin, the choice is either change to an ecommerce platform that does integrate or hire a service for custom integration. Eventually all shopping cart and ecommerce platforms will add bitcoin or provide a plug-in for easy adoption.

Generally, the smaller the business and the fewer the products or services the easier it is to set up bitcoin payments. An online business with a few products could scrap its legacy shopping cart for a solution like Shopify.com, which has a Coinbase.com integration. Braintree, a full-stack payments platform, makes it easy for merchants to accept payments on an app or website with dozens of shopping cart, ecommerce and billing integrations like FoxyCart, Shopify or U-Commerce. Braintree's Coinbase integration allows merchants to accept bitcoin along with Apple Pay and PayPal, thus creating a merchant-friendly, single integration solution. Bitpay. com's single bitcoin payment button can be dropped anywhere on a website, making it one of the fastest ways to get set up.[138] These are just some examples of the variety of solutions available for accepting bitcoin.

If you're starting a new business from scratch you can create a website on Wix.com, a user-friendly website builder, plug Shopify. com into Wix for accepting bitcoin and link Shopify to Quickbooks. com accounting software with a sync app. Now you have an online, end-to-end, easy-to-set-up, bitcoin-accepting business covering marketing, sales, payments and accounting. If you already have a website and shopping cart, your business is almost guaranteed a path to accepting bitcoin considering the wide range of overlapping options. Professional service businesses who bill by the hour and send unique invoices typically have no website integration issues because they can fire up GoCoin, BitPay, Coinbase or many others and send invoices in minutes.

**Proudly display the "bitcoin accepted here" logo when your online or brick-and-mortar business is set up to accept bitcoin.**

Image courtesy of bitcoin promotional graphics wiki

Go to BestBitcoinBookEver.com/bonus right now to get best practices and feature updates on various platforms.

## Bitcoin Success Stories

Tigerdirect.com brought in $250,000 worth of bitcoin sales on its first day of acceptance and $1,000,000 within a few weeks.[139] Similarly, Overstock.com reached $1,000,000 in sales within two months with 60% of the purchases made by new customers.[140] Australian online retailer, Millennius, experienced 5% of sales in Bitcoin and Litecoin, significantly more than Overstock's 1% of sales. In some cases, retailers had average bitcoin sales more than twice that of credit cards with a fraud rate of 0% and 2.7% respectively. [141]

The power of bitcoin comes from impacting profit rather than just reducing transaction fees and headaches. According to Bain & Company, many retailers operate on notoriously razor-thin profit margins of 1-4%. For example, a retailer with a 1% profit margin and 3% credit card fees can use bitcoin's role-reversing magic to gain a 3% profit margin and 1% in processing fees. If a company's bitcoin sales totaled $1,000,000, the profit would triple from $10,000 to $30,000. Businesses with higher profit margins won't experience the same results, but every business can benefit by eliminating the headaches and hidden costs of credit card chaos. [142]

## Transaction Fees and Profit Margins Example

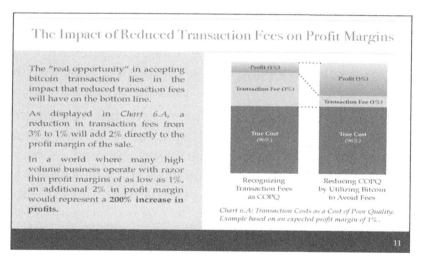

Image courtesy of Ryan Walker

## Bitcoin Merchant On-Ramp Takeaway

There's a wide range of solutions for accepting bitcoin in your business. Payment service providers offer dashboards, invoicing, shopping cart plug-ins and more. Getting set up to accept bitcoin can be as fast as a few hours, but could be longer depending on the size and type of business, and whether it's a web store or a bricks-and-mortar operation. Microbusinesses and publicly traded companies alike should create a plan to proactively promote and incentivize bitcoin adoption among their customers. For example, consider passing on savings from credit card fees to customers. Your customers will become more loyal, bitcoin-adopting fans of your business. Over time the B2B or B2C relationship will strengthen as the additional benefits of Bitcoin technology are realized. It's so easy to accept bitcoin there's no reason not to accept it.

Manage the risk in your business separately from your investments; accepting bitcoins and choosing how much to cash out is a separate consideration from investing in bitcoin. Use the same discretion and due diligence for bitcoin and cryptocurrencies as you would for any other investment, business strategy or cash flow management decisions. A business can always choose to cash bitcoin into fiat currency without having to manage, store, understand, be subject to volatility, or account for bitcoin transactions. Your business may get more customers this way, but it can't take advantage of other opportunities available with bitcoin. A full cash out also doesn't support the bitcoin ecosystem.

Sign up for accounts at multiple payment service providers to become familiar with their respective platforms. Choose a merchant service provider with the best integrity, transparency, security and feature set that fits your business. Coinkite.com has set the standard with full disclosure about every part of their service. This way you'll find out which ones have the best tool set, the most intuitive dashboard, and the best customer service that also matches your risk management strategy. Alternatively, Gocoin could be set up on a website while Coinbase could be used for email-based invoicing and recurring payments. These platforms provide APIs allowing them to be customized and adapted with new and existing services. By using and test driving multiple payment service providers, you can also take advantage of unique features only available on specific platforms while having the option to switch to an alternative should an issue arise.

Early adopters have a steeper hill to climb but the first ones to the mountaintop always reap the rewards. So start accepting bitcoin as soon as possible, then make calls to the press for as much free, once-in-a-lifetime publicity as your business can get. Restaurants or other retail establishments would be great for this strategy. Be creative and set up something like "Bitcoin Wallet Night" where your staff trains customers on setting up a wallet that entitles them to special promotions for spending their first bitcoins. Staff training is the key when it comes to retail customers. Generally, the smaller the business the easier it is to adopt bitcoin because of fewer decision makers, locations or custom integrations. Dell proved it could be done in two weeks while effectively eliminating any reasons why a business shouldn't accept bitcoin. Remember bitcoin is like having a birthday party for your business—complete with the gift of reducing expenses and eliminating headaches. Don't be the last adopter in your industry.

# Bitcoin Microtransactions & Paywalls

## Micro Opportunity

Microtransactions, or micropayments, are now possible thanks to bitcoin. A microtransaction is simply a charge for a small chunk of information for a very small payment (usually less than one dollar), or any other amount where credit card fees would otherwise make a sale cost prohibitive. If a business charged customers $.30 to access an article, then PayPal's 2.9% plus $.30 per transaction would never make sense. Micropayments can also be used for tipping.

## Paywalls

Bitcoin paywall sites such as bitmonet.com, coinwall.co and bitwall. io, offer microtransactions, generally without any account signup for the business. Traditional paywalls offer subscription access to web content but businesses have to create an account to use the service. The bitcoin paywalls are free and easy to use; however, some of them interface with a payment processor like BitPay.

## As You Like It

Bitmonet.com caters specifically to the publishing industry while the overall concept is best suited for images, content and music. The bitcoin paywalls provide maximum versatility for customers by charging per article or view, by the hour, by the day, or in the case of bitwall.io, by the tweet to access content. *The Chicago Sun Times* used Bitwall in the first notable case study that successfully used microtransactions.

## Easy Setup

The setup is as easy as adding your bitcoin wallet address, the price per delivery method, the hook copy and the corresponding content that's released when a micro payment is made. Then a snippet, hosted URL or plug-in is available to install the bitcoin paywall. In addition, Bitwall provides merchant analytics to track how customers interact with the paywall. More of these features are likely to develop over time.

## Love Button

ChangeTip.com allows people to show appreciation for the value of any Internet content like a love button instead of a like. Their tagline sums it up, "Building a micropayments infrastructure for giving and generosity on the Internet." Whether it's a podcast or an article, ChangeTip provides an easy way for passionate people who provide content to receive micropayments in support of their efforts. This use case would have been previously cost prohibitive with old rail models like credits cards and demonstrates a brilliant application of Bitcoin technology.

ChangeTip makes tipping with words of appreciation as easy as a tweet, either directly through the ChangeTip platform or with Twitter. Tipping monikers are like a menu of appreciation with predefined words of love and tipping amounts used to represent money where a "Thank You" is $5 in bitcoin and "Quality Work" is a $20 tip. Users can click on a moniker and send a tip in seconds or create any tip amount on the fly. For example, a simple tweet such as, "Hey @TheBitcoinCPA your insight is excellent. Here's $4 on me @ChangeTip," is automatically detected by ChangeTip bots and sent to the recipient. Unlike other bitcoin payments the tip is cancelled if it's not accepted within seven days. Other social media platforms such as YouTube, Facebook, reddit, Google+, tumblr and more can be used in the same way. Every user gets a unique link such as http://thebitcoincpa.tip.me, which can be inserted anywhere such as within the website copy or email signature blocks, thus providing another way for fans to show appreciation. Code is also available to embed a ChangeTip link on a website. Everyone should set up an account and engage the law of giving and receiving!

## Auto Tipping

ProTip is a web browser plug-in-based wallet designed to grab bitcoin addresses from frequently used sites. It automatically makes bitcoin payouts every seven days based on user-defined settings, including a total amount for payout. Users can also set up favorites by subscribing to a bitcoin address for inclusion in the weekly payout. "This is all about building tools that help facilitate conversations in markets," says ProTip creator Chris Ellis. This is a great tool for overcoming the mental obstacle of tipping multiple times throughout the day or week. It's like a "set it and forget it" tool for passively tipping content creators who provide the most value. Contrast this with ChangeTip which requires intentional, active tipping on behalf of the user. Both approaches can be useful while serving different purposes. Paywalls and in-app messaging are forthcoming features of the ProTip plug-in. [143]

## Paid by the Minute

Streamium.io allows users to stream live video while getting paid instantly by viewers. Just create a live stream, add a bitcoin address, enter the rate per hour (for example, $60 per hour), and share the Streamium video link. Private lessons, live podcasts, consulting and educational courses are great use cases. If someone watches for 37 minutes, you get paid $37 worth of bitcoins—instantly, with no fees, and most importantly, no banks or middlemen. [144]

## Bitcoin Microtransactions & Paywalls Takeaway

Microtransactions are one of the most important breakthroughs resulting from Bitcoin technology. A whole new world of value transfer is possible that wasn't possible before by changing not just the way payments are made, but the way people interact. This model is perfect for Internet marketers and infopreneurs and relevant for any business that sells information or content. Merchants should ask themselves how they can use these tools to monetize existing products as well as new products, get more customer engagement or a combination of these things. Whether you want to add a paywall for content on an existing site, add tipping to a website or blog, or get paid for a one-off video, versatile tools are already available to make it happen. The tweet for access, pay as you like it, and yet-to-be-created features open up a new way to deliver customer value. Brand new business models will also emerge from microtransactions. Will your new business idea be one of them?

# Bitcoin Directories, Forums, Reputation & Identity

The Bitcoin social sphere comes in a variety of forms including bitcoin business directories, bitcoin-focused social media sites, bitcoin forums and combination sites or as features of another platform. All of these platforms are a great way to connect with the global bitcoin community which includes everyone from beginners who want to learn more about bitcoin to developers interacting with enthusiasts and businesses engaging with the community.

## Bitcoin Forums & Social Media

There are several bitcoin subreddits on Reddit.com that generally mirror the bitcoin ecosystem. Bitcointalk.org is an online community forum similar to the subreddits except the entire site was created just for bitcoiners. Similarly, many Bitcoin 2.0 projects such as Counterparty and Bitshares have their own forums called counterpartytalk.org and bitsharestalk.org, respectively. Anyone with an interest in bitcoin can find a way to engage with others who have a similar interest. The forums can also be used to get more information on a topic or to research business opportunities and engage with like-minded people to solve problems or start new ideas. There are also numerous Facebook pages on everything bitcoin. The one and only Let's Talk Bitcoin, a multi-medium platform known for its signature podcasts and unique peer-to-peer interactions, is covered later in the chapter on Beyond the Coin.

Zapchain.com is a bitcoin-centric social media platform whose tagline is "the best place to learn about bitcoin." Here, beginners as well as bitcoin experts can engage with each other by answering questions, liking a comment, following another member or tipping another for sharing good info. New members engage by answering questions and getting influence points until they get enough points to start asking their own questions. Zapchain also has a podcast and uses the platform to gather interview questions for guests of the show. The question and answer format is the distinguishing feature of the platform.

## Bitcoin Directories

Several free bitcoin business directory sites exist with combination social media or other features. If a business can say "bitcoin accepted here" then it can be listed in a directory. This isn't always required or verified, but users search these directories with the assumption that only businesses accepting bitcoin are listed. Any business category from services and products to online and retail can get listed, generally for free. This is also a great way to claim a top listing spot in a particular category, depending on the platform. Airbitz.co is a combination mobile wallet as well as a business directory that helps people find bitcoin-accepting businesses near them via GPS. If you have a hankering for pizza in New York City, simply log in and find the nearest bitcoin-friendly pizza shop. Airbitz also sources and creates a high-quality business listings for free, making this a unique proposition among directories.

Bitcoinyellowpages.com, btcpages.com, bitcoindir.com, and bitcoiney.com are examples of basic business directories. Bitcoinada.com is geographically focused on businesses accepting bitcoin in Canada. Some directories only have a few hundred listings, which makes it a great time to get listed and promote a business.

## Hybrid Platforms

Bitcorati.com is an example of a platform that's a combination business directory and social media platform. It's a convergence of bitcoin-accepting businesses, bitcoin enthusiasts and contributors to the bitcoin ecosystem. Members can post public or private messages, join groups and post blogs among others.

Bitscan is another example of a social networking and business directory site with an eBay-like classified platform. Several thousand businesses were listed in 2015 as well as thousands of regular members called "bitscanners" making it one of the largest directories. Individuals set up a profile with a corresponding 236-maximum point scale representing a trust score that other bitscanners can use within the platform or elsewhere within the bitcoin ecosystem as a gauge for conducting business with someone.

For example, the 236-point scale includes fields for name, address, email, mobile phone, social media links, bitcoin wallet address, etc. Voluntarily supplying information results in a higher Bitscan score for trust and credibility. Personal profiles and business profiles can be set up with descriptions about the stuff you're up to, the services you provide and social media links with an option to have Bitscan spread those profiles into the social media universe. Bitscan has a social networking and linking feature, which allows members to connect and form communities. Writers can also post articles and get paid based on the interest an article generates. Businesses can advertise on the site and get paid referral fees from advertising revenue.

## The Value of Bitcoin Reputation & Identity

Bonafide.io is a reputation scoring system linked to a user's existing social media profiles such as Facebook and Twitter, and bitcoin platforms such as ChangeTip and Coinbase. A system for credibility is welcome in a space where bankruptcies, fraud and bad actors give bitcoin a bad name. This could help spark merchant adoption and be valuable in all transactions, including B2B, B2C and peer-to-peer. "What we've found is that people need to identify with something, whether it's a person or entity in the bitcoin ecosystem. People need to be able to see what's out there," says Brian Moyer, Bonafide.io co-founder. Users build reputations by sending and receiving bitcoins and leaving reviews so this platform can be used for any and all transactions as desired. [145]

Bitrated is an identity reputation and trust platform discussed later in the Practical Bitcoin Business Tools chapter, related to the smart contracts and multisig features. The reputation part of the platform, however, is similar to Bonafide, providing value across the bitcoin ecosystem.

Onename.com released the first blockchain-based identity service by registering users' existing profiles in the bitcoin blockchain. For example, my Facebook profile can be verified by sharing a public post such as "Verifying I am +thebitcoincpa on my passcard. https://onename.com/thebitcoincpa." Your passcard ties your Facebook post and others into the blockchain and this approach may eventually replace traditional login credentials. A Onename blog declared, "Today, we're giving the user profiles more meaning and power, something that you could truly call your personal digital identity. We're calling them passcards and they're much more than profiles." These approaches to identity and reputation make it infeasible to create false personas and thus become more valuable for others to rely on. [146]

## Bitcoin Directories, Forums, Reputation & Identity Takeaway

A bitcoin-accepting business strategy must include getting listed in every business directory and social site available. It's often valuable to claim you're the first at something. Being the first to claim you accept bitcoin in your niche or industry is no different. Your business could add new bitcoin-related service offerings or focus existing services on bitcoin startups, for example. This is another once-in-a-lifetime opportunity to define your business in the early stages of this technology so don't limit your exposure to just accepting bitcoin.

Knowing what you know now, don't you wish you could roll back the clock when LinkedIn had only 300 members? New directories only have a few hundred listings, which presents a great opportunity to lock in a first place listing in a business category. List your business early and often because some of these sites will gain serious traction. Bitcoin startups should do the same thing so that traditional businesses get exposed to the awesome new platforms transforming the way business gets done.

Niche social media platforms provide a huge opportunity to connect with the bitcoin community from promoting your business to understanding the issues. The bitcoin community is relatively small and obsessed about Bitcoin making it easy to reach out and connect. It's also important to develop a reputation for trust inside an otherwise trustless technology; therefore, the bitcoin social, reputation and identity sites are more important than simply getting your business in multiple listings. Sign up and start building your reputation today.

# Bitcoin Wallets

## Bitcoin Safekeeping

Businesses and individuals are 100% responsible for their bitcoins, an ongoing theme that bears repeating. Keeping bitcoins safe requires a thorough understanding of bitcoin wallet strategy, thus making it the heart and soul of bitcoin from a user perspective.

There are several types of bitcoin wallets such as desktop wallets, web wallets, mobile wallets, hardware wallets, paper wallets, vaults and others. All bitcoin wallet types are either hot wallets or cold wallets. A cold wallet is generally "Internet free" meaning it was never used or generated on a computer with an Internet connection, also known as an air-gapped computer. It can also be any other offline medium. A hot wallet is used on an Internet-connected device and is defined as any wallet that's not a cold wallet.

One type of wallet is not necessarily better than another because each one serves a particular purpose. The benefits of the different wallet types are more valuable when they're used in conjunction with one another. Generally speaking, bitcoin wallets have an inverse relationship between convenience and security. The more convenient your bitcoin wallet is for buying and selling stuff, generally the less secure it is and the greater the risk of losing bitcoins for various reasons discussed later. Conversely, the more secure a bitcoin wallet, the less convenient it is.

## BIPs

Bitcoin Improvement Proposals, known as BIPs, are a set of standards used by bitcoin developers. A new proposal is accepted with mutual consensus from the developer community. Each one is like a special tool that can do something unique and many BIPs are breakthrough improvements on the original bitcoin protocol. There are dozens of BIPs, which can be reviewed at the BIPs wiki, but for purposes of this book we'll be looking at BIP 32, BIP 38 and BIP 39. These BIPs relate to wallets and the following discussion highlights the different types of storage methods and specific platforms.

## BIP 39: Mnemonic Code for Generating Deterministic Keys

This breakthrough BIP creates an easy way to use computer-generated randomness in the form of a mnemonic sentence also known as a passphrase such as: *"loser cross purpose jealous innocence haunt button trick essence scream proud excuse"* instead of managing a very long seed or a private key such as: KziXBfNy 2eZEKHdZeBZQ3ZyW3joXcv2k66yHuKPaDgNwEX76wMPU. A mnemonic passphrase is obviously easier to write, save, speak and transcribe. The mnemonic sentence is cleverly derived from an algorithm and then processed through another algorithm to generate a seed which is used by BIP 32 described below to create a master key. Basically users only need to be concerned with storing the passphrase. [147]

## BIP 32: Hierarchical Deterministic Wallets

Old-style bitcoin wallets generated new private keys and their respective bitcoin addresses independent of each other, thus requiring regular backups to capture newly added addresses and transactions. BIP 32 wallets use a seed generated by BIP 39 to generate a master private key, unlimited child keys and related bitcoin addresses. If a computer fails or you otherwise can't access your wallet, then a properly stored passphrase can regenerate the seed, the master key and the wallet, with all the addresses and transactions, just like nothing happened. This is once-and-done storage of one piece of information in lieu of having to make continuous backups. A master public key can produce all the addresses in a wallet while a master private key can produce all the private keys in a wallet, like a tree trunk extending to all its roots. The master public key can be used to view the balance of all addresses but can't spend any bitcoins.

The hierarchical nature of BIP 32 gives users a choice to produce new addresses for every transaction, which allows for greater privacy instead of using a publicly viewable, single address showcasing all your transactions. Many platforms have integrated BIP32 as part of their feature set. BIP 32 can also be applied in a corporate structure where the CFO maintains supreme control of the master private key and generates subsequent child keys for regional controllers. This application has limitations but highlights the capabilities of the standard. [148]

## BIP 38: Passphrase-Protected, Private Key

Private keys can be encrypted with a passphrase using platforms like bitcoinpaperwallet.com that have a BIP 38 encryption tool. This passphrase is like putting a deadbolt on your private key and should not be confused with the BIP 39 passphrase mentioned above. Many people refer to BIP 38 as password protection instead of referring to it as passphrase protection. This feature is excellent for creating two-factor security; combining something you have with something you know. With these tools you can either generate a new paper wallet or encrypt an existing wallet. Always test the passphrase by successfully decrypting it using the decryption feature in the same tool set. Otherwise your bitcoins will be trapped if you send them to a freshly created wallet with a bad passphrase. Several physical wallet companies produce "paper wallets" using wood, stainless steel or synthetic paper for a more durable wallet in lieu of using paper. For example, BIP 38 allows you to submit a private key and public key pair with your purchase without compromising any security. If you didn't passphrase protect the private key, then in theory anyone at these companies could later steal your bitcoins. Paper wallets with bitcoins could also be sent via mail as a payment to a person or company while the passphrase could be communicated over a different channel such as email or by phone.

Bitcoinpaperwallet.com, Bippy.org and many others provide BIP 38 password tools. [149, 150]

## Making Change

It's important to visualize how bitcoin transactions work in the context of change addresses and related risk management while providing an easy to understand cash transaction analogy. A change address is the address used to receive change from a bitcoin transaction. It's generally the address used to spend bitcoin or a new bitcoin address that hasn't been used before. New bitcoin change addresses are used to enhance privacy and security.

Let's look at a fiat cash transaction example to better understand change addresses. If you buy office supplies for $22.39 you either have to use exact dollars and coins or overpay with the expectation of getting change. Paying with a $10 and a $20 bill for a total of $30 results in change of one $5 bill, two $1 bills, two quarters, one dime and one penny for a total of $7.61. The same holds true for bitcoin except coins and dollars are substituted for unspent outputs, which is simply the bitcoin "change" received from a previous transaction, a bitcoin payment for goods and services, or a bitcoin transfer. Inputs are the bitcoins used to send a bitcoin payment or make a bitcoin transfer. Conversely, the bitcoins received are the unspent outputs, which then become the inputs of future transactions.

## Transaction Privacy

The blockchain is a public ledger of all transactions and related details without the corresponding identity of the people making the transaction. It's a great example of pseudonymity, or partial anonymity. If the bitcoin change received from a transaction goes back to the sending address instead of a newly created, never before used change address, the identity of one or both parties in the transaction could be exposed at a later time. Different wallets and platforms have varying degrees of security and privacy, which can be quite complex, so it's important to consider privacy as part of an overall bitcoin and cryptocurrency strategy. Individuals may have to exercise a higher degree of care because individuals have the right of privacy while businesses have the duty of transparency.

## Desktop Wallets

Desktop wallets are installed and maintained on, you guessed it, a desktop computer. Users have complete control and responsibility over their wallets with desktop wallet software. This wallet type is more secure by nature because you don't rely on third parties, but it's only usable when you're at the computer. Desktop wallets are generally used in online mode except for Armory's unique approach, which makes them an Internet-connected hot wallet. However, users have options to make their desktop wallets more secure. Examples of desktop wallets include the bitcoin core wallet, bitcoinarmory.com, electrum.org and multibit.org, which are all open source, free, downloadable software. Free user software comes with a cost of maintenance and development offset by the generous support from donations from readers like you.

The typical desktop bitcoin wallet comes standard with these simple features:

- Wallet backup for saving an encrypted or unencrypted file copy
- Encrypt wallet with a passphrase (sending bitcoins and other actions can't be performed without the passphrase)
- Change passphrase
- Send bitcoins
- Receive bitcoins
- Transactions list
- Address list and new address button
- Sign message to verify wallet ownership

# Example of a typical desktop wallet based on bitcoin core

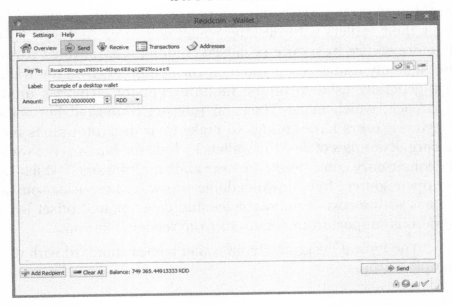

Image courtesy of the Reddcoin and Bitcoin developers

The open source nature of the bitcoin core wallet means many altcoins such as Syscoin, Infinitecoin, Vertcoin and Reddcoin, to name a few, have copied the source code so their respective wallets look essentially the same as bitcoin core. Once you understand and get comfortable with one of these wallets you already know how to use them all.

## Armory

The bitcoin core wallet must be downloaded at bitcoin.org to run in conjunction with the Armory wallet, bitcoinarmory.com, making it a "thick" client. Bitcoin core takes a while to install; installation includes a full download of the bitcoin blockchain while users get the benefit of becoming a network-supporting node. Armory is installed on both an Internet-connected computer and a non-Internet-connected computer (an air-gapped computer), which work in conjunction with one another in a unique desktop cold storage scheme. First, a new wallet is generated on the offline computer keeping the private keys in permanent cold storage. Then a "watching only wallet" backup file is saved to a USB drive and imported on the online computer. Sending bitcoin is done in three simple steps using a USB drive as the liaison between the two computers:

1. Create an unsigned bitcoin transaction (using the online computer)
2. Sign the transaction (using the offline computer)
3. Broadcast the transaction (using the online computer)

Armory's website sums it up like this, "Armory pioneered easily managing offline Bitcoin wallets using a computer that never touches the Internet. Everything needed to create transactions can be managed from an online computer with a watching only wallet. All secret private key data is available only on the offline computer. This greatly reduces the attack surface for an attacker attempting to steal bitcoins. By keeping all private-key data on the offline computer only someone with physical access to the offline computer can steal your Bitcoins. Plus, Armory employs many security practices so that even if someone physically stole your offline system then it still may take centuries for them to get through the advanced wallet encryption!"

This is similar to the cold storage technique used by several bitcoin vault services described later. An unlimited number of wallets can be created while Armory's recommended one-time-only paper backup can recover any forgotten wallet password made possible by a technology similar to BIP 32 hierarchically deterministic (HD) wallets mentioned earlier. It requires more computer resources, more work to understand and set up, and comes with more features and security than any other desktop wallet, making it the recommended choice for enterprise grade business use or individuals needing to store large amounts of bitcoin. Hands down, it's one of the best self-serve cold storage methods available. [151]

## Thinner Versions

Electrum.org and Multibit.org are "thin" clients that don't require a full download of the blockchain. They require fewer computer resources, less work to understand and set up and therefore less robust than Armory, which makes them great for experimenting with smaller bitcoin amounts. Both have many great features but it always comes back to convenience and security trade-off.

The Electrum wallet About tab states, "Electrum's focus is speed, with low resource usage and simplifying bitcoin. You do not need to perform regular backups, because your wallet can be recovered from a secret phrase that you can memorize or write on paper. Start times are instant because it operates in conjunction with high-performance servers that handle the most complicated parts of the bitcoin system."

General attributes of and best practices for desktop wallets include the following:

- Private keys are encrypted on your computer, not external servers.
- Encrypt wallets with a passphrase.
- Back up passphrases and private keys on paper for bitcoin wallet recovery.
- Alternatively, store passphrases and private keys in a secure note of a password manager.
- Create a wallet backup file of the wallet data file (.dat for example).
- Save the backup file to USB or computer hard drive, or attach the file to a secure note as mentioned above.
- Either the private key or the passphrase of an encrypted wallet has to be properly stored and managed (i.e., There is always a final end point of information must always be managed with care).
- Paper backups are defenses against computer failure, forgotten passphrases and stolen computers.
- Combine physical security of a safe with digital security.

- Transactions are signed on an air-gapped computer for best security.
- Bitcoin transactions are sent or broadcasted from a different second computer.
- More security equals less convenience and vice versa.

## Desktop Wallets Takeaway

Businesses should manage desktop wallets and other cold storage strategies discussed later to minimize risk by keeping bitcoins in an appropriate wallet matching low frequency of transactions and higher bitcoin amounts with more security. Desktop wallets should be encrypted using the encrypt wallet feature with a corresponding backup of the wallet file. If your computer crashes or you have to uninstall and reinstall the bitcoin client then both are needed to restore your wallet. Desktop wallets can be used without encrypting the wallet; however, the wallet file should still be backed up. An unencrypted wallet with no passphrase is more convenient and would be acceptable to use in a manner like petty cash. Strong passphrases provide more security and should be backed up on paper and kept in a fireproof safe and/or stored in a secure note of a password management system.

Most desktop wallets are free and heed the warning "this is experimental software," which is another reason to follow security procedures in the event anything goes wrong. Larger organizations should apply chain of custody procedures for desktop wallets and other types of cold storage. These wallets range from a thin client like Electrum to an enterprise class workhorse like Armory. The former could be used in the unencrypted petty cash example while the latter can be set up on dedicated hardware security modules to secure the Fortune 500. The features also range from simple send and receive commands to distributed, auditable, enterprise security for multi-national operations.

## Web Wallet and Mobile Wallet Tandem

Web wallets or online wallets are simply hot wallets used as an online platform. Web wallets exist in tandem with the creation of an account on a bitcoin or cryptocurrency exchange or they can be a stand-alone service. Many wallet services also exist in tandem as a web wallet service and corresponding mobile wallet app. Some web wallets have no sister app and some mobile wallets have no sister web wallet. (Bitcoin exchanges and their related wallets are discussed in another chapter.)

Both web wallets and mobile wallets are generally less secure and more convenient than desktop wallets; however, mobile wallets are more secure than web wallets because smart phones don't get infected with viruses and malware like desktop computers. Web wallet-mobile wallet duos usually recommend using the mobile app whenever possible. The convenience of logging into a wallet anywhere, anytime, creates web wallet risk; the risk that login IDs, passwords or private keys could be breached or hacked the same as any other online account. Web wallet platforms have many innovative security features to minimize this risk, but cold storage methods still provide greater security.

Mobile wallets are hot wallet apps on your smart phone that can be a stand-alone app or an app provided by an exchange. Mobile wallets make sending and receiving bitcoin as easy as tapping a few buttons, scanning a QR code or pasting someone's bitcoin address. For example, Coinbase is an exchange and merchant service provider that also has a mobile wallet. Hybrid platforms like this one show how challenging it can be to categorize services in the bitcoin ecosystem. Mycelium.com and airBitz.co are examples of pure mobile wallet apps while web and mobile wallet tandems include blockchain.info, hivewallet.com and greenaddress.it. Wallet apps provide easy guidance for backing up in addition to other security features.

## This image depicts the joy of a mobile bitcoin wallet.

Image credit: iStock-Thinkstock (merznatalia)

## Web & Mobile Wallet Examples

**Mycelium.com** is an Android-based app with a rich feature set and easy-to-use, intuitive interface. Sending bitcoins is as easy as tapping a saved contact and choosing the send amount while receiving bitcoins is as easy sharing your bitcoin address or having someone scan a QR code. Private keys always remain on the smart phone until they're backed up to an encrypted PDF. The keys are encrypted using a 15-character password that must be stored in a safe or password manager. The spend-from cold storage feature allows users to spend bitcoin from a paper wallet while immediately erasing private keys from device memory after the bitcoins are spent. Multiple bitcoin addresses including watch-only or view-only addresses can be set up in a Mycelium wallet and displayed as an aggregate total. [152] Business, personal and specific-use bitcoin addresses can be easily maintained with this wallet. Mycelium also has additional features and related products as follows:

- Address book for saving send-to bitcoin addresses
- Wallet PIN for extra security
- Local Trader that helps people find and trade bitcoins using an encrypted chat
- Entropy, a special USB device for securely printing paper wallets separate from the app

**airBitz.co** is a pure mobile wallet and business directory combo available for both the apple iPhone and Google android platforms. The airBitz website is for informational purposes only and doesn't act as a web wallet companion site. Its easy-to-use, intuitive interface is packed with features and security. No personal info is required to set up and use this free bitcoin wallet with automatic backups, client-side encryption and easy access. A simple username and PIN are needed to use the app while a password is also required to set up the wallet and make changes to the settings.

## The airBitz app screenshots show the login, business directory and wallet features.

Image courtesy of airBitz.co

The business directory is a no-brainer for finding places to spend your bitcoins while merchant info is automatically added to transactions for business backup documentation. The blue tooth feature eliminates QR code scanning for sending bitcoins while requests for money can be made via email, text, QR code or copy and paste. Pre-populated expense categories provide easy tracking for bitcoin purchases and multiple export formats are great for accounting system importing. The settings also provide per day and per transaction spending limits along with a host of user preferences and security settings. The complete feature set makes this a must-have, business-ready mobile wallet.

**Hivewallet.com** is "a human-friendly digital token wallet for multiple platforms." It is ultra-simple and easy to use with no account setup required. Anyone can start using a new bitcoin wallet in seconds by clicking "create new wallet" which generates a passphrase and corresponding user-created, four-digit PIN allowing users to quickly log in without having to type a 12-word passphrase every time they want to buy a cup of coffee. Five failed PIN attempts results in a lockout that can be unlocked by entering the backed up passphrase, similar to how greenaddress. it works. Hive currently supports Bitcoin and Litecoin with more forthcoming. The coins are not stored on a server and the wallet doesn't require a backup. The passphrase should be securely saved in a password manager and saved as a paper backup. The sister hive web wallet can be accessed from the web, but the mobile version is recommended.

**Blockchain.info** is a free platform with a bitcoin block explorer, bitcoin charts, stats, market information and a web wallet that's been downloaded over three million times in 2015. It easily pairs with all smart phone applications by scanning a simple QR code. The private keys are encrypted with a user-controlled password and stored on platform servers. Blockchain does not store the password and can't access bitcoin wallets, which allows users to retain full control. Double security can be set up to allow one password for login and a second password for sending transactions.

Continuous wallet backups can be set up automatically whenever a transaction takes place. Many bitcoin-related crowdsales require participants to send bitcoins from a web wallet like blockchain.

The Blockchain.info block explorer can used to search the details of any bitcoin transaction as shown below.

Image courtesy of Blockchain.info

Some additional features of blockchain.info web wallets include the following:

- Two-factor authentication is set up via SMS, email, YubiKey or Google authenticator.
- Encrypted wallet backups can be made via download, Dropbox, Google drive, email or paper.
- You can easily send bitcoins with Facebook, email or SMS.
- An address book is available for convenience.
- You can restrict access to specific IP addresses.
- Login level can determine unauthorized access with a privacy trade-off.
- The mobile app has a four-digit PIN for easy access.
- Wallet files can be imported.
- Watching-only wallets can be set up.

- Numerous additional security features are available.

**Greenaddress.it** has woven convenience and security together in a web wallet full of features with a corresponding smart phone app and an optional Chrome browser plug-in. "Greenaddress provides an easier, safer and faster way of transacting and storing bitcoin," says Lawrence Nahum, the company's founder. Greenaddress combines two-factor authentication with two-of-two multisig signed both greenaddress.it and the user for sending bitcoin. This provides additional security so the person receiving the bitcoins can trust the funds as an "instant green address transaction" that can't be double spent. The user's private key is derived from a 24-word mnemonic passphrase so a securely stored passphrase is a once-and-done backup. [153] Users can log in with a four-digit PIN without having to type in the 24-word passphrase; however, three failed PIN attempts results in a lockout that can only be unlocked by re-entering the backed up passphrase. It includes BIP 32 wallet address for added privacy.

The GreenAddress wallet tandem screenshot shows the mobile wallet on the left and the web wallet on the right. Both have a nearly identical user interface. This shows how sending bitcoins is as easy as entering a PIN, the recipient's bitcoin address, the amount, an optional memo, and clicking send.

Image courtesy of GreenAddress

Some additional features of greenaddress.it include the following:

- Two-factor authentication via SMS, phone, email and Google authenticator is used for every transaction.
- Watching-only address login is available via Facebook, Twitter or custom login.
- You can easily send bitcoins with Facebook, Twitter, email or SMS.
- A new bitcoin address is used for each incoming transaction.
- Private keys are never stored on Greenaddress servers.
- nLockTime feature unlocks funds from multi-sig, reducing third-party failure risk.
- It can be used in conjunction with the Trezor hardware wallet.
- Exchanges and other platforms can use Greenaddress technology on the back end.

## Strong & Easy

Strongcoin.com is an example of a pure web wallet with many robust features and a long track record. Private keys are encrypted on the client side or on your computer while only an encrypted backup is stored on the platform's servers. Strongcoin claims to be the longest running online bitcoin wallet since 2011. Coinpunk.com and easywallet.org are also examples of no-frills, donation-driven web wallets. "We do not aspire to be a bitcoin bank and as such can only provide a medium level of security. Do not store more than some spare change here," reads a statement on easywallet.org's home page.

## Web Wallet and Mobile Wallet Tandem

Mobile wallets are great for easy, on-the-go, bitcoin purchases. Reduce the risk of loss or theft by keeping and replenishing only a few hundred dollars' worth of bitcoin, depending on your business policies and comfort level. Businesses can use mobile wallets as petty cash for small purchases in the field like meals and entertainment.

A separate mobile wallet should be created for personal and business use, further reducing risk while avoiding commingling of transactions. This can be achieved by either creating two wallets within the same app or using two different mobile wallets, all depending on the platform. All wallet apps are free and easy to install so be sure to create multiple wallets and take them for a test drive. Most mobile wallets apps have a four-digit PIN code for easy access; however, if you fumble and temporarily lock yourself out, you can simply use one of your other apps. Mobile wallets will be the most widely used wallets around the world as the most practical way to buy things on the most widely adopted device. Therefore, massive innovations, including security and convenience, will continue in this area.

Web wallets are so easy and convenient it makes sense to use them for online purchases by stashing a few hundred to a few thousand dollars' worth of bitcoin, similar to mobile wallets. After a new wallet is created, send a small amount of bitcoin as a test transaction.

Exchange accounts come with a web wallet, but these platforms should be thought of as a temporary, third-party conduit for buying and selling bitcoins while your other wallets are for spending and storing bitcoins. Sending bitcoins from an exchange wallet to another wallet like blockchain.info reduces counterparty risk. Web wallets with a sister mobile app make a great hot wallet combo for convenience and ease of use. Experience and practice is the best teacher of this new 21st century value transfer.

## Hardware Wallets

A hardware wallet is a small, single-purpose computer or device used for making secure bitcoin transactions. The private keys are generated by the device and stored in its microcontroller preventing the keys from being transferred out. Hardware wallets are offline therefore malware can't compromise private keys. The code used by the device is also open source and verifiable.

"Hardware devices like the Trezor that cannot be infected by malware will make holding bitcoins as easy and secure as holding paper money. They are an exciting step in the evolution of bitcoin from experiment for geeks to a payment system anybody can use," says Gavin Andresen, bitcoin core developer.

## Ledger Wallet

The Ledger Nano is a USB hardware wallet combining the aluminum, plastic and silicon elements of a smart card into the familiar size and ease of use of a USB stick. The smartcard is the secure element, a piece of malware-proof hardware that stores private keys for signing bitcoin transactions. Therefore, it can also be used on an infected, untrusted computer. LedgerWallet.com provides a free, matching, Google chrome app as the interface for managing bitcoins. Just plug the Nano into your computer, create a four-digit PIN and a 24-word recovery seed, and you're ready to securely send and receive bitcoins.

Image courtesy of Ledger Wallet

A recovery card is included to permanently document the recovery seed for storage in a safe or safe deposit box. A verification code must be entered using a credit card-sized security card to send bitcoins from the Ledger app. Every Nano comes with a security card, a secret code of sorts (where the letter W, for example, corresponds to the number 7) typed into the app. This extra layer of security outsmarts man-in-the-middle attacks. If the PIN is incorrectly entered three times, the recovery seed is wiped out and must be re-entered from the recovery card to restore a bitcoin wallet. Ledger Wallet is another example of combining a hardware device, a software app and physical safekeeping elements for comprehensive bitcoin security.

## The Bitcoin Trezor

Also known as The Bitcoin Safe, Trezor.com, was one of the first hardware wallets developed. Its key fob-size display has two easy buttons to confirm or deny an action for sending and receiving bitcoins while working in conjunction with its web wallet interface, the Trezor browser plug-in. A small dongle (software protection device) connects the Trezor to a computer, and its malware-proof design allows transactions to be signed offline and visually verified on the device screen without exposing the private keys. Therefore, it can also be used on an infected, untrusted computer. It's a deterministic wallet with an unlimited number of bitcoin addresses and private keys. A lost or stolen device can be securely restored on a new one using the recovery seed written down on the Trezor-provided recovery card upon setup. Trezor's PIN code system squares the wait time after an incorrect entry so a hacker making 20 failed PIN attempts would require six days of waiting. 30 failed PIN attempts would require 17 years of combined waiting, making it infeasible to brute force the PIN.

## The Trezor fob style hardware wallet

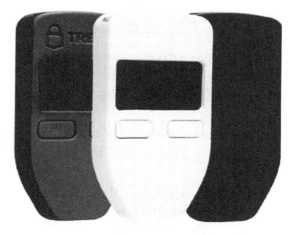

Image courtesy of bitcointrezor.com

## A Case for Bitcoin

ChooseCase.com, a first of its kind, on the go, mobile bitcoin hardware wallet, is unlike other hardware wallets that need to be tethered or plugged into a computer. It's a self-contained device the size of credit card, combining security and ease of use by sending bitcoin with a biometric fingerprint and QR code scan. The initial setup requires interfacing with an app that generates a bitcoin private key on the device via thermal noise randomness. The Case hardware wallet scans and encrypts bits and pieces of your fingerprint profile without storing an image on the device or servers. The fingerprint encryption file is stored on Case servers while the decryption key is stored in the wallet. This is the heart and soul where security meets ease of use. Your fingerprint, the first authentication factor, signs and sends bitcoin to the Case servers which verifies the transaction by decrypting the fingerprint file, the second authentication factor. When everything checks out, Case also signs the transaction as the second signer of a 2/3 multisig scheme and the bitcoin is on its way. If you lose your Case hardware wallet it's no problem. Peace of mind is part of the package because a third bitcoin private key is stored by an institutional grade, third-party key recovery service. Most importantly, only you have control of your bitcoins. [154]

Other features include:

- Combines three private keys and three factors of authentication
- Third Key Solutions provides backup for the third private key
- No mobile phone or computer needed for Internet access
- Uses GSM one-way communication technology to send transactions
- Malware and anti-virus proof dedicated hardware
- Buy and sell bitcoins directly on the device
- No monthly subscription plan
- Uses inductive charging and no cords required

## Keep Your Keys

KeepKey.com is a small black USB device with a sleek OLED display allowing users to securely store and spend bitcoins with a four digit PIN and browser plugin. The private key is generated securely upon setting up the device even if it's plugged into a malware infected computer. A twelve-word KeepKey recovery sentence is also generated for restoring bitcoins in case the device is lost or stolen. The device will lock out a thief upon multiple incorrect PIN entries rendering it useless. The recovery sentence is displayed one time, must be written down and stored in a safe similar to other cold storage hardware wallets. If you purchase a new safe from Overstock, the browser will automatically populate the transaction details which can be reviewed and confirmed with the click of a button on the KeepKey device. You can trust KeepKey cold storage because it's nearly impossible for virtual attackers using malware or viruses to steal your valuable bitcoins. "KeepKey is a device that gives you control of your money. Bitcoin transactions don't require third parties, but they do require good security so most bitcoin users let custodians handle it for them. KeepKey gives you great security without having to trust third parties," states KeepKey Founder Darin Stanchfield.

## Hardware Wallet Takeaway

The Ledger, Trezor, Case and KeepKey are four examples of different hardware approaches to cold storage and security with price points from about $30 to $200 USD at the time of publication. All four are worth the investment considering that paper wallet generators, desktop, mobile, web, multisig and vault services are either free or at least have a level of free service. They all use a type of secure element, a mini force field of sorts, keeping the private keys disconnected from the digital world while maintaining the ability to sign transactions (similar to the benefit of an "air-gap" strategy used in desktop wallets). The PIN feature adds a level of convenience like mobile wallets do. In addition, Ledger and/ or Trezor can be used in conjunction with other wallets such as GreenAddress, Electrum and Coinprism.

## Bitcoin Cash Flow Determines Wallet Strategy

If a business accumulates bitcoins from sales, then the excess bitcoins should be moved into cold storage or sales can be paid directly into cold storage using Armory, for example. The security and convenience risk trade-off should also be considered in the context of a business receiving and spending bitcoins. Most businesses would likely use a payment service provider allowing sales to be paid out into 100% fiat, kept 100% as bitcoin, or a combination of the two. If bitcoins are not converted to fiat currency, they can be automatically sent to a cold storage address from the payment service provider.

Coinbase, for example, allows merchants to both receive and spend bitcoins from the same wallet in addition to providing a cold storage vault within the platform. Bitcoin inflows and outflows could match up so bitcoins would not accumulate and a hot wallet may suffice. Customer returns and general business expenses could be spent from a hot wallet with just enough bitcoins to cover the outflows. Some combination of receiving bitcoins in wallet A, moving bitcoins to wallet B or C and spending or transferring bitcoins among A, B or C, as appropriate, is a general framework similar to minimizing risk with bank accounts and debit cards.

These strategies are also consistent with best practices using traditional bank accounts. Debit card and credit card usage carries its own risk as seen from multiple credit card breaches. A debit card used for purchases should be tied to bank account A that only has enough cash to cover those purchases. Operating bank account B, with no corresponding debit card, would transfer the necessary cash to bank account A. Bank account B would also be used to receive cash inflows or sales of products and services. Bank account C could be used as a money market savings account for excess cash and for transfers only to other accounts. If only one bank account was used then all your cash would sit in one bank account waiting for a debit card hack and sale of card info to a fraudster.

## Fiat Strategy Failure

We can learn bitcoin wallet strategies by observing the simple strategy violation in traditional banking. A local Pennsylvania, USA, bank with fewer than 20 branches, went into receivership in 2013 resulting in an FDIC raid which instantly shut down the bank. A long-time branch manager shared several stories about customers in their golden years that lost most of their life savings. The manager advised his clients to open up additional accounts at his bank or at a competitor bank to make sure their deposits did not exceed the $250,000 FDIC limit. As long as the accounts at the same bank have a different name, for example one account in one name, the second account titled as a joint account with a spouse or even a business account, then $250,000 of protection is available for each additional account. Bitcoin doesn't have any governmental insurance guarantees because it's not issued by a government, but this example demonstrates how bitcoin could identify and contain risk where fiat fails.

## Extremely Painful

The most painful story involved a 75-year-old woman who sold her house and deposited $950,000 of proceeds into her one and only account at that bank about two weeks before the FDIC raid. She was waiting to settle on a house in Florida only to lose $700,000 and a retirement dream. This is like permanent sick-to-your-stomach syndrome. Three simple bank accounts would have safeguarded her $950,000 under the FDIC rules and prevented this nightmare. There are several hundred bank failures in the United States, even during good years of supposed non-financial crisis, but most of them are averted by an acquiring bank and nobody knows their bank was ever in crisis mode.

This story from our current system demonstrates the power of reducing wallet and exchange risk in a way that everyone understands. When bitcoin disappears it's gone for good and there are just as many stories about evaporating bitcoins from lost private keys and forgotten passphrases as there are theft from hacking. Keep bitcoins in multiple wallets and on multiple platforms based on frequency of use and amount. Bitcoin also gives you the choice to avoid third parties so there's no bank to trust and no surprise banking blow-ups.

## Multi Signatures, More Control

A bitcoin multisig wallet is simply a nickname for a wallet requiring multiple signatures to send bitcoin. This is a wallet security innovation addressing hot wallet risk and cold storage inconvenience. Regular bitcoin wallets require one signature so the best custody system for a single private key such as a private safe, safe deposit box or paper wallet could still result in a single point of failure regardless of how well it's secured. Attacks can happen on all fronts inside and outside a business from employee dishonesty to hackers, thereby increasing the need for higher-level security.

## Golden Rule of Wallets

The golden rule for wallet risk and security bears repeating so be sure to embrace what may seem like redundancy: the more secure a bitcoin wallet, the *less convenient* it is; the *more convenient* a bitcoin wallet, the less secure it is. This inverse relationship is addressed in multisig by requiring two or more private key signatures to spend bitcoin, similar to a checking account that would require any two signatures on a check from three different authorized people. Multisig wallets are based on an M of N scheme where M is the number of private key signatures required for spending bitcoin and N is the number of private key holders who are authorized to sign. A private key is simply a digital pen used for electronic signatures and businesses can use multisig keys to reduce wallet risk and increase internal controls. A multisig bitcoin address starts with a 3 and looks like this:

3Eskmssx9agvG5iHzChyLpuchArb9fMPCP

Whereas, regular bitcoin addresses start with a 1. For example, a company may want to create four private keys and any three of four are required to make a large bitcoin transfer. This multisig feature is far superior to any traditional internal controls currently used for managing funds. See diagram below comparing risk and convenience of the various wallet types.

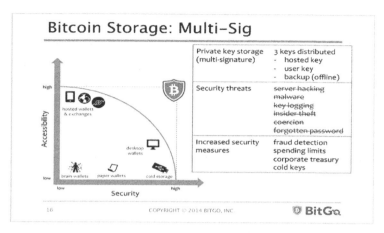

Image courtesy of BitGo

## Internal Controls are Needed Everywhere

Traditional internal controls are used in all functional areas of a business whether it's two or more signatures for a payment, two or more approvals to pay an invoice or two or more approvals for purchases. Internal controls are absolutely necessary to reduce the risk of fraud and abuse. Even more sophisticated enterprise-level settings can be set up via multisig to match a company's existing policies and procedures.

For example, the CEO may be authorized to make unlimited transfers with the approval of the CFO and the accounting manager may be authorized for smaller bitcoin payments using a 2 of 2, 2 of 3 or any multisig scheme that reduces risk to an acceptable level.

## Policies vs. Controls

Multisig wallets enable technology to match company policies or help create new policies. In many cases business policies establish threshold amounts for payments or transfers requiring more than one authorization; however, technology platforms don't provide automatic policy enforcement, which increases the risk of policy circumvention by employees. For example, a business policy limits Jim's transfer authority to $5,000 but the online banking system doesn't provide enough controls thus allowing Jim to transfer $10,000. This doesn't mean that Jim will transfer $10,000 and a circumvented policy doesn't mean fraud occurred but it does mean there's more risk hanging around with a higher susceptibility for fraud. If multisig was applied to this example, the $5,000 transfer policy becomes automatically woven into the technology, thus eliminating trust with better controls than the old model.

## Armory Multisig and Multicrypt Enterprise Security

The free version of the BitcoinArmory.com desktop wallet can be used in conjunction with its multisig feature called lockboxes. Multisig signers can be created up to a 7 of 7 signing scheme where all seven signers are required to spend funds from a lockbox. Any other variation can be created such as 3 of 5, 4 of 7 and so on as long as each signer has his or her own version of Armory. Multisig is most often used in the context of spending funds; however, Armory lockboxes have an awesome breakthrough innovation called simulfunding. This is just as valuable on the funding side of the equation as multisig is known for on the spending side of the equation, which could also be thought of as simulspending. Simulfunding creates a commitment among signers called a promissory note that simultaneously funds a lockbox when all parties have signed the transaction. For example, three founders are working on a startup and agree to fund the company lockbox with 6 BTC, 3 BTC and 3BTC matching their ownership percentages of 50%, 25% and 25% respectively, as reflected in their company operating agreement. This invisible hand forces everyone to commit funds at the same time compared to the old model where one party funds a bank account and the other parties make excuses instead of bank deposits.

Armory Quorum is an enterprise powerhouse version of the Armory desktop wallet. It combines Armory's Multi-Sig technology with a new MultiCrypt layer to provide a distributed, auditable, enterprise level of security for banks, bitcoin exchanges, investment funds and large, multinational companies. It provides the most value when an organization has a very large stash of bitcoins, a large number of people responsible for those bitcoins, and those people being spread out around the world. In a traditional multisig scheme, when one signer in an N of M multisig scheme leaves the company, bitcoins have to be moved from the old wallet to a new multisig scheme to maintain appropriate internal controls. MultiCrypt eliminates this scenario by allowing the signer's encrypted key fragment to be swapped out for a new one without having to move bitcoins or create a new multisig wallet. Otherwise, without MultiCrypt, the larger the multisig scheme, say 7 of 9 for example, the more likely a signer has to be replaced and the more painful and frequent new multisig schemes would be created to compensate. Quorum would be installed on a series of hardware security modules, or specialized computers dedicated to enterprise security. Armory's consulting arm provides custom development, key creation ceremonies and auditable security models. [155, 156]

## Armory's Multi-Sig MultiCrypt Quorum enterprise solution diagram shows the power of the distribution of the Multi-Sig keys and the auditability of the MultiCrypt fragmented signers responsible for a key or keys.

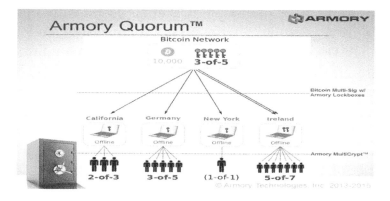

Image courtesy of Armory

## Go Bitcoin Go

BitGo.com is an enterprise-level, multisig platform designed to provide internal control and risk management features in a clean intuitive interface. They have a 2 of 3 multisig scheme where Bitgo holds one encrypted private key and the user holds the second private signature key and a third backup private key. Two of these signatures are required to spend funds from a BitGo wallet so BitGo cannot spend your company's bitcoin without one of your private key signatures. If BitGo breaks down for some reason, your private key and backup private key can be used to move funds from your BitGo wallet. BitGo describes their enterprise architecture as a multisig, multi-user, multi-institution scheme providing an equilibrium point for bitcoin risk management. The triple play combines the power of multisig, an administrator dashboard of treasury user controls, and BitGo additional risk monitoring. [157] BitGo also offers insurance that covers errors and omissions of the technology, including external hacks and employee theft, while the customer gets reimbursed as a loss payee.

Your company's private key signature is coupled with additional internal controls on the administrator's or CFO's dashboard, including multiple users, spending limits, and a bitcoin address whitelist. Users can be setup by the administrator with either admin, spend-only or view-only access. Per transaction and per day maximum-spending limits can also be set up for additional controls. Address whitelisting prevents users with spend-only authority from sending bitcoins to an unapproved vendor bitcoin address. BitGo provides third-party benefits including various fraud monitoring techniques similar to traditional bank fraud monitoring. For example, if a spend-only user logs in from a new IP address, BitGo will flag the transaction and potentially notify the administrator. The multi-institutional play combines your company's internal controls with BitGo's monitoring for additional risk reduction.

## Multikite

Coinkite.com added multisig functionality to its platform in addition to merchant services, consumer wallets, and developer tools. Coinkite's multisig features include a robust M of N scheme with up to 15 of 15 signers. They love giving users options including five different ways to create a private key depending on the golden rule of wallets. The choices range from the simple method by which Coinkite manages the key on your behalf to the "generate key" and "import key" methods where users create and manage keys while maintaining full control. Once again the simple method comes with less work to set up and manage as demonstrated by the diagram below, which shows three stars for ease of use, yet Coinkite can access the bitcoins. Conversely, the import key method shows one star for ease of use yet it's impossible for Coinkite to access your bitcoins. The latter requires more technical skill and time to set up. Users have multiple choices and in many cases the easier method is still a very good method.

## Coinkite's 5 Multisig Key Creation Choices

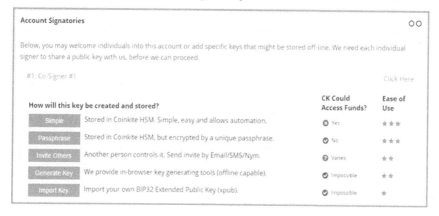

Image courtesy of Coinkite

## Multiple Multisigs

Several other multisig options were developed in 2014 known as "the year of multisig." BitPay assembled a team to create an open source project called Copay as a free, self-serve multisig tool.

Coinbase also added vault services and multisig capabilities, further expanding as a universal platform. Multiple multisig options will continue to be developed, likely as extensions of existing platforms.

## Bitcoin Multisig Takeaway

Both individuals and businesses benefit from multisig wallets requiring an M of N private key distribution to multiple people. A special degree of care is required to maintain continuity of bitcoin access in certain situations. Private key safekeeping should include a plan for bitcoin access when someone dies, becomes incapacitated or incarcerated, whether it's a spouse or more importantly a business partner. Unlike getting access to a bank account after someone dies, bitcoin cannot simply be retrieved by presenting a death certificate and power of attorney to a third party. A surviving spouse or business partner with no private keys may end up with irretrievable bitcoins.

A business partner or employee with access to a bitcoin wallet with a single private key or passphrase could fraudulently send bitcoins to his or her personal wallet. The risk that bitcoins die along with a person, or that a company's bitcoins die along with an owner is bitcoin legacy risk. Multisig wallets offer seamless access to bitcoins when a multisig signer is not available or in any of these situations as long as the number of private key signatures required is at least one less than the total number of people authorized. In addition, any size business needs internal controls to reduce risk of fraud and abuse with business bitcoin wallets. Multisig technology creates versatile internal controls while simultaneously reducing risk and the cost of enforcing policies scalable from microbusiness to Fortune 500 companies.

## Ice Cold Storage & Vaults

Cold storage or a cold wallet is any offline method for safekeeping of bitcoins. Bitcoins stored on a computer are considered in cold storage if the computer is not connected to the Internet. The cold storage exercise is worth the effort because hot wallets, the opposite of cold wallets, come with the inherent risk that private keys could be hacked from your Internet-connected computer or online wallet. Bank vault-level cold storage is another method for managing hot wallet risk.

Cold storage examples include:
- Vault service
- Hardware wallets
- Brain wallets or using your brain to remember a passphrase
- Paper wallets or private keys and addresses printed on paper
- Wallet seeds and passphrases stored on paper
- Paper wallets on alternative materials like stainless steel
- USB drives with wallet backup files
- Internet-free laptops
- Private safes for storing paper wallets, USB drives or laptops
- Safe deposit boxes

Cold storage is either self-serve or service for hire. Everything on the list above is self-serve cold storage except vault services, which are great for businesses, or individuals who don't want to manage their own cold storage. Users create an account on one of the vault service platforms and send bitcoin to their new vault. The services take care of all the offline bitcoin storage behind the scenes so users have peace of mind without having to install or learn any software.

Vault services use some variation of offline computers maintained in bank vaults or tier 3 data centers to sign and save transactions on USB drives to facilitate network broadcasting with an online computer, similar to desktop wallets described previously. Each service has a proprietary security method usually partially disclosed due to insurance contracts or other reasons. The private keys are the things stored in the vault since they are used to move bitcoin from one wallet to another. Bitcoin is not actually stored in the vault but it's easier to refer to it that way. Bitcoin vault services such as xapo.com, elliptic.co and icevault.ch generally offer bank vault-level security with the ease of making an online bank transfer.

Elliptic.co vault service is focused exclusively on custom, enterprise-level solutions. The company became the first to receive security and compliance accreditation from a Big-4 auditing firm. It's based in the United Kingdom, a leading financial capital ripe for digital currency businesses. The service is tailored to larger businesses and institutional investors with custom solutions and pricing based on the customer's need. Any type of multi-signature authorization can be set up for retrieving bitcoins. For example, three company executives have to authorize retrievals greater than £75,000.

Other features of elliptic.co include the following:
- Insurance against internal theft, external theft and company negligence
- Unlimited bitcoin retrievals
- A solution expected of a regulated institutional custodian
- Service appropriate for customers storing more than £50,000 of digital assets
- Private keys always maintained offline
- Vault-only service

Icevault.ch, a cold storage vault service located in Switzerland is subject to strict banking security and privacy laws. The bank vaults used for cold storage are located in the comfort of the Swiss Alps. Bitcoin is sent into your new icevault wallet using one of your already existing bitcoin wallets. The private keys are fragmented or split into pieces requiring three parties to sign a transaction before the bitcoins are sent from the vault. This service is meant for long-term storage because bitcoin retrievals are limited based on service plans. Other features of icevault.ch include the following:

- Private key fragmentation stored in separate safe deposit boxes
- Segregation of customer accounts
- Altcoin storage in the near future
- Subscription pricing levels with a free account up to two

bitcoins
- Bitcoin retrievals limited to up to three, based on subscription plan
- Custom, enterprise-level plans have unlimited bitcoin retrieval

Xapo.com offers a unique combination of convenient online wallet storage and the security of offline cold storage by including an online wallet with each "vault." Simply transfer bitcoin into Xapo from any other bitcoin wallet or buy bitcoins on the platform. Then bitcoins can be transferred back and forth between the Xapo hot wallet and the Xapo vault as shown in the screenshot.

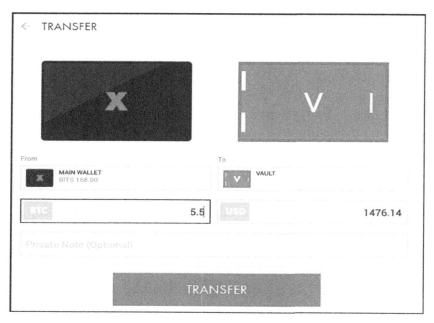

Image courtesy of Xapo.com

Transfers from the vault take up to 24 hours because of the extra security measures while transfers to the vault are instantaneous. This is an excellent example of a platform that reduces wallet risk by design. For example, bitcoin for everyday purchases of 10% can be held in the hot wallet and bitcoin reserves of 90% can be "held" in the vault until needed at a later time. Either an individual or institutional account can be created with a corresponding Xapo Visa debit card. Other features of Xapo include the following:

- Fully insured bitcoins
- Underground tier 3 data centers with armed guards and biometric security
- Locations on three separate continents for "jurisdictional security"
- Bitcoins segregated and held in full reserves
- Two-factor authentication required for withdrawing bitcoins
- Email and text notifications for withdraws
- Bitcoins can be purchased via wire transfer or ACH
- Bitcoin debit card compatible on the Visa network

## Xapo Institutions

Xapo's business suite is the first to combine a vault service with treasury controls, multisig and a debit card. It's designed to help businesses and large institutions control and audit their funds. The administrator can easily create multiple wallets and vaults with permission levels for specific groups of employees within a company such as marketing and accounting departments in larger companies. This creates internal controls for initiating, approving and viewing transactions or setting approval limits which can be turned on and off by the administrator. New users are invited by email so it's best to create a new email used only for access, not communication, for this and other bitcoin platforms. This is the Golden Thread Rule discussed in the Digital Identity Management chapter.

## Ice Cold Storage & Vaults Takeaway

Vault storage provides peace of mind value by reducing the risk of storing large amounts of bitcoin to a level that will help accelerate adoption by institutional investors, financial firms, high-net worth individuals, businesses and anyone who doesn't want to deal with cold storage. Individuals and small businesses can still use services like Xapo or Icevault while Elliptic focuses on larger institutions. Many of these services are offering some level of insurance to minimize the level of perceived or actual risk expected with traditional financial services, such as with FDIC and SIPC insurance in the United States.

Self-serve cold storage is more management intensive with a higher learning curve. Vault storage is not necessarily better than other cold storage methods; however, consistent with other bitcoin storage and security strategies, multiple cold storage methods should be deployed to work in conjunction with one another. The cost of a cold storage vault may be well worth the value for its ease of use, but users have to forego some control to get the convenience.

## Paper Wallets

A paper wallet is a physical piece of paper used to print or write down a new public address and private key. Paper wallets are classic cold wallets created from wallet generators such as bitaddress.org, bitcoinpaperwallet.com or offlineaddress.com. These sites are free, open source services that also accept donations. Always review their recommendations and instructions for best practices in creating paper wallets, which is one of the safest ways to store bitcoins when it's done correctly. It seems counterintuitive to use paper for security in an electronic world of emails and PDFs. However, the main purpose is to create a wallet for your eyes only that is never stored on a computer. The proper format and randomness of characters needed for generating public and private keys requires some considerations, described here for creating secure paper wallets.

Bitaddress.org is a free, open source, client-side bitcoin wallet generator. This platform has a straightforward user interface with multiple wallet options including a single wallet in a simple format as shown below which displays the bitcoin address, the share, and the bitcoin private key, the "secret." Additional wallet options include a paper wallet similar to paper money, a bulk address wallet, brain wallet, vanity wallet, or a split key wallet. The wallet details feature is great for entering in a private key and getting the bitcoin public address, public key and private key in multiple key formats. The single wallet feature is shown below.

Image courtesy of bitaddress.org

Offlineaddress.com is another example of a free bitcoin wallet generator that prompts users to disconnect from the Internet before generating new addresses. It also offers three formats for printing wallets such as printable notes, individual addresses, and raw public and private keys. Printable notes are like beautiful artwork while the individual address style displays the essentials with QR codes and plain English. The raw format produces the basics such as the public address and private key.

Bitcoinpaperwallet.com allows users to create free paper wallets with a unique tri-fold design for hiding the private key, which can be further secured with hologram stickers available for sale. They recommend downloading and using the local version after disconnecting form the Internet, although a safer, live CD version is available. A passphrase option is available for encrypting a private key into a meaningless phrase using BIP 38. This feature can also be used to create a BIP 38-encrypted wallet to purchase a BIP38wallets synthetic paper or stainless steel Bitkee wallet described later.

# Bitcoin paper wallet front side example from bitcoinpaperwallet.com

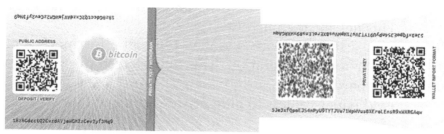

*The public address is on the left side while the private key on the right side is folded over and concealed.*

Paper wallet back side with important instructions including sweeping the ENTIRE BALANCE when sending bitcoins from the wallet.

Image courtesy of bitcoinpaperwallet.com

It's fun to create new wallets by either typing random characters in a box or moving a mouse around and watching cascading dots resulting in a message like "randomness complete, click here for wallet." The format is designed to create the most secure private keys possible using human randomness. General tips for using paper wallets include:

- Create paper wallets only when disconnected from the Internet.
- Do not save a PDF of any wallet format to a hard drive. This defeats the purpose.
- Run a live CD with a wallet generator for more secure paper wallet generation. This is preferred over download to a hard drive.
- Fold paper wallets to hide private keys from view.
- Also keep in mind:
- Print spools may store wallet info just like a computer hard drive does.
- Wallet generators may offer a secure print feature.
- Undetected malware can't scrape information when a live CD is used. [158]

## Entropy

Mycelium developed a USB device called Entropy that generates secure paper wallets by plugging the device directly into a printer. Randomness is generated from the "noise" within the USB stick. It cuts out the computer from the paper wallet equation I've referred to in the examples above. Paper wallets are printed directly from the printer without the risk of being first generated on a computer or being connected to the Internet. The wallet file is destroyed when the Entropy device is removed from the printer, reducing the risk of creating a secure paper wallet to just a few minutes. A paper wallet can also be created with M of N split keys where two of the three parts are needed to retrieve the bitcoins. The three paper slits can be stored in different locations for a higher level of security. [159]

## Funding and Single Send Paper Wallets

Bitcoin wallets are simply a collection of addresses. Some wallets may use one address, automatically generate a new address for each transaction or allow the user to choose whether to create a new address for each transaction. (Better privacy and security is achieved when a new address is used for each new bitcoin transaction.)

Fund a paper wallet by sending bitcoins from a hot wallet to a new paper wallet for longer-term safekeeping. Paper wallets can be funded by sending multiple bitcoin transactions, but only a single-send or withdraw transaction should be used to remove 100% of the bitcoins. The life of a paper wallet should consist of the bitcoins that fund the wallet and a single withdraw of the total amount. The old zero balance paper wallets should be discarded as the cycle continues.

For example, if you have 3.456 BTC in a paper wallet and need to spend 2.345 BTC, then the total amount should be sent to a wallet such as blockchain.info via importing the keys thus getting the bitcoins from an offline paper world into an electronic means for spending. After the 2.345 BTC is spent, the remaining 1.111 BTC should be sent to new paper wallet. Paper wallets are for one-time use and one should never assume that the 1.111 BTC in the above example is sent back to the same paper wallet. Always assume the 1.111 BTC in change has to go to a new address and just make sure you know what that address is, whether it's going to a new paper wallet or another wallet. [160] It's more important to be aware of how change addresses work than to be concerned with the often unusual circumstances of losing bitcoin with a change address. Change addresses increase privacy, and the benefits of using them far outweigh the risks. Several paper wallets should be created at the same time and stored in a safe or safe deposit box to make use of setup time.

## Wood, Stainless Steel and Other Physical Wallets

Several companies produce physical wallet mediums providing a more durable cold storage alternative to paper wallets. Customers have to create their own wallet with a BIP 38 passphrase-protected private key before submitting an order on one of the websites. Generally, private keys and public keys can be ordered as separate wallet cards or they can be ordered as a front and back of the same piece of wood or stainless steel. Think of the private keys as a passphrase card and the public keys as an address card. In addition, a single address card can be ordered without having to use the BIP

38 encryption process for encrypting private keys to produce and order a passphrase card.

## Metal Wallets

Bitkee.com offers a metal version of paper wallets the exact size of a credit card. Public addresses and password-protected private keys come standard on both sides of the same wallet with an optional custom title for front and back. The metal, laser-engraved, corrosion-proof bitcoin wallets are available in titanium, stainless steel and anodized aluminum, which have three distinct melting points of 3000, 2000 and 1200 degrees Fahrenheit, respectively. Passphrase cards are produced using encrypted private keys provided by the customer in BIP 38 format. Multiple Armory-fragmented backups can also be ordered in the same form as passphrase cards, taking enterprise cold storage protocols to another level in lieu of using paper to record fragmented backups. The Bitkee product line also includes keychain and dog tag wallets for maximum coolness. [161]

Below, a Bitkee stainless steel wallet is shown on the left and multi-colored anodized aluminum keychains are shown on the right. You can show off your bitcoin knowledge and generate some conversation with these great products.

Image courtesy of Bitkee

Cryobit.co makes stainless steel wallets the size and thickness of a credit card available in black or stainless. They demonstrated the durability of the printed keys and the metal by blasting a wallet with a high temperature torch, thus eliminating the degradation issues with paper wallets. Fires, floods and fading are no match for stainless steel. Private keys and public can be ordered on both sides of the same wallet or as separate pieces.

## Synthetic Wallets

BIP38wallets.com makes grease-proof, tear-proof, water-proof durable wallets from synthetic paper. The wallets are approximately the size of paper money and are available for dozens of altcoins with multiple design choices. Users have the option to customize their wallets by uploading images and including 180 characters of text.

## Once Wooden Wallets

Woodwallets.io, no longer in existence at the time of publication, made wood wallets smaller than the size of a credit card. The maple wood wallets were produced using a laser cutter where the keys, QR Codes and words were etched into the surface like a branding process. The wood is just another medium substituting for a paper wallet and could be thought of as the wooden version of metal wallets.

## Paper Wallets Takeaway

Paper wallets are born in a non-Internet world and stay in the physical world in the form of any medium, from paper to metal, until the time comes to retrieve the bitcoins.

Bitcoin passphrases and private keys are first secured from the digital Internet world by existing in physical form, and secondly, secured in the physical world by using safes, safe deposit boxes or a secret hiding place. Keep in mind that a metal bitcoin wallet with a "receiving only" address, for example, doesn't necessarily have to be secured because the bitcoins can't be stolen. Make sure paper wallets are generated using the most secure offline method you are technically comfortable with. Paper wallets will be secure when you combine best practices for both creation and custody.

Every business whether a microbusiness or a large company should have at least one physical safe or similar method for securing important papers, debit cards, checks or other valuable assets. Individuals should take the same precaution and any business that doesn't have a safe and/or safe deposit box should get one, regardless of bitcoin.

Paper wallets require a special degree of care; therefore, depending on the size of the business and number of employees, a second bitcoin-only safe should be dedicated to isolate custody risk. For example, either business owners or specific financial officers would only have access to the crypto safe, separating its access from employees who shouldn't be responsible for crypto assets and thus avoiding commingling of important business assets. Chain of custody controls should be also be implemented to log access to the safe and identify any issues that may arise. The same approach could also be applied to bitcoin hardware wallets.

## Headstrong

A brain wallet is a way to store bitcoins in your head by creating a user-generated sentence and then using brain wallet generators such as brainwallet.org to turn it into private keys and bitcoin addresses. For example, a silly passphrase like, "Eat dinner getting dressed upside down while jogging backwards in the park" is easier to remember than a string of characters. A BIP 39 passphrase is a way for humans to use computer-generated randomness in the form of a group of meaningless words. Conversely, a brain wallet could be thought of as a human-generated passphrase. [162]

## Hybrid Wallets

Kryptokit.com is a free Google chrome browser extension with a one-click, one-second install. It's like a desktop wallet with the convenience of a web wallet. All private information is client-side on your own computer and Kryptokit stores no information and has no access to bitcoins. There is no traditional username and password setup required although just a password is optional and recommended. Secure messaging is included similar to the security of sending bitcoins except with Kryptokit information is exchanged instead of bitcoins. Bitcoin Google headlines, reddit news feeds and bitcoin charts are also included, rounding out Kryptokit as a nice package tool.

You can randomly generate new wallet addresses by moving your mouse in circles and it's easy to understand when you're using it firsthand. Brand new wallets can be easily funded from another bulging bitcoin wallet and one-click verified via blockchain.info. Brain wallets can also be set up within Kryptokit or existing ones can be imported. It's critical to remember that creating of a new wallet wipes out an existing wallet so be sure to get settled on a wallet before sending in bitcoins. Kryptokit automatically picks up site payment information turning it into a one-click payment for easy online shopping without having to copy and paste wallet addresses. It can also be used on any computer including one that you don't own. [163]

## Bitcoin Wallets Final Takeaway

Each type of wallet has its own set of risks and benefits that revolves around convenience to the user. The age-old cliché "Don't put all your eggs in one basket" is a great strategy for managing bitcoin wallets. Create two to three accounts or wallets for each type of wallet since a test drive is the best instructor.

It's also a good time to get a team involved for splitting up the work and collaborating on what combination of wallets works best for your business. Each person could also experiment on a personal level and bring his or her experience back to the team. Of course if you wear all the hats then you'll have to do all the test driving. Go to BestBitcoinBookEver.com/bonus right now for step-by-step guides to setting up your wallets.

Mobile wallets and web wallets should be used for convenience and contain only a few hundred dollars' worth of bitcoin similar to the way most people manage their own leather fiat wallet. Desktop, paper wallets and vaults work in conjunction with hot wallets to reduce risk with longer-term storage of bitcoin. Cold wallets are more secure, used less often, used to store more bitcoin and require more work. Hot wallets are less secure, used more often, used to store fewer bitcoins and require less work. Larger bitcoin amounts held in reserve need cold storage and small amounts needed for frequent purchases are best for hot wallet convenience.

Company polices and internal controls should be updated to reflect the overall bitcoin wallet strategy employed by a given business. This will be an ongoing, ever-evolving strategy considering the speed of innovation and technology improvements. The number one reason bitcoins evaporate is forgotten passphrases and lost private keys; thus, 100% responsibility comes with a great degree of care. The whole process becomes easy when you start with the fundamentals.

# Bitcoin Exchanges

## Buy & Sell

There are generally five ways to get bitcoin including mining, peer-to-peer trade, accepting bitcoin as a merchant, receiving bitcoin tips (like an online "tip jar") or buying bitcoin from an exchange. Bitcoin exchanges are online platforms for buying and selling bitcoin and cryptocurrencies similar to platforms for buying and selling securities, commodities and fiat currency. Floating point or market exchanges match customers' buy orders and sell orders, which means the market sets the price. The order-matching system will complete the bitcoin trade when a buy order is higher than the lowest sell order which means that the buyer is willing to buy it for at least as much as the seller is willing to sell it for. Fixed-rate exchanges quote bitcoin prices for buyers and sellers and the broker sets the price.

Buyers can instantly acquire bitcoin and altcoins at market price or place an order to buy or sell at a certain price. There are dozens of both market and fixed rate or broker exchanges. Depending on the exchange, multiple fiat currencies can be used to buy multiple cryptocurrencies. Many exchanges cater to a specific country or region based on where the exchange and the owner-operators are physically located although others hold themselves out for business on an international level. [164]

## Exchange Account Setup

Make sure you have chosen and activated your password management system before setting up new bitcoin exchange accounts. The sign-up process varies from one exchange to another. The following discussion refers to funding accounts; however, users create accounts on an exchange platform and every account has an online wallet with a bitcoin address used for buying and selling bitcoin. Signing up can be as simple as creating a username/

212 THE ULTIMATE BITCOIN BUSINESS GUIDE

password combo and adding an email address like you would on a simple subscription site or it can be as complex as having to supply a driver's license, proof of address and other documentation. Many exchanges give users a choice to supply as little or as much information as desired. Supplying the maximum amount of information is similar to getting a bank account.

## Account Verification

Opening new bank accounts generally requires identity verification including driver's license, social security number, physical address and usually physical presence. There are no physical bitcoin locations and every account is created virtually, thus identity verification is a significant component of bitcoin exchanges in order to comply with regulations depending on the region. There are many different exchanges and each one seems to have its own unique identity verification method, request for information and documents as well as the methods for submitting them. Obviously the more information required the longer it takes to verify the account, ranging from a few minutes to a few days.

Users may be given a choice to supply information corresponding to a level such as level one using the simple username and email example above or a higher level with full verification. Each exchange uses different names and information types for each level of verification. For example, a basic verification may limit withdraws to $1,000 per day with a monthly maximum of $5,000. The next level may limit withdraws to $5,000 per day and $20,000 per month maximum and so on. Some exchanges may only distinguish between an unverified account and a verified account requiring full documentation.

The following documents and information may be needed depending on the exchange and level of service. Add these files in a new folder called bitcoin exchange documentation for easy reference when opening multiple accounts.

1. Setup
   - Create an account
   - Username and password
   - Name and address
   - Email and phone number

2. Identification
   - Government-issued ID
   - Driver's license
   - National ID card
   - International passport

3. Proof of residency
   - Utility bill
   - Bank statement
   - IRS letter or tax authority letter
   - Voter ID card

4. Business Verification
   - Articles of Incorporation or business organization documents
   - By-laws or similar documents
   - Business utility bill
   - Business bank statement
   - Business-related IRS letter or tax authority letter
   - Certificate of Good Standing

5. Other Requirements
   - Debit card, credit card and bank account info for account funding
   - High-resolution .jpeg or PDF files required
   - Front and back of all ID and debit cards as separate files
   - Picture or video of you holding the ID next to your face
   - Document addresses must match each other on all

documents
- Random profile validation questions may be asked

Compliance officers often get tripped up by virtual mailbox addresses or post office boxes. Banks require a physical address but a different address can be used as a mailing address while driver's licenses and passports require physical addresses. Bills and correspondences can typically be sent to the address of your choice such as a physical, virtual or post office box address. The standard compliance review includes matching the address listed on a driver's license or passport with bills and bank statements for both individual and business accounts. If you strategically receive your mail at an address other than a physical address, compliance officers may initially deny your account unless you have a bank letter signed by a banking manager identifying both your physical address and mailing address. Request this letter from your bank and add it to your bitcoin exchange documentation folder. Be proactive when submitting your verification documents and explain how the letter ties your addresses together between your identification and bank statements. This is an example of an old rail, know-your-customer, anti-money-laundering model ripe for transformation by blockchain technology.

## Verification Example
The following Bitfinex verification process and corporate account requirements screenshot shows the type of documents needed as well as the document format required for upload. Also notice how Bitfinex offers both individual and corporate accounts.

## Verification Process

Whether you wish to deposit or withdraw US dollars funds to/from your Bitfinex account, your account must be verified in order to comply with relevant anti-money laundering (AML) and counter terrorism financing (CTF) laws and regulations.

Bitfinex has adopted an online verification procedure which will require you to complete an online questionnaire and attach certain documents as support. You will also need to download, sign and upload a declaration form confirming the accuracy of the information provided and authorizing Bitfinex to verify the information.

Bitfinex offers two types of accounts:

* **Individual account** - an account in the name of an individual
* **Corporate account** - an account in the name of a corporation/partnership/trust

### Verification Requirements: Corporate Account:

* Complete online form
* Corporate Documents: please see link here for complete list of required documentation.
* Director Information: each director, significant shareholder and controlling officer(s) are required to provide identification. Please review the online form for complete details.
* **After completing the corporate verification form, an individual form for each director, significant shareholder(s) and controlling officer(s) will be required to be completed.**

**Please note:**

* All documents provided must be in Roman/Latin alphabet or a certified English translation is required.
* All files uploaded must be in pdf, jpeg, png, text (txt), msword
* All fields in the following verification form are mandatory (NA for Non Applicable can be used)
* To avoid possible delays please check the correctness before submitting documents, please double check you do not send the same document twice and possibly forget one.

**Continue to Corporate Verification**

Image courtesy of Bitfinex

# Golden Rule of Accounts

Most exchanges offer default personal accounts meaning they don't distinguish between business and personal accounts. However, some can morph into a business account through additional documents and verification. The golden rule of accounts states that business and personal transactions should never be commingled for any transaction in bitcoin or fiat currency. Commingling creates an accounting nightmare and tends to weaken the corporate veil. Many exchanges allow multiple funding accounts including both business and personal; however, the transactions are still comingled. Separate your business and personal transactions by creating separate accounts or bitcoin wallets for each one. This has the added benefit of reducing bitcoin concentration risk when bitcoins are spread out in multiple wallets.

## Blazing Fast Verification

Several bitcoin exchanges use third party online technologies to verify customer accounts in real time. Jumio's Netverify is an example of an identity verification service with video verification technology using your computer's video cam to match your face with an official ID card and or debit card to support instant verification. Platforms like Identity Mind Global provide sophisticated and automated back end anti-fraud, merchant risk, know your customer and anti-money laundering tools required by regulations in most countries for ongoing risk management of user transactions.

## Fiat Funding

Once an account is set up and verified, it can be funded with fiat currency (directly from your bank account) to buy bitcoin and start using it. Any method used for buying things can also be used to buy bitcoin, including cash, money orders, cashier's checks, credit cards, debit cards and wires. Credit card and debit card deposit features are usually less prevalent than other funding methods.

## Credit & Debit

Credit and debit card transactions are reversible and bitcoin transactions are not. Therefore, a customer could fund an account, buy bitcoins, dispute the transaction and get his or her money back leaving the exchange out in the cold. This explains why some exchanges do not accept cards and those that do are usually bearing the risk as a convenience to the customer. All other methods are more inconvenient, time-consuming and fee-intensive to the customer, but it is likely that all exchanges will take cards in the future. For example, coin.mx takes debit cards and coinbase.com takes credit cards but only as a secondary backup to a primary funding bank account. Circle.com also has easy no-fee, debit card funding. Payeer is an example of an adjunct payment service used by several bitcoin platforms to facilitate debit and credit card deposits.

## Bank Trips & Cash

Some accounts can be funded by depositing cash directly into the business account of the exchange. For example, Coincafe.com a New York City-based exchange and mobile web wallet, will exchange cash for bitcoin when deposits are made at Bank of America by snapping an iPhone picture of the deposit slip and emailing or uploading the jpeg to their site. Trips to the bank may seem counterintuitive to the virtual nature of bitcoin, but this is likely to be a temporary growing pain that fades into a better process over time. Many folks still operate cash-intensive businesses so any bitcoins-for-cash method will likely have strong user support into the near future. Other platforms such as localbitcoins.com and bitquick.co mentioned later are specifically designed for exchanging cash for bitcoin. It is mostly individuals who use these services, but a business could still use them for a cash-to-bitcoin exchange.

## Wires, ACH and Money Orders

Exchange platforms generally accept money orders, cashiers' checks or bank wires for account funding. A significant deposit amount is needed to justify the expense of a wire fee and requires a higher degree of trust. ACH funding increases convenience with lower fees by automatically connecting a bank account. Money orders and money remittance services will eventually fade away as ACH and debit card funding is offered on more exchanges. Wires will continue to be a funding tool because most exchanges accept international wires in USD allowing individuals or businesses in one country to use an exchange based in another country.

## Bitcoin-Ready

Once an exchange account is funded with fiat currency you're ready to buy bitcoins. Exchanges generally accept the same fiat currency used in the country where the exchanges are based. Other widely used currencies such as the Chinese yuan, euros, British pounds and U.S. dollars may also be accepted. For example, U.S.-based exchanges typically accept U.S. dollars or euros, European-based exchanges typically accept SEPA payments, a Eurozone payments initiative, euros and USD while Chinese exchanges accept yuan and USD. Otherwise, accounts generally must be funded by international wire in USD. If you already have bitcoin, it can be sent to an exchange, sold and withdrawn for fiat currency essentially doing the funding process in reverse.

## Funding Fees

Funding or depositing money into an exchange account usually comes with a range of fees depending on the exchange of choice and the fiat currency used to fund the account. Exchange fees may range from 0% to .5% and be charged for both funding accounts and withdraws from accounts in fiat currency. When bank wires are required, the exchange may charge a wire fee in addition to your bank wire fee, but funding can usually be done without wires.

Funding costs may be comprised of both exchange funding fees and bank fees depending on the type of deposit such as money order, wire, or credit card. Getting in and out of bitcoin and fiat currency can be a three to five day standard legacy process on either end. Ironically, bank wires may take the same amount of time to credit to an exchange account even though wires are typically used for one-day payments. Therefore, the shortest time to create an account, fund it with fiat, buy bitcoin, sell bitcoin and withdraw fiat could take a week or more not considering the account verification process. Some platforms such as Circle.com have removed the legacy delay by bearing the clearing risk as a convenience to the user. If you take bitcoin out of the equation, you get the same legacy delay as using fiat to go into and out of any other asset. Getting bitcoin is worth the wait so be patient while you stumble through the old model on your way to the Promised Land.

## Trading Fees

Once an account or online exchange wallet is funded, fiat currency is traded for bitcoin or altcoins, which triggers an exchange trading fee, also around .0% to .5% of the transaction depending on the exchange and monthly trading volume. This is similar to exchanging one currency for another through a currency exchange kiosk at an international airport. In some cases a minimum deposit amount and or minimum deposit fee may apply. Bitcoin to altcoin purchases may be free or incur a very small transaction fee. Competition among exchanges is shifting funding and trading fees towards zero in a race to accelerate user adoption, provide convenience and gain new customers.

## Maker Taker Scheme

Many bitcoin exchanges have adopted the maker-taker fee scheme designed to incentivize liquidity on the exchange platform. Traders who provide liquidity, the market makers, get a transaction rebate or reduced fees while traders who take liquidity, the market takers, pay a fee or premium over the market maker fees. For example, if you place a bid (or ask) order, and there's a matching ask (or bid) order in the existing orderbook, it'll be executed immediately. You are the taker and the matching order is the maker. If there's no matching order in the current orderbook, your order will be added to the orderbook, waiting for someone else to place an order to match with you. If it gets executed some time later, you are the maker and the new order is taker. [165]

The following LakeBTC deposit, withdraw and trading fee schedule is an example format of what every bitcoin exchange should disclose. Notice how fiat currency deposits are free, but this does not include any third-party bank fees such as a wire fee charged by your bank.

Image courtesy of LakeBTC

## Commission Tricks

A commission-trading fee of 1% sounds easy enough to understand if you know what it's multiplied by. "The first thing someone almost always asks me is, 'What's your commission?'" says David Moskowitz of Coin Republic, "when the better question is, 'Where do you base your rate, and how does this compare to Coinbase or other major exchanges?' I can tell you right now, that one site is quoting a rate of $663.23, while the Coinbase price is $648.62."[166] Pay attention to integrity and transparency as you develop relationships and have experiences with exchanges.

## Transparency & Exchange Risk

As with anything else in life and in business, do your due diligence and make sure the exchanges pass the smell test before doing business with them. Transparency is the number one thing to look for in any online business like a litmus test for integrity and tone at the top. With all else being equal, the higher the integrity the lower the risk of a third-party exchange failure. Customers have to judge transparency and integrity before signing up, while test driving, and throughout the business relationship of a given platform. There are many websites and businesses of all sizes and flavors that have varying degrees of transparency. For example, some of them don't identify themselves with an about page, location or any backstory while others have an extensive profile about the people behind the business, along with profile pictures and geographical location.

## Full Disclosure

If you have nothing to hide, why are you hiding? When doing your due diligence, things like how the platform works, fee structures, security, compliance, privacy policy and FAQs should be standard review procedure. Contact information such as phone numbers, emails and chat features are also signs that management wants to engage with customers and not hide out in the background. All of these factors are part of a platform's transparency and integrity fingerprint. Test the responsiveness of the help desk by contacting an exchange via all methods provided. Bitcoin is part of a new paradigm so the level of transparency should be at the highest end of the spectrum when it comes to businesses. For example, bitcoin exchange, BTC-e.com, doesn't disclose anything on its website, such as an about us page or business location and they ignored a help desk inquiry requesting full disclosure. BTC-e.com may be a great business operating with full integrity, but they don't pass the transparency test, which is the complete opposite of bitreserve's approach. Repeat the following natural law when setting up and using any and all bitcoin-related platforms.

## KIRK's LAW:
## Consumers have the right of privacy;
## businesses have the duty of transparency.

## Fluctuation-Free Exchange

The Bitreserve.org motto is "Change Money, Change the World." This platform offers an easy, frictionless way to exchange value between fiat currency and digital currency, reaping all the benefits of bitcoin without the volatility. Users can send bitcoin to a bitcoin address or a number of other fiat currency-denominated bitcoin addresses. Bitcoin can be held as U.S. dollars, Japanese yen, Chinese yuan, euros, British pounds and even gold. For example, LMN Company sends 100 bitcoins to the bitcoin address of its U.S. dollar card allowing them to hold bitcoins as U.S. dollars until they want to spend it as bitcoin, thus eliminating price fluctuations during the holding period. Bitreserve does this by selling bitcoins for U.S. dollars or other fiat currency and conversely buys back bitcoins when LMN Company wants to spend or transfer the U.S. dollars as bitcoin.

Bitcoins are held on bitcoin cards, U.S. dollars on U.S. dollar cards, and euros on euro cards etc. in lieu of using the terms "bitcoin addresses" or "bitcoin wallets." However, each card has its own bitcoin address for easily sending and receiving value. The cards are just non-physical representations on a user's account and no physical cards are issued. Bitreserve has "no fees forever" for all money conversion and exchanges, which all happens invisibly behind the scenes for an easy-peasy user experience.

## Transparency Reserves

Bitreserve claims it is the first financial service company in the world to provide verifiable, real-time proof of solvency. Its Reservechain feature allows customers to trace transactions from the start of their account to the present. The Reserveledger feature publishes real-time obligations owed to customers and assets held in reserve. Halsey Minor, founder and CEO of bitreserve, proclaims, "What you do with your money is your business, what we do with your money is everybody's business." Bitreserve's published assets held in reserve exceed its customer obligations. Good-bye fractional reserves, the new age of transparency and positive net reserves has been ushered in.

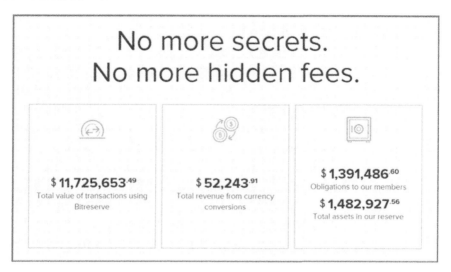

Image courtesy of bitreserve

## Catapult Your Coins

Coinapult.com is an online wallet and payment service provider for merchants, featured in this section for its price stability tool called Locks. The merchant tools have zero fees to accept bitcoin and zero exchange rate risk similar to other payment service providers who give you $249 when you get paid $249. Locks does what it sounds like by allowing users to lock in their bitcoin balance, which is pegged to the value of U.S. dollars, euros, pounds, gold or silver on a given day, and unlock them for the same amount a week, a month or a year later. Locks works much like Bitreserve and also includes an exchange fee to guarantee a bitcoin price during the lock period.[167]

Coinapult is a Panama-based business primarily focused on Latin America and available to U.S. customers while identification is optional upon signing up. Ironically, volatility-busting tools are more valuable to people and businesses in developed countries because they're used to a very stable, fiat currency. The price fluctuations of fiat currency in high-inflation or developing nations can be more radical than bitcoin, making this digital currency seem like a very stable medium of exchange.

## Gold Stability and Bitcoin Agility

Vaultoro.com, the bitcoin gold exchange, does one thing well as stated in their first motto, "combining the oldest store of value with the newest store of value." This bank independent platform allows customers to make bitcoin deposits up to $5,000 U.S. per day without identity verification. You can literally turn bitcoin into gold or turn gold back into bitcoin in a matter of seconds. The tiny trading and storage fees also support frequent trades and small holdings which was never possible with old gold platforms. Everyone in the world now has access to gold with one milligram purchase minimums. Vautoro's second motto, "combining the stability of physical gold with the agility of bitcoin" sums up the power of the platform. Your business can hedge against bitcoin volatility by keeping bitcoins in quasi cold storage in the form of gold. Just trade the gold back into bitcoin and it's ready for spending in seconds. In addition, the gold is insured in a high security vault in Switzerland and audited by CPA firm, BDO. Some other amazing features of Vaultoro include:

- Instant buy settings allow for automatic buys of gold when bitcoins are sent to the platform.
- You can buy gold with leading altcoins using the built in ShapeShift button.
- Instant bitcoin deposit features no waiting for bitcoin confirmations.
- Bitcoin miners can effectively mine real gold using the instant buy setting.

## Bitcoin Price Index

The coindesk.com bitcoin price index (BPI) is a widely used source for bitcoin pricing. The BPI is comprised of the top exchanges by trading volume to create a representative price for bitcoin at any point in time. Bitstamp, Bitfinex, BTC-e, LakeBTC and OKcoin make up the pricing index as of 2015. Many securities may be listed in one place such as NASDAQ resulting in only one asset price; however, bitcoin is listed on multiple exchanges and therefore has multiple, slightly different prices at any one time.

## Specialized Altcoin Exchanges

Altcoin or cryptocurrency exchanges specialize in trading one type of altcoin for another such as Bitcoin for Litecoin. These trades may have a tiny fee depending on the platform while the protocol of a particular altcoin usually determines whether or not a transaction fee or miner's fee is required to complete the transaction. For example, a token called NXT requires one NXT to complete a trade. Cryptsy, poloniex and ShapeShift are examples of platforms that specialize in trading hundreds of altcoins. Get set up on multiple exchanges because your favorite altcoin may be available on one exchange but not another.

Cryptsy.com is one of the original and largest U.S.-based pure altcoin exchanges founded in 2013. They specialize in trading several hundred different cryptocurrencies, including bitcoin, hence the name cryptsy. Users can trade peer-to-peer for free and make fiat currency deposits to start buying and trading altcoins although sending bitcoin to a cryptsy account is the best way to use the platform. Cryptsy points are earned for regular trading activity and are redeemable for weekly drawings. The platform has an excellent user interface and clean design. Cryptsy's sister platform Mintsy offers mining contracts so users can participate in mining coins without technical know-how or having to buy equipment. The mined coins can be automatically sent to a linked Cryptsy account.

# Cryptsy example of an NXT token purchase with BTC in three steps

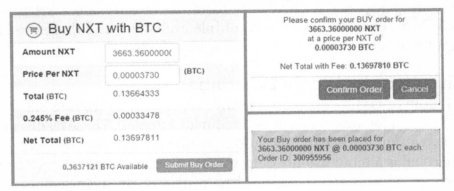

Image courtesy of Cryptsy

Bleutrade.com is a pure cryptocurrency exchange based in Brazil. The user interface is friendly to the eye with the easiest navigation and least clutter of altcoin exchanges. Fiat deposits can be made with a Payeer account using 150 different worldwide payment systems. Payeer.com also works with other platforms like EXMO and cointopay and is one of the few traditional payment systems that accepts U.S. debit and credit cards. After the initial Payeer setup, debit and credit cards deposits are instantaneous, making this a great tool to get from fiat to crypto in a few minutes, despite the fiat fees. Anyone can open a Bleutrade account without supplying personal information and start trading instantly by sending bitcoin to your bleutrade address. There are no business or corporate accounts so users should set up separate accounts for business and personal use to avoid commingling transactions.

Users can participate in the growth of the platform by buying bleutrade shares (BLEU). All fees generated from over 100 cryptocurrencies on the Bleutrade platform are automatically distributed as dividends every 12 hours on a pro rata basis. For example, if you own 5% of all bleutrade shares then you receive 5% of the fees earned from each coin traded on the platform, which allows you to own dozens of altcoins within 12 hours. This is a unique feature among altcoin exchanges and a great example of blockchain technology applied to real-time revenue sharing.

ShapeShift.io requires no account setup, no passwords and no emails to use this pure altcoin exchange with no fiat currency features. Put Peercoin in and get bitcoin out in less than 10 seconds. It's the fastest, most private and convenient way to exchange dozens of altcoins. Simply enter your address for the coins you want to receive and the system generates a deposit address for the coins you want to exchange. ShapeShift is a low-risk conduit because you can't store coins on the platform. As the name implies, you send one type of altcoin from your wallet through ShapeShift back into another one of your altcoin wallets. It's like sending bitcoin from one wallet to another except it magically changes into an altcoin of your choice. The API turns ShapeShift into a great business tool for sending or receiving multiple cryptocurrencies with instant conversion to and from bitcoin. With ShapeShift, customers are no longer limited to paying you in bitcoin.

## Bitcoin Exchanges Around the World

*European Exchanges*

Safello.com is a European bitcoin exchange based in Sweden with services available in more than 32 countries. Instant account funding of fiat currency is primarily made with SEPA, which stands for "single euro payment area," an initiative to simplify bank transfers made in euros. Other methods such as Faster Payments, Swish and international wire are also available. The exchange is not available to U.S. residents as of 2015.

EXMO.com is incorporated in the U.K. and headquartered in Spain. They accept deposits in euros, U.S. dollars and Russian rubles using deposit methods such as Payeer.com and bank wires. The Bleutrade About Us page has profile pictures of the entire team assembled from eight countries around the world. EXMO's incorporation document and corporate address with street photo is also posted on their website, further demonstrating a good commitment to transparency. Customer service is available 24 hours a day via chat, email and country-specific phone numbers.

The platform has an intuitive user interface that's easy on the eye while boasting the lowest fees in the industry.

In Bitcoin We Trust is a U.K.-based exchange offering bank withdraws and deposits for U.K. residents but anyone who can get an OKpay account can also fund an account with fiat currency. U.S. residents can't use the platform because OKpay is not available to anyone in the U.S. as of 2015. Transparency gets a big thumbs-up for having tabs on well-defined areas including verification, legal, terms, privacy, company registration, compliance and an about us page. They have three levels of verification with a corresponding transaction limit and one standard fee for all transactions.

The IBWT team states, "The current state of the U.K. government's view towards Bitcoin is a 'wait and see' approach, allowing Bitcoin time to grow and mature. The IBWT team keeps itself apprised of the developing regulatory framework and will be adhering to any relevant regulation as it appears." U.S. regulation often precludes foreign exchanges and other financial services from being offered to U.S. residents and businesses, a stark contrast to the U.K. approach.

Bitstamp.net, one of the oldest exchanges founded in 2011, is headquartered in the U.K. It accepts U.S. dollars via international wire and SEPA payments, which stands for single euro payment area, an initiative to simplify bank transfers made in euros. All euros and wires received in other currencies are automatically converted to USD free of charge for buying bitcoin. Users can also make deposits via Astropay, a fiat payment platform; however, similar to OKpay, U.S. residents cannot open an Astropay account as of 2015. Bitstamp has a Ripple payment gateway deposit alternative as described in the LakeBTC section.

The following terms and conditions excerpt is an example of an FATCA compliance disclosure further discussed in the BSA and FATCA chapter. "With respect to U.S. residents, we also may share your information with other financial institutions as authorized under Section 314(b) of the US Patriot Act, and with tax authorities, including the U.S. Internal Revenue Service, pursuant to the

Foreign Account Tax Compliance Act ("FATCA"), to the extent that this statute may be determined to apply to Bitstamp Ltd."

## U.S. Exchanges

Exchange.Coinbase.com is a U.S.-based bitcoin exchange only available in limited states upon launch in 2015 due to the myriad of individual states' money transmitter licensing requirements. Top tier investors including the NYSE and USAA have backed the exchange. Insurance against hacking, internal theft and accidental loss of bitcoins is provided, which is something few other exchanges disclose.

Coinbase.com, its simpler affiliate, is a universal platform for both merchants and individuals where bitcoin can be purchased with a bank account or bitcoin can be received as payment for customers. Everyone should add a Coinbase account to his or her bitcoin toolbox. Be patient as you endure the standard hurry-up-and-wait old rail banking model taking up to five business days to get your bitcoin after making a USD purchase.

Kraken.com is a pioneering U.S.-based bitcoin exchange built on credibility. The Bitcoin Blog summed it up by saying, "Kraken is an exemplary institution that the rest of the bitcoin world should look up to. One of the first exchanges to pass an independent audit, they've consistently shown themselves to be leaders on security practices." This robust platform offers multiple order types, margin trading and fiat currency deposits in USD, euros, pounds and yen. Good luck being able to use Kraken in your state as of 2015 because U.S. state regulations are making the rollout a slow process. Ironically, U.S. residents can use some foreign exchanges to buy and sell bitcoin but they can't use a U.S.-based exchange depending on their state of residence. Kraken is also a leader in creating a framework for exchange auditing, as disclosed on their website.

Bityes.com a U.S. trading platform affiliated with Hong Kong-based bitcoin exchange Huobi. Multiple deposit methods are available for fiat currency and 24-hour customer support includes live chat, Skype, phone or email to handle all your questions on this FAQ-less platform. They offer a standard order book to buy and sell bitcoin, margin trading and peer-to-peer lending. All customers have to get verified in order to make fiat currency deposits; however, their simple verification includes a government-issued ID and a proof of residence with a one-to two-day approval process.

## Chinese Exchanges

LakeBTC.com, a Shanghai-based exchange, is the self-proclaimed marketplace for all users including individuals, merchants, miners and institutional investors by providing great customer service, liquidity and security. The platform offers unverified, individual and corporate accounts. Their Ripple gateway makes this a truly universal exchange because anyone can create a RippleTrade account in conjunction with SnapSwap to deposit USD almost instantaneously. Ripple users can easily trade fiat currency and cryptocurrency opening a possibility that anyone can use LakeBTC by exchanging their local fiat into USD on the Ripple platform. LakeBTC also provides comprehensive FAQs.

Bitfinex.com is another Hong Kong-based exchange offering three types of services: change bitcoin, margin trading and liquidity providing with three corresponding dedicated bitcoin wallets, exchange wallet, trading wallet and deposit wallet, respectively. Change bitcoin is a standard order book for buying and selling bitcoin, margin trading is for investors who borrow USD to buy bitcoin, and liquidity providing is for lenders who offer funds on their own terms for margin traders. Both individual and corporate accounts are available and users must get verified to make fiat currency deposits. Bitfinex has taken a voluntary audit approach similar to Kraken. Other Chinese exchanges include Huobi.com, ANXBTC.com and BTCChina.com, China's oldest bitcoin exchange.

## Latin American Exchanges

In Argentina, online brokers and over-the-counter methods are more common than exchanges due to the regulatory climate and the negative view of peso alternatives. Bitcoin has gained traction in this high-inflation country with high credit card fees and long clearing times to get cash from sales. However, several Latin American bitcoin exchanges have emerged such as Bitex.la, meXBT.com,

Unisend.com.mx and coinbit.it. LocalBitcoins.com and Bitquick.co are examples of peer-to-peer bitcoin platforms that connect people on a local and regional level who want to exchange bitcoins for cash.

*Local and Worldwide*

LocalBitcoins.com is the worldwide local marketplace bringing buyers and sellers together from over 7,000 cities. Simply type in your city and choose whether you want to buy online or in person for cash. Sellers can also post bitcoins for sale and choose an online payment method or sell in person for cash. The listings are separated by buyers and sellers as well as online versus cash payments. Users can easily submit a trade request and communicate via the Local Bitcoin messaging system. A built in escrow system releases a secret code to both the buyer and seller after the seller sends bitcoins to the buyers wallet. This works great for in person cash sales when both parties verify the code which releases the bitcoins with a text confirmation. Local Bitcoins is a great example of a peer-to-peer marketplace; however, bitcoin sellers should investigate engaging as a money service business to avoid stepping into quicksand with law enforcement.

## Quick and Easy

Bitquick.co combines the power of convenience and privacy in a platform where buyers and sellers can exchange bitcoins for cash in less than three hours depending on the country. This peer-to-peer bitcoin exchange platform is available in the U.S., India, Taiwan, the European Union and other countries. No personal identifying information or account setup is required to use the service. Bitcoin buyers simply choose the amount of bitcoins they want to buy and the bank where they want to make the deposit, and enter an email address to start the trade. The buyer is matched up with a seller who already put bitcoins in escrow, and entered a bank account and email address. A three-hour timer starts ticking for the buyer to make a cash deposit at the seller's bank while the deposit slip has to be uploaded to complete the trade. For example, a buyer lives a few blocks away from Bank of America and prefers to make all deposits at a nearby bank; therefore, only sellers with Bank of America bank accounts are matched up with the buyer. Buyers and sellers don't have to meet in person as necessary for cash purchases using LocalBitcoins.com. Other payment methods are available such as SEPA transfers in the EU, but depending on the country and the payment method, there may be a longer wait time to get your bitcoins.

## Bitcoin Exchanges Takeaway

The exchanges mentioned here are centralized functions in an otherwise decentralized, cryptographic model. Centralization and transparency have a direct relationship so the more something is centralized the more it should be transparent. Bitcoin's decentralized, built-in blockchain transparency is a trustless system spread among thousands of participants instead of centralized inside of one. There are several decentralized exchange and peer-to-peer marketplace models evolving as alternatives to centralized models. This is another example where Bitcoin technology gives users a choice and a good business strategy will likely encompass both centralized and decentralized exchanges.

Find out who is behind an exchange and where it's located in addition to considering all the other factors mentioned above. Reduce third-party exchange platform risk or the risk of exchange failure by conducting business with an exchange that is based in your home country. If your business is in the U.S., there are several exchanges based in the U.S. and pairing puts both players in the same jurisdiction in case something goes dreadfully wrong. The likelihood of recovering any type of currency in a total failure is remote but it's magnified if the exchange is in a different country. Filing a cross-jurisdictional lawsuit would be time and cost-prohibitive. If an exchange is not available in your region or if you live in an unstable region, then choose one located in a country you trust.

As with all bitcoin ecosystem platforms, the best strategy is getting on the court, signing up for multiple accounts and funding them with small amounts of fiat. A small amount is defined as an amount that wouldn't bother you if you never saw it again. There is no better way to gauge transparency, integrity and trust than testing the waters by putting money into play, contacting support, making trades and so on. Reviewing a website without signing up is like buying a car without test-driving it. Test drive exchanges, then choose two or three go-to platforms. This spreads the risk by using multiple baskets to carry your eggs. If an exchange or any other bitcoin platform doesn't pass the transparency test, then don't use it, regardless of how popular or how good the pricing may be. There are many other options where your business can find a home. (Bitcoin storage strategies are discussed in the chapter on wallets.)

Be sure to visit BestBitcoinBookEver.com/bonus for step-by-step guides to get set up on various exchanges.

# Bitcoin Accounting & Reporting

## Triple Play

Businesses have three distinct challenges in accounting for bitcoin transactions. First, the sale of goods and services for bitcoin will flow through bitcoin payment service providers for most businesses. Sales transactions have to be moved from the provider into an accounting system. The profit on the sale has to be captured for accounting and tax purposes; however, there may or may not be a corresponding gain or loss from holding bitcoin or another tax-related calculation, depending on the jurisdiction. If bitcoin sales are immediately cashed out into fiat currency, then the gain or loss is zero in the case of U.S. taxpayers since bitcoin was held for a zero amount of time.

Second, whenever bitcoin is received from a sale and held in a wallet for more than one day, gains and losses must be calculated when bitcoin is sold. In other words any combination of sales, purchases and exchanges of bitcoin or other cryptocurrencies for fiat money has to be accounted for. Wallet aggregation and tax reporting platforms do a great job summarizing this kind of information. (Also refer to the chapter on taxation for more detail.)

Third, bitcoin purchases of goods and services are considered the expenses or assets of a business and they have to be captured in an accounting system. This creates a bigger challenge because the reporting platforms are designed to capture transactions for gain and loss tax purposes as well as provide a dashboard of crypto-holdings but generally not for calculating the profit and loss of a business for income tax and accounting purposes. For example, ABC Corp. records two bitcoins worth $1,200 as revenue from consulting services. Bitcoins are worth $500 one month later when they decide to purchase a computer for $1000 in bitcoins. ABC records a $200 capital loss ($1,200 basis in the bitcoins received as revenue less the $1000 purchase price). The computer is recorded on the company's books for $1,000. Generally, the reporting platforms track the $1,200 as the basis of the two bitcoins received for calculating the loss, but it doesn't keep track of the bitcoin as $1,200 in revenue or the $1,000 basis in the computer the same as a full blown accounting system. Reporting platforms are great for summarizing information but they are generally not double-entry accounting systems.

## Accounting Exercises

Larger companies have the resources to solve these challenges with customized solutions within their existing accounting systems while small and medium businesses will have to use one of the great new bitcoin reporting platforms. Most payment service providers, exchanges and wallets offer some kind of exporting feature into a CSV file or other file type, which can be imported back into most accounting systems or bitcoin-reporting platforms. Businesses that cash out bitcoin into fiat currency and don't hold any bitcoin won't create any potential gains and losses, which thereby minimizes their accounting and tax reporting. In this case, a business may simply export sales transactions from its payment service provider into a CSV file for its accounting system without needing to first use a bitcoin transaction-aggregating and tax reporting platform as mentioned above. Businesses that accept and hold bitcoin should use a reporting platform to centralize transactions for accounting and tax purposes.

Bitcoin accounting and reporting platforms use a combination of methods to get transactions from bitcoin payment service providers, exchanges and wallets into their respective systems, ranging from automatic to manual transaction importing. There are generally four ways to import transactions as follows:

1.   Accounts are automatically linked by user granted permission. For, example a Coinbase.com and Blockchain. info account can be automatically linked to Libratax.

2.  Users manually connect accounts with their unique API keys and the transactions are automatically imported. For example, a user logs into a Cryptsy.com account, generates an API key and enters it into bitcoin.tax.

3.  Users download a CSV transaction file and drag or upload the file. Circle.com transactions only have a CSV download and have to be managed this way.

4.  Users manually import transactions using the CSV format required by the reporting platform such as Cointracking. info. Multiple transactions from multiple wallets can be assembled together and imported as one file.

The transaction importing exercise will vary from person to person and business to business depending on the number of accounts and wallets you have, which impacts the number of transaction sets requiring importing. If all your transactions go through one platform like blockchain.info then importing will be easy. Conversely, if you have every type of wallet and account then you will have a lot of transaction management. Following a few methodical steps can make this a pain-free process.

The following steps demonstrate an example of a U.S. business taxpayer going through a daisy chain of transaction management steps from transaction source to tax calculation and finally accounting system importing. If having one account and one set of transactions automatically linked to a reporting platform is on one end of the spectrum, then this example is on the other end of the transaction management spectrum.

1.  Create an inventory of all wallets and platforms with bitcoin transactions. The fewer platforms and wallets, the less complicated the exercise will be.

2.  Export CSV files on a monthly, quarterly or annual basis for consistency and cut-off. Track the file downloads on the inventory worksheet.

3.  Clearly name files using platform name, dates and report type (e.g., ABC, Co. Blockchain Transaction History Report

1-1-2015 to 12-31-2015.csv).

4.   Save and rename the platform CSV files to modify the format while maintaining an unaltered copy of the original file (e.g., ABC, Co. Blockchain Transaction History Report (Libratax Import Format) 1-1-2015 to 12-31-2015.csv).

5.   If your business has seven import files, they can be imported one by one or consolidated into a master import file.

6.   Reorganize data into a reporting platform import format; e.g., columns and headers required by bitcoin.tax (see example below).

7.   Import the adjusted and renamed service provider CSV file into the transaction-aggregating and tax reporting platform.

8.   Adjust or code transactions as income, sale, etc., including any manual transaction entry required.

9.   Calculate, download and save the tax calculations report for tax filing (e.g., ABC, Co. Libratax Capital Gains Tax Report 1-1-2015 to 12-31-2015.csv).

10.  Save and rename the tax report CSV file to modify the format for accounting platform importing (e.g., ABC, Co. Libratax Capital Gains Tax Report (Xero Accounting Import Format) 1-1-2015 to 12-31-2015.csv).

11.  Reorganize the tax report columns into the accounting platform import format (e.g., columns, dates and headers). Delete the gains and losses because only bitcoin translated to USD is needed for importing; i.e., A computer was purchased for 3 bitcoins worth $1,125 USD. The capital gain or loss isn't needed; only the U.S. dollar amount of the computer is needed for this exercise.

12.  Import the adjusted tax CSV file into the accounting system to capture the USD or other fiat currency as if the transaction had been imported from a bank account.

A required CSV importing format varies slightly from platform to platform but looks something like this:

- Date (format can vary i.e. YYYY-MM-DD, DD-MM-YYYY or MM-DD-YYYY)
- Source (optional, such as platform name or gift, donation, etc)
- Action (BUY, SELL or FEE)
- Coin type (BTC, LTC, DOGE, etc)
- Amount (number of coins traded)
- Currency (fiat currency such as USD, GBP, EUR or coins, BTC or LTC)
- Price (per coin price in currency)
- Fee (transaction cost)
- Memo

Coinbase.com has multiple report types such as transaction history, merchant order history, cost basis for taxes and more. Every report type should be saved and clearly named as described above regardless of whether the report type is used. This approach allows personal and business files to be clearly distinguished from each other by platform, type of report and date. It's also best practice for naming and saving files in general, but this practice becomes more valuable with multiple bitcoin platform and wallet files. Individuals would only be concerned with the steps, including the tax calculation, because they generally are not required to file and produce a balance sheet. Businesses have to complete all the steps because they need a full accounting for internal management and external reporting purposes, including preparation of a balance sheet. Individuals who operate their personal affairs like a business would go through this exercise. Many countries have different tax treatments for bitcoin so the tools used and the calculations may be different, but the exercise of managing transactions will be the same.

## Short-Term Challenge

Businesses may have to perform a combination of manual entries and multiple importing and exporting of transactions to get the proper information. These are challenging, short-term, multi-step processes for accounting that will eventually give way to seamless integrations and more robust, innovative platforms. Bitcoin Transaction Coordinator (btc4erp.com) is a subscription-based module that integrates with Netsuite, a middle market accounting system. The platform manages payments and creates the appropriate accounting entries, thus minimizing the need for exporting transactions into other platforms. Both unrealized gains and losses for accounting and realized gains and losses for taxes are calculated within the system. The transaction coordinator plug-in is limited to handling bitcoin but not altcoins, which will change as the plug-in gets more robust. In other words, the process closely mirrors bank account linking with accounting packages eliminating the above steps for managing multiple transaction files. [168]

Netsuite is an expensive accounting package and doesn't make sense for most businesses until they have sales in the neighborhood of $5 to $10 million. Therefore, you can't use the plug-in unless your business already uses Netsuite. A large company may already be invested in a different accounting package and migrating to Netsuite might not be practical.

## An Easy Way

Intuit launched paybycoin.intuit.com, a service that allows QuickBooks Online users to invoice and accept payment in bitcoin. All bitcoin sales are immediately cashed out with the help of Coinbase thus allowing businesses to get the benefits of bitcoin without any exchange risk or additional accounting exercises. [169] The transactions are recorded directly in the system because no separate payment service provider account is necessary. This is better than a merchant not accepting bitcoin at all, but fiat cash-outs don't allow merchants to keep bitcoin in the ecosystem. Bitcoin sales are relatively small for most merchants in 2015 and most of them won't feel a volatility impact by holding a modest amount of bitcoin.

## Tricky Tracking

How do you keep track of all your wallets, bitcoin addresses and bitcoin transactions? A review of the bitcoin wallets chapter demonstrates the wide variety of bitcoin wallets available. Wallets are a collection of bitcoin addresses; therefore, one wallet can have more than one bitcoin address. There are as many different reasons to have multiple wallets as there are wallets to choose from.

Desktop wallets, vault wallets, smart phone wallet apps, wallets coupled with exchange accounts and wallets coupled with payment service providers, are examples of the many wallets needed for business strategy and risk management. There are hundreds of different altcoins (and counting) making it even more necessary to keep it all organized. Multiple wallets on multiple platforms in multiple cryptocurrencies require a lot of tracking for both individuals and businesses. Just keeping track of bitcoin alone can be challenging enough.

Individuals and businesses are required to file and pay taxes, but only businesses have to account for every transaction, including all income and expenses. Most individuals aren't motivated to track their own income and expenses and don't have the same accounting challenges as businesses.

## A Platform and A Place

Fortunately, there are several platforms designed specifically to centralize and summarize bitcoin transactions. They also generally track the basis or purchase price and the corresponding sales amounts translated to fiat currency for reporting gains and losses for both personal and business tax purposes. In addition to tracking actual gains and losses, the features may also include the increase or decrease in value of your overall bitcoin and altcoin portfolio in the fiat currency of your choice, similar to the way TD Ameritrade or Fidelity Investments report gains, losses and asset appreciation.

All of these platforms are information compiling, read-only services in the form of watch-only wallets that don't store coins or private keys. Bitcoin addresses are simply added to facilitate the data linking. These platforms generally offer automatic data importing as well as manual entry for transactions. Multiple charts with data analysis, prices, trading volume, and stats may also be available for the altcoin market and your specific portfolio.

In general platforms are continuously adding new features to strengthen customer loyalty by providing as many tools as possible. For example, Coinbase.com is an exchange and payment service provider that released a tax-reporting module. Bitgo.com multisig wallet provider displays multiple, watch-only bitcoin addresses in a dashboard format.

## Dashboard & Reporting Platform Examples

Several specialized dashboards and reporting platforms include Nucleon.io, CoinTracking.info, Libratax.com, Bitcoin.tax, Tapeke. com and Coyno.com. CoinTracking and Nucleon provide a dashboard that compiles multiple altcoins with a simple cost basis, real-time value and real-time gain-loss summary while Libratax and Bitcoin.tax specialize in tax reporting.

Tepeke.com and Coyno.com are like Mint.com platforms for bitcoin and cryptocurrencies. These platforms are read-only and do not store private keys or hold coins. Both individuals and businesses can use these platforms, but it's important to create separate accounts, the same as with bitcoin exchanges and other platforms, to avoid commingling transactions. For example, ALT, Inc. accepts bitcoin and multiple altcoins for services and chooses to hold most of the altcoins in lieu of cashing them out to fiat. ALT, Inc. holds bitcoin and 21 altcoins including Bitshares, Vertcoin, Peercoin, Mastercoin, Counterparty, NXT, Maidsafe, Dogecoin and others. It hold 121 bitcoins worth $33,275 as of June 30, 2015, with a cost basis of $51,444, resulting in a potential loss of $18,169. The dashboard displays this potential gain and loss for each altcoin allowing for strategic decision making to sell coins at a loss to offset taxable gains or sell losers that may be on a downward slide. The tax calculations and reporting features capture transactions from the past and the dashboard features provide decision making for the future.

Cointracking.info is a real-time portfolio dashboard and tax tracker for hundreds of digital coins, commodities and fiat currencies. The value of each altcoin can be displayed in the fiat currency of your choice including a total portfolio value and the respective gain or loss if an altcoin was sold on a given day, which represents the increase or decrease in value from the purchase price. The tax-reporting feature calculates gains and losses from sales or exchanges of altcoins that require tax reporting, depending on your jurisdiction. The tax-reporting module also has settings for tax rates and methods to calculate tax for several countries around the world with FIFO being the most common method. Users can see the performance of their portfolio in multiple chart, graph and list formats. Cointracking Founder, Dario Kachel says, "This tool tells you automatically and in real time what your coins are worth and what your current potential profit and loss is." The transactions can also be exported for tax reporting and accounting system importing for balance sheet and income statement purposes. [170]

The CoinTracking Realized and Unrealized Gains dashboard example shows potential profits in green and potential losses in red for a given coin.

**Realized and Unrealized Gains**

The following page displays information which shows you whether you would be at a profit (indicated by the color green) or a loss (indicated by red) if you sold those particular coins. [How does the calculation work?]

**Purchase value of your coins**

| Coin | Ø Purchase value | | Current sales value | | Profit / Loss | | |
|------|---------|---------|---------|---------|---------|---------|---------|
| | for 1 coin | ∑ all coins | for 1 coin | ∑ all coins | for 1 coin | ∑ all coins | percent |
| BTC | 79.530725 $ | 208.86 $ | 266.600000 $ | 700.25 $ | 187.134275 $ | 491.39 $ | 235.27% |
| DVC | 0.000187 $ | 239.76 $ | 0.000019 $ | 23.96 $ | -0.000168 $ | -215.80 $ | -90.01% |
| FTC | 0.312597 $ | 158.96 $ | 0.005837 $ | 2.97 $ | -0.306760 $ | -155.99 $ | -98.13% |
| IXC | 0.009186 $ | 75.17 $ | 0.017877 $ | 146.24 $ | 0.008688 $ | 71.07 $ | 94.55% |
| LTC | 4.314824 $ | 368.33 $ | 4.037232 $ | 344.64 $ | -0.277592 $ | -23.70 $ | -6.43% |
| NMC | 0.983096 $ | 157.89 $ | 0.538653 $ | 88.31 $ | -0.424442 $ | -69.58 $ | -44.07% |
| NVC | 3.775540 $ | 210.32 $ | 1.303667 $ | 72.64 $ | -2.471873 $ | -137.68 $ | -65.46% |
| PPC | 0.261317 $ | 156.01 $ | 0.455889 $ | 272.23 $ | 0.194672 $ | 116.22 $ | 74.50% |
| TRC | 0.529764 $ | 147.91 $ | 0.004483 $ | 1.25 $ | -0.525282 $ | -146.66 $ | -99.15% |
| XAU | 1750.000000 $ | 350.00 $ | 1107.306153 $ | 221.46 $ | -642.694847 $ | -128.54 $ | -36.73% |

Image courtesy of CoinTracking

Nucleon.io is also a crypto dashboard and tax-reporting platform. Its text and email alert feature sends notifications when balances rise or fall based on settings of your choice. Users can setup free accounts and add multiple bitcoin and altcoin addresses. Transactions can be automatically linked with the major exchanges, depending on the availability of APIs, or imported as a CSV file. "Our mission is to provide our customers with tools that make cryptocurrency a part of their everyday lives and foster adoption of this amazing new technology," says Nucleon.io founder and CEO, Brock Wood. The platform takes a snapshot every five minutes of the user's portfolio of addresses and displays cost basis as well as increases and decreases in value in a graphical format. Nucleon is actively building out its offerings to include a more advanced set of features. [171]

Libratax.com is a tax reporting-focused platform that offers capital gains and losses calculations and reporting for U.S. taxpayers as well as automatic linking with Coinbase, Blockchain, Bitgo and other services. Various cost basis methods such as LIFO, FIFO, Average Cost and Libra Optimized, can be selected for calculating gains and losses. Jake Benson, Libratax CEO and founder, told a SXSW audience that, "The blockchain is simply an accounting ledger and nothing more. Libratax is built with this mentality in mind." The service is free to use for individuals and the tax reports can be downloaded for a fee. Libratax for business provides enhanced reporting capabilities including a tax report, balance report, acquisition report, disposal report and custom reporting as well as an integration with leading payment processor, Bitpay. Libratax also has a tax professionals network to serve taxpayers who need professional services. [172]

Bitcoin.tax is a complete tax solution for calculating gains and losses as well as mining income. This tool calculates and summarizes the numbers that specific tax rates are applied to. Bitcoin businesses and individuals are responsible for maintaining their own records for every bitcoin and crypto transaction including cost basis, sales and purchases, an otherwise recordkeeping challenge if you don't have a tool to manage it. Bitcoin.tax can handle calculations for bitcoin and thousands of altcoins with choices for average cost, FIFO and LIFO cost basis methods, including an option for like kind treatment known as 1031 exchanges in the U.S. This platform is suitable for taxation methods of various countries and advisors who may differ in opinion on tax treatments. Multiple exchanges and payment processors are supported for data importing or API linking thus eliminating many of the aforementioned reformatting scenarios. Transactions can also be formatted to the CSV bitcoin. tax import format. IRS Form 8949 is produced for U.S. taxpayers as an attachment includable in tax returns. In addition, Bitcoin.tax supports importing from Turbo Tax and Tax Act.

Tapeke.com is a free bitcoin transaction service, much like a Mint.com for bitcoins. Multiple wallets and bitcoin addresses can be set up to track bitcoin transactions in a view-only dashboard format. It provides expense categories and transaction history, including beginning balance, ending balance, income and expense. Bitcoin balances can be viewed in total, by wallet or by bitcoin address. Tapeke does not provide tax reporting or altcoin support; thus, it's not designed to track altcoins or other assets purchased with bitcoins. It's more of a profit-and-loss summary platform and not a balance sheet platform, and it's more suited for individuals than businesses.

Coyno.com is an overview and control tool for cryptocurrency. It sits like a watch-only layer on top of a user's bitcoin services and tracks all transactions on behalf of users, thereby providing them with an easy-to-use, graphical user interface to their crypto-holdings. Furthermore, Coyno converts transactions into fiat values, which can be used for crypto-bookkeeping. "If you use multiple wallets and exchanges, which is often the case, it can be difficult to keep the overview, a problem that Coyno aims to solve," explains Erasmus Hagen, Berlin-based Coyno.com co-founder.

## Bitcoin Accounting & Reporting Takeaway

Several platforms have been developed to consolidate multiple coins into a single dashboard with complex reporting including tax features. A wide variety of market information for coins is also provided. Features are continually being improved and added while the number of platforms is also expanding. Sign up and test-drive the free versions to figure out which platform has the best presentation and features for your situation. Maintain a separate business account and individual account on each platform to avoid commingling, for reporting purposes. Many bitcoin wallet services and platforms don't make the distinction between business and personal so users need to be intentional with their respective purpose.

There isn't a single utopian accounting solution and the challenges presented here should not be a reason to forego accepting bitcoin in your business. Every business is unique and creating a customized strategy for business processes is like a work of art. It's no different when bitcoin is added into the equation. The benefits of accepting bitcoin far outweigh any additional work to account for bitcoin transactions. Most businesses already face the challenge of managing disparate systems; therefore, integrating bitcoins from an accounting perspective will be a marginal exercise in effort that gets better over time. Light speed innovation within the bitcoin space will eventually result in the emergence of multiple superior accounting solutions. The sooner your business implements bitcoin the sooner it will benefit from these innovations in the short and long term. Go to BestBitcoinBookEver.com/bonus right now to get more help with your accounting and tax reporting, including step-by-step guides and platform updates.

# Bitcoin Taxation & The IRS

The taxation of bitcoin varies from country to country as much as other bitcoin regulation and continues to develop into taxation schemes ranging across the spectrum. Covering the tax treatment in every country is beyond the scope of this book; however, the U.S. Internal Revenue Service guidance is a good example of the unique challenges presented by the application of an existing rule set.

## NOT Legal Tender Therefore Property

The United States Internal Revenue Service (IRS) issued guidance on the taxation of bitcoin and convertible digital currency in March 2014. The IRS stated that bitcoin is not legal tender in any jurisdiction thus defaulting it to property status. Therefore, all the rules regarding the taxation of property apply to bitcoin. Convertible digital currency is defined by FinCEN as "digital currency that can be traded or bought and sold for government-issued fiat currency or legal tender." Some digital currency used in online worlds and gaming can't be turned into cash so it's not convertible and not part of the IRS rules and definition. [173]

## Bitcoin Chameleon

All bitcoin is considered property whether owned by an individual or business. It may be taxed differently, however, depending on the nature of that property in the hands of the taxpayer. This means different tax types and tax rates apply depending on what you plan to do with your bitcoin. Individuals or businesses that buy bitcoin as an investment have capital assets like gold, collectibles, stocks or mutual funds. A capital asset is the IRS term for property held as an investment. A business such as a bitcoin broker or exchange that buys and sells bitcoin has inventory just like any store selling physical products. Property not considered an investment or inventory is personal property used productively in a business.

Personal property used by a business has tax benefits of depreciation while the same personal property used by an individual does not have the same depreciation benefits.

## Bitcoin's Not Personal Property

Personal property, called section 1245 property by the IRS, purchased for productive use in a business such as computers, office furniture and automobiles, can be depreciated or deducted as an expense from income. Bitcoin is not tangible personal property and can't be placed in service or depreciated in the context of a productive machine therefore these rules don't apply. It also doesn't have a determinable useful life like computers, which typically depreciate over three years. Bitcoin's useful life is essentially infinite.

## Capital Assets and Capital Gains

When capital assets are sold or traded the result is a capital gain or capital loss. A long-term capital gain comes from selling a capital asset owned for more than one year with a special tax rate from 0% to 20%. The same capital asset sold in one year or less is a short-term capital gain taxed at higher ordinary rates as high as 39.6% as of 2015. A specific ordinary tax rate for short-term gains depends on an individual's tax bracket or marginal tax rate for a given year.

For example, Bobby bought bitcoin as an investment on April Fool's Day 2015 for $5,000 making it a capital asset. One month later he sold it for $6,850 resulting in a short-term capital gain of $1,850. If he sold it more than a year later, it would have been a long-term capital gain. There is no short-term capital gain tax rate for short-term capital gains. If a gain is short term then ordinary tax rates apply and if a gain is long term then the special long-term capital gain tax rate kicks in. Let's say the April Fool's joke is on Bobby and he bought bitcoin for $5,000 then sold it a month later for $3,900. The result is a short-term capital loss of $1,100. The loss is a bummer, but it can be offset or netted with short-term or long-term capital gains, respectively.

## Bitcoin Inventory

Bitcoin exchanges or brokers in the business of buying and selling bitcoins and altcoins have property that is considered inventory instead of capital assets. This is the same as Wal-Mart buying and selling household items that most people think of as inventory. When inventory is sold or traded it's considered a sale of goods with a corresponding cost of goods sold. The sale price less the cost of goods sold is the gross profit taxed as ordinary income. Inventory status will not apply to the majority of businesses that buy and use bitcoin and it would not apply to individuals. Diving deeper into inventory is beyond the scope of this book and not necessary due to its limited application.

## Bitcoin Salaries & Wages

Any business that pays its employees or independent contractors in bitcoin must account for and report those payments as if they were made in U.S. dollars. For example, if Fran was paid 5 bitcoins on four different dates for a total of 20 bitcoins, and the value of each bitcoin payment translated to U.S. dollars was $250, $325, $510 and $375, respectively, then the total of $1,460 is reported to the IRS. The first payment of 5 bitcoins was made on April 26, 2015, when the U.S. dollar value was $250 and each successive payment is therefore translated the same way. Any employer withholding taxes would also be calculated from the U.S. dollar translation. The sum of all U.S. dollar to bitcoin translations within a given tax year are added up and reported on W-2 forms for employees and 1099s for independent contractors. Payments in bitcoin don't change the nature of the relationship or the reporting. Everything else is the same except that bitcoin payments or any combination of altcoins have to be translated to U.S. dollars. For example, if an employee was paid in Feathercoin, Mastercoin, Startcoin and bitcoin, then a U.S. dollar translation is made just like the example above. The substance of the transaction and its related taxation—payment in exchange for work done—is not changed by the form of medium of exchange. Therefore, whether a person is paid by a company in gold, eggs, wood, bitcoin or fiat currency, the tax applied will be the same. The only issue is determining the fair market value of the goods received. Many crypto price indexes exist, such as coinmarketcap.com, for market prices of hundreds of altcoins that can be used in the translation to U.S. dollars.

## The Payroll Problem

Payroll is made up of three parts: 1) the employee's net pay, 2) the employee's tax withholdings, and 3) the employer's payroll tax, a premium paid by the employer for the privilege of having employees. The total business expense results in a hypothetical 120% of an employee's salary or hourly wage while each employee's payroll calculation is unique. For example, a business paying employees 100% in bitcoin actually pays 70% to the employees while 30% of the employee's withholding together with 20% of business' payroll tax premium is paid to various federal, state and local tax authorities. The challenge is making payroll tax payments in bitcoin resulting in a combination digital currency and fiat currency transaction. Payroll solutions will address this problem and taxing authorities will eventually accept digital currencies.

## Payroll Solution

Bitwage.co is the first startup to deliver a bitcoin payroll solution which can also work in conjunction with traditional payroll services. They leverage the bitcoin protocol to reduce payroll processing time and cost. Payment friction is already bad enough with international money transfers so Bitwage provides a huge advantage for paying workers internationally in our increasingly global business world. Their breakthrough flagship product, real-time payroll, allows employers to pay employees on a daily or hourly basis that was previously cost-prohibitive. For example, weekly payroll is the most frequent time period using traditional payroll services because the old model is too expensive and time consuming to pay out more frequently. Meanwhile, employees can avoid high-interest check cashing services for better personal cash flow management. Employees can also get paid in bitcoin without employer participation in Bitwage.

## Bitcoin Mining Income

A miner receives 25 bitcoin on New Years' Day 2015 for his supercomputing efforts in validating a mega block of bitcoin transactions. If bitcoin was trading for $600, the miner has a resulting $15,000 worth of taxable income. A miner is in the business of supplying computational power in the same way any other business supplies goods or services where the corresponding revenue is taxed as ordinary income. The ordinary tax rates vary based on the type of business entity but at 39.6% they can be almost twice that of long-term capital gains. Miners may have to cash out bitcoin to fiat currency in order to pay their tax liability and other operating expenses.

## Buying Stuff with Bitcoin

When you buy something with bitcoin you are exchanging property for property or property for services. For example, Billy purchased a flat screen TV for $699 with bitcoin he bought seven weeks earlier for $499 resulting in a $200 short-term taxable gain, the difference between the two amounts. These everyday purchases result in short-term capital gains or losses from the sale of property.

If Billy bought the same flat screen for use in the business conference room then the same short-term capital gain would still apply. Individuals report the short- and long-term gains and losses on Schedule D of IRS Form 1040. Businesses on the other hand report sales of business property on IRS Form 4797 included with the respective business tax return such as IRS Forms 1120, 1120S or 1065. The business is also entitled to depreciate the $699 TV over several years or as a one-time deduction depending on tax strategy and then report a capital gain or loss on the TV when sold or disposed.

## The Coffee Problem

The flat screen TV example applies to every transaction made with bitcoin including coffee from your favorite coffee shop. Therefore, a $2 coffee purchased using bitcoin with a basis of $3 results in a $1 short-term taxable gain. If Jennifer averages five purchases a day or 1825 purchases per year, a 100% bitcoin lifestyle would result in 1825 reportable gain or loss transactions to the IRS. Within the existing framework, a 100% bitcoin-based business could have thousands of bitcoin transactions and related gain or loss calculations. Either way, this is a minor inconvenience considering all the tremendous benefits of bitcoin. The IRS may eventually modify its rules, but the reporting platforms addressed in the Bitcoin Accounting and Reporting chapter make these calculations easy.

## Brand New Coin

The IRS property rules are easily applied to convertible digital currencies with readily determinable market values. Bitcoin's U.S. dollar value can be easily obtained from multiple sources for making the calculation. What happens when hypothetical, newly issued Brand New Coin is paid to a subcontractor for services? How long will it take for Brand New Coin to have a readily determinable market value? How is Brand New Coin accounted for and taxed in the meantime? These are all brand new questions inside the new paradigm of digital currency.

Brand New Coin must achieve two things to be easily accounted for and taxed like bitcoin. It must have a readily determinable market value and it must be convertible into fiat currency. Both of these things could likely happen around the same time when the price discovery process determines the price of Brand New Coin through the interactions of buyers and sellers. [174] Brand New Coin may start out trading peer to peer for goods and services or exchanged for fiat currency while eventually getting listed on an exchange platform. It's during the transition process from first distribution or mining of coins to being listed on multiple exchanges where valuation becomes tricky. As stated by the IRS, "Taxpayers will be required to determine the fair market value of virtual currency in U.S. dollars as of the date of payment or receipt."

## Brand New Brainteaser

Company B pays 10,000 Brand New Coins obtained in a first round distribution from Coin Issuer C to Alicia for preparing annual tax returns for which she normally charges $1,000. Brand New Coin has no market value because it was just issued therefore you have to look at the value of the services to determine a taxable value. Every transaction has an exchange of value and the IRS will look for some way to put a value on it. This could also create a situation where the taxpayer thinks property or services is worth X while the IRS thinks it's worth 3X leading to the proverbial fist fight and a resulting compromise somewhere in the middle.

Let's assume there is no dispute in the above example. Alicia will receive a 1099 for $1,000 of income and Company B will have a corresponding $1,000 expense for the services. In addition, Company B originally got the coins as a promotion from Coin Issuer C with a corresponding zero basis resulting in a $1,000 short-term capital gain. Alicia will report the $1,000 payment for tax services are ordinary income in her business. Company B has both a $1,000 gain and a $1,000 expense, but it can't net short-term capital gains with ordinary expenses because they have different tax treatments. Alicia can use her cost basis of $1,000 in 10,000 Brand New Coins or $.10 per coin to calculate capital gains and losses when she spends or sells the coins.

Alternatively, if Company B had provided marketing services worth $2,500 to Coin Issuer C in exchange for 10,000 Brand New Coins then Company B would receive a 1099 from Coin Issuer C for $2,500, unless a value for the 10,000 coins can be established to justify a different amount. Let's assume a $2,500 value was established and reported on Form 1099. Company B has $2,500 of ordinary income and a $2,500 basis in the 10,000 Brand New Coins. Now when Company B pays the 10,000 coins (after the value has gone down) to Alicia for tax services worth $1,000, Alicia still has $1,000 of ordinary income and Company B still has $1,000 of expenses; however, Company B has a $1,500 capital loss ($2,500 basis in the coins less the $1,000 paid for tax services.) A single transaction can seem like a moving target resulting in multiple calculations for both parties involved in the transaction, which certainly makes this section worth rereading!

## Bitcoin Taxation & The IRS Takeaway Part I

Although examining tax scenarios for every country is beyond the scope of this book, the same general principles can be applied in order to understand the challenges and benefits that come with new technologies. Please visit BestBitcoinBookEver.com if you need additional help with your tax reporting and compliance.

Bitcoin's store of value and medium of exchange combo creates two distinct user groups. Many early adopters and other investors are holding significantly appreciated bitcoin while the average consumer is enjoying ease of use benefits for everyday purchases. The coffee problem is an obvious pain in the rear for consumers and businesses; however, bitcoin's property status is a slam-dunk for long-term bitcoiners who may be holding close to 100% unrealized capital gains. The benefits of long-term capital gains are more valuable relative to folks in the highest tax bracket because a fixed tax rate is generally applied to long-term capital gains while an ever-increasing tax rate is applied to ordinary income. A taxpayer in the highest tax bracket of 39.6% feels like they are getting a 50% discount on long-term capital gains taxed at 20%. Meanwhile, a low-income taxpayer may have the same tax rate for both ordinary income and long-term capital gains. New tax regulations may be good for some and bad for others while the benefits depend more on the unique circumstances of both individual and business taxpayers.

Convertible virtual currency taxation presents unique challenges for business and investment transactions for both taxation and business strategy. Coins with no established market value create a subjective valuation challenge and businesses using new coin to compensate for services should carefully establish the classic employee vs. subcontractor relationship with up-front written agreements. In addition, company policy for the taxation of bitcoin and altcoin payments, including Form W-9, taxpayer ID request, Form 1099 and W-2, should be clearly communicated to vendors and employees to avoid any misunderstanding and confusion.

Bitcoin and digital currency enthusiasts may find this topic disappointing, but changing the medium of exchange generally does not change the taxable nature of transactions, a principle that will probably be applied consistently in most taxing jurisdictions. In other words, if U.S. dollars, Canadian dollars, euros or yen are substituted for bitcoin in the same transaction, there's no magical tax treatment exempting the transaction from taxation. Look for and take advantage of the tax benefits instead of focusing on drawbacks and challenges.

## Deferred BitGains

When it comes to taxes every individual and business owner wants to pay the least amount possible. Infrequent and sometimes large capital gains are no exception. An IRS Section1031 exchange allows otherwise taxable gains to be temporarily deferred into the future. Many bitcoin owners are holding highly appreciated bitcoin as highlighted by the price appreciation in bitcoin milestones. For example, bitcoins purchased at $60 with a current value of $600 have a 90% potential taxable gain. The 1031 is a great strategy for exchanging a highly appreciated asset for something irresistible like bitcoin. Ironically, bitcoin holders already own that next awesome thing and want to continue holding it. The world of cryptocurrencies offers a realm of equally exciting opportunities where a tax deferred strategy of exchanging bitcoin for altcoin makes sense. Examining whether other jurisdictions may or may not have a similar rule is beyond the scope of this book even though the principles for navigating the risk can be applied to other situations.

## 1031 Wildcard

Section 1031 of the U.S. Tax Code provides an exception to paying tax on gains by swapping one like asset for another while deferring the gain into the future. The question is whether or not bitcoin qualifies for 1031 tax treatment since it's already classified as property. The IRS' Internal Revenue Bulletin released in March 2014 did not address section 1031 exchanges, however the application to bitcoin is examined below.

The property given up and the property acquired in a 1031 exchange must meet the following two tests to qualify for deferred tax treatment:

- Both assets must be like kind property.
- Both assets must be held for investment or business use.

A 1031 exchange can be one of two types of exchanges:
- A simultaneous exchange
- A deferred exchange

A 1031 exchange can involve two types of property:
- Tangible property
- Intangible property

In a simultaneous exchange the property given up and the property acquired are one in the same transaction. Instead of selling property for cash you are essentially selling one property for another property, except it's considered a trade instead of a sale. When you sell something for cash, the thing you sell and the cash are one in the same transaction. On the other hand, when it comes to real estate, private jets and intangible assets, it would be nearly impossible to exchange two pieces of like-kind property in a simultaneous transaction.

Fortunately, the deferred exchange method allows one property to be sold before another property is identified and purchased. Deferred exchanges must also happen within the following timeframe:

- The property to be acquired is identified within 45 days.
- Both transactions are completed within 180 days.

Finally, like kind exchanges are mandatory and not elective so a transaction would have to be intentionally structured to fall outside the requirements of Section 1031. For example, a piece of manufacturing equipment is sold for cash and the proceeds are used to acquire a better model. Once the taxpayer has control and possession of the cash it's considered "constructive receipt." Therefore, even if the taxpayer intended to get 1031 tax treatment the transaction would be automatically disqualified. Sometimes recognizing a gain is a good thing if it can be offset with a loss, or if it creates another tax benefit better than a deferred gain. A simultaneous exchange of like kind property is inherently mandatory, such as a car for a car or perhaps an altcoin for an altcoin.

The IRS says bitcoin is property therefore the property held-for-investment test can be easily met for both individuals and any type of business entity. The question is whether or not virtual currencies could be considered like kind. Certain property doesn't qualify as property under this definition. For example, inventory, stocks, bonds or partnership interests don't qualify as property and bitcoin doesn't fit into any of these exclusions. The IRS could later classify bitcoin as digital currency, but for now it hasn't been specifically excluded.

## Like Bitcoin and Like Kind

The IRS states, "Like-kind property is property of the same nature, character or class. Quality or grade does not matter." [175] Real estate is commonly traded in a 1031 exchange even though it's heterogeneous. Real estate comprised of land and a building can be exchanged for vacant land while the rules for what qualifies as like-kind personal property—that is, any property other than real estate—are more restrictive. [176] For example, a car is not like-kind property to a truck.

Does bitcoin have the same nature, character or class as its altcoin cousins? Is bitcoin like-kind property to NXT? It's more likely than not that bitcoin is the same as its altcoin kin for 1031 purposes; however, the IRS could arbitrarily make it an exclusion or specify scenarios where digital currency isn't considered like-kind. For example, bitcoin's proof of work algorithm is deemed not the same as NXT's proof of stake algorithm. Personal property can also be tangible such as aircraft and cattle or intangible assets such as copyrights, trademarks and patents. Intangible property must be nearly identical; therefore, bitcoin and NXT would have to be the same as much as the copyright of a book is the same as the copyright of another book. Conversely, the copyright of music is not the same as the copyright of a book. In the meantime a court case may set a precedent before the IRS provides more clarity. The IRS is notorious for taking 10 years or longer to issue final regulations.

Let's assume Ted purchased 21.5 bitcoins for $2,150 and a planned 1031 exchange is set up to acquire 31,000 ExampleCoin in a private transaction. ExampleCoin is not yet available on the altcoin exchanges; therefore, Ted wants to avoid constructive receipt of cash. The $2,150 basis in the bitcoins becomes the new basis in the ExampleCoin for computing tax at a later time. If the 21.5 bitcoins are worth $22,150, then a $20,000 unrealized gain is deferred until a future taxable event occurs. Now let's assume Ted sold the bitcoins for $22,150 instead of exchanging them, resulting in a $20,000 capital gain. At a 20% capital gains rate Ted would have to pay $4,000; thus, the 1031 exchange allows him to keep $4,000 in the game. Five years later, ExampleCoin hypothetically explodes in value to $100 and the 31,000 coins are now worth $3,100,000. Approximately 20% of this newfound wealth, or $620,000, was created by leveraging $4,000 that would have otherwise gone to Uncle Sam.

Ted also is also a power trader on Cryptsy, Bleutrade and Poloniex. He is constantly buying 12 of his favorite altcoins using bitcoin he mined in 2011. These crypto-to-crypto purchases are a simultaneous exchange because no fiat currency is used in the transaction. Ted is parlaying his gigantic, unrealized bitcoin gains by hoarding massive amounts of altcoins, which he believes will explode in price like bitcoin. He will have to track all these transactions and likely report them on Form 8824 Like-Kind exchanges after he consults with his tax advisor.

## Hand-Cuffed Proceeds

A taxpayer can't touch the cash proceeds that will be used to buy like-kind property even if the cash stays untouched in the taxpayer's bank account until the new property is acquired. This is the aforementioned constructive receipt doctrine. The entire transaction, including the proceeds, has to filter through a third-party qualified intermediary (QI) specializing in 1031 exchanges. Your real estate agent, attorney or accountant generally can't be a third-party intermediary. For example, a real estate exchange can be completed within 180 days including 45 days allowed for new property identification. The trade-off for getting a deferred gain and generous time allotment is having to forego the ability to play around with your own money until the new property is acquired. The QI should also provide Form 8824 for inclusion in tax returns.

## The Swapper

Qualified intermediaries specialize in providing 1031 exchange services and many of them consider bitcoin exchange worthy, however finding one who could pull off an exchange without losing your bitcoin is the real challenge. Fortunately, a new platform called swapper.io aims to solve this challenge by creating a crypto only 1031 exchange platform. Swapper would act as the Qualified Intermediary and facilitate the exchange. [177]

For example, Jimmy bought 1,000 bitcoins in 2012 for $9 with a basis of $9,000. In 2015 his bitcoins are now worth $300,000 when the price of a bitcoin is $300. Jimmy is fired up about buying Bitshares but doesn't want to pay 20% or $58,200 in capital gains tax on his $291,000 gain. Swapper magic allows him to buy $58,200 more of Bitshares while deferring the tax to another day. Users have to provide identifying information as required by 1031 regulations in the process of setting up the transaction. If the exchange transaction timeline if blown then the tax has to paid and the power of tax deferral gets lost.

## Bitcoin Taxation & The IRS Takeaway Part II

A 1031 exchange is not a magic wand for avoiding taxes but it can be a great tool to defer gains by keeping more of your assets in play. There's already a lot of uncertainty and a lack of guidance regarding these types of exchanges with both tangible and intangible assets. One way or another you are venturing into unchartered territory even if the IRS provides more clarity. A bitcoin exchange for property other than altcoins or vice versa is likely out of the question. Tracking all of your altcoin to altcoin exchanges could be trickier than tracking capital gains and losses because the basis of one altcoin will get rolled into the next in a daisy chain of tax deferrals. Some reporting platforms have a "like-kind" exchange calculation feature for simultaneous altcoin exchanges. Consult your tax advisor to discuss the finer details of your business and or individual tax situation regardless of whether you have a simultaneous or deferred exchange.

A qualified intermediary is needed in a deferred exchange scenario. It's possible a service like Bitrated would suffice as a qualified intermediary because it's already designed to hold funds in escrow. The good news is swapper aims to use bitcoin technology to specialize in 1031 exchanges including reporting requirements. Transactions involving larger blocks of coins could be exchanged on this platform with other individuals or businesses looking to do the same thing.

# Bitcoin AML, BSA and FATCA Quicksand

## Bitcoin Money Transmitters

Almost everyone will end up buying bitcoin from an exchange so it's important to understand the financial crimes risk that money transmitters have to manage while individuals and businesses have to assess their own risk in dealing with an exchange. Many countries have similar anti-money laundering laws governing financial institutions and banks; however, an extensive coverage of global regulations is beyond the scope of this book. Please seek competent legal counsel for information on regulations affecting your jurisdiction. The U.S. has one of the most regulatory-intensive environments on a federal and state level regarding money transmission and anti-money laundering laws, which generally cover businesses physically located in the U.S. and any business that services a U.S. customer. Therefore, a review of these regulations will provide a basic understanding related to bitcoin exchanges on a global level.

## FinCEN Regulation

United States bitcoin businesses may be subject to money transmitter regulations of the U.S. Treasury's Financial Crimes Enforcement Network known as FinCEN issued on March 18, 2013. A money service business, or MSB, is a money transmitter if it collects money or digital currency from party A and transmits it to party B, or if it exchanges fiat currency for digital currency or vice versa on behalf of another person. "Accepting and transmitting anything of value that substitutes for currency makes any person a money transmitter." Bitcoin and digital currency exchanges are subject to complying with these rules. Any business that accepts bitcoin or digital currency for goods and services is not subject to the rules; however, every individual and business will likely use an exchange in the normal course of business, making it an important topic for due diligence and risk management purposes. [178]

Any business falling within the definition of money transmitter must register at fincen.gov after reviewing the "Application of FinCEN's Regulation to Persons Administering, Exchanging or Using Virtual Currencies" and consulting with legal counsel. Registering a business is the easy part; compliance is the hard part. FinCEN regulates money transmitters through the Bank Secrecy Act (BSA) and the Patriot Act, requiring both anti-money laundering (AML) and customer identification program (CIP) policies, respectively, for purposes of assisting in possible criminal investigations.

A BSA AML compliance program must include the following:[179]

- Written, board-approved policies
- Internal controls to assure compliance
- Independent review to assure compliance
- A designated individual responsible for ongoing monitoring and compliance
- Training for relevant employees
- Filing suspicious activity reports based on dollar thresholds
- The "three Rs": Registration, reporting and recordkeeping

Additional requirements of The Patriot Act [180], an amendment to the BSA, must include the following:

- A customer identification program (CIP) a.k.a. know your customer (KYC) program
- Verification of a customer's identity (also covered in the account verification section of exchanges)
- Maintenance of records of information used for verification
- Cross-referencing of the customer with a list of known or suspected terrorists
- Conducting a risk assessment of the customer

These regulations require bitcoin exchanges to collect the same bunch of information collected by traditional financial institutions. In addition, each state has its own set of money service business and money transmitter rules; therefore, if an exchange wants to conduct business in all 50 states it has to potentially go through the same regulatory exercise 50 times over.

## Canada's National Law

Canada pioneered the first national bitcoin law focusing on the anti-money laundering aspects of bitcoin businesses. Any business "dealing in virtual currencies" will be subject to registration as a money service business with FINTRAC, the Financial Transactions and Reports Analysis Center of Canada. The requirements of the law are similar to the US Bank Secrecy Act and FinCEN registration, including recordkeeping, customer verification and suspicious activity reporting. It also encompasses Canadian businesses physically located in Canada and foreign companies targeting Canadian customers—a far-reaching law with global consideration similar to the extraterritorial reach of the BSA.

At a minimum the nationalization of bitcoin law in Canada brings regulatory clarity to businesses. That's certainly better than the same bitcoin exchange in the U.S. having to jump through the same hoop 50 times to do business in all the states. A clear definition of "dealing in virtual currencies," the most important part of the law, was somehow left out of the equation, leaving businesses wondering if it applies to them even though it won't be in full effect for some time. [181, 182]

## Other Approaches

In the United Kingdom, the Financial Conduct Authority (FCA) has stated it doesn't regulate bitcoin and has no intention of regulating it. The UK's anti-money laundering laws don't require any preventive measures, information gathering or reporting for dealings in bitcoin—a stark contrast to the US and Canada. It's a global financial center with a reputation for self-regulation evidenced by bitcoin exchanges implementing policies as if they had to comply with regulations, including anti-money laundering. This is also a logical, proactive approach should UK regulators make an about face on bitcoin.

If the Mt. Gox bankruptcy had happened in the U.S., the bitcoin equivalent of the PATRIOT Act would have quickly made its way through Congress. Japan's decision to remain hands-off after the post-Mt. Gox hearings on bitcoin regulation was a shocking reminder of the varied regulatory landscape. [183]

## Far Reaching Reporting

Every bitcoin enthusiast is watching tax authorities around the world for positions on the taxation of bitcoin. However, regulations that require informational reporting require an equal amount of guidance and understanding. Let's review the filing requirements of a pair of U.S. statutes to see how bitcoin and cryptocurrencies may have to be reported.

More than 90% of all countries around the world tax income at the source. Conversely, the United States considers all income "from whatever source derived" earned by the taxpayer as U.S. taxable income. The following regulations, though unique to the U.S., are extra-territorially far reaching in nature, requiring every financial institution in every country to comply with most of these regulations. This potentially impacts multiple stakeholders regardless of country of residence or business nexus. You could be affected directly or indirectly, so if one of your investors, business partners, vendors or advisors steps into quicksand, the financial impact on them could be a financial impact on you or your business. The main intention of the regulations is to close a nearly $450 billion tax gap of unreported income estimated by the IRS. [184]

## Pair of Jacks

U.S. citizens and businesses that hold financial accounts at foreign financial institutions are required to comply with both the Bank Secrecy Act (BSA) and the Foreign Account Tax Compliance Act (FATCA) when the dollar value of the account exceeds a certain threshold. For example, a U.S. citizen visiting a second home in Ireland several times per year opened foreign bank accounts at an Irish bank for convenience of traveling and for additional investments which makes the person subject to the BSA and FATCA. The institutions that hold these accounts always have custody of the funds. The question is whether or not bitcoin is being held in a foreign account and who has custody of the bitcoin.

## Bitcustody
Bitcoin custody could be in the hands of the account holder or in the custody of a third-party institution depending on the nature of the wallet. As a general rule, custody will probably come down to who holds the private key and has direct control over the bitcoin. Online wallets storing private keys on your behalf would be considered third-party custodians subjecting the account owners to reporting whereas desktop wallets requiring users to manage private keys could be considered non-custodial, non-foreign accounts and therefore probably not subject to the reporting requirements.

## Foreign, Everywhere and Nowhere
If an online wallet meets the third-party, institutional custody test as a financial account but the site operator is based in the U.S., there's no filing requirement because the operator is not foreign. Conversely, if the site operator is based in another country under the same scenario then the filing requirement is met based on thresholds described below. In addition, the third party institution is considered a foreign financial institution (FFI) relative to a U.S resident.

A non-custodial wallet, one where the owner controls and has custody of the private keys, resides wherever the owner resides. As previously mentioned, bitcoins are actually stored in the bitcoin blockchain and simply transferred from one bitcoin address to another with the private keys. One could even argue that the blockchain has custody of bitcoins. Even though the owner controls the right to move bitcoins, the bitcoins essentially reside everywhere and nowhere at the same time because bitcoins live on the blockchain and the decentralized network. It can't be considered a foreign account when it defaults to residing wherever the bitcoin wallet holder resides. The wallet owner, custody, private keys and bitcoins become one in the same location.

## BSA Rules

The reporting forms required by both statutes are for informational reporting only and are not used to calculate any tax liability. They are simply requirements giving notice to the federal government about the nature and amount of foreign accounts. The Bank Secrecy Act (BSA) requires filing of FinCEN Form 114, Report of Foreign Bank and Financial Accounts (FBAR), electronically at fincen.gov. Taxpayers were not subject to reporting bitcoin on the FBAR for tax year 2014. [185]

The rules state, "A United States person who has a financial interest in or signature authority over financial accounts must file an FBAR if the aggregate value of the foreign financial accounts exceeds $10,000 at any time during the calendar year."

A U.S. person is:

- A citizen or resident of the United States
- A domestic legal entity such as a partnership, corporation, estate or trust

## BSA Quicksand

The penalty for not complying can result in expensive pain and agony depending upon whether or not it was a willful failure to file, which includes a civil penalty for the greater of $100,000 or 50% of what should have been reported. Criminal penalties can also be imposed on top of civil penalties with fines up to $250,000 and imprisonment up to five years. For example, Omar steps into quicksand by willfully failing to file an FBAR report when his 17 altcoins were worth $30,000 U.S. resulting in a $100,000 fine thus evaporating 100% of his altcoins as he scrambles to cover the remaining $70,000 in penalties while facing a possible criminal liability bonus. Fortunately, non-willful violations are only up to

$10,000. In 2014, Carl Zwerner of Florida, USA was slammed with a 150% penalty totaling more than $2.2 million dollars for willfully failing to file FBARs for three consecutive years. The record fine by percentage wiped out the value of his Swiss account of approximately $1.5 million. "As this jury verdict shows, the cost of not coming forward and fully disclosing a secret offshore bank account to the IRS can be quite high," said Kathryn Keneally, U.S. Assistant Attorney General. [186]

## FATCA Rules
The Foreign Account Tax Compliance Act of 2010 (FATCA) requires the filing and attaching of IRS Form 8938, Statement of Specified Foreign Financial Assets, to an individual tax return when the total value of all financial accounts held by a specified person exceeds $75,000 at any point during the year or $50,000 only on the last day of the year. In addition, Foreign Financial Institutions (FFI) are required to enter into an intergovernmental agreement with the IRS to report information about accounts held by U.S. taxpayers. The IRS strategy uses information from FFIs to match against what they expect to receive from taxpayers, much like a prisoner's dilemma. IRS information matching is one of the oldest plays in the playbook.

A specified person includes:
- A U.S. citizen
- A resident alien of the U.S.
- A non-resident alien who elects to be treated as a resident alien

## Extra Caution
The IRS states domestic legal entities are not required to file Form 8938 as of 2015, but it anticipates issuing regulations in the future that will require businesses to comply. FACTA compliance also includes specified foreign financial assets (SFFA), which are NOT in the custody of a foreign financial institution such as securities, other financial interests or ownership interests in a business entity, all of which are originated from or issued by a foreign entity. This

is a dangerous tripwire considering a business ownership interest in a bitcoin company could easily appreciate beyond reporting thresholds, even though valuation is subjective and doesn't show up on a monthly statement like other accounts. The penalty for failure to file Form 8938 is up to $10,000 with an additional $10,000 for every 30 days of non-filing after the IRS gives notice of the same. The filing requirement is much higher than the BSA and the penalty much lower at a maximum $50,000. [187] Please refer to the chapter on bitcoin reporting for tools that can help determine the value of bitcoin and multiple cryptocurrencies.

## Regulatory Warning

The U.S. regulators have made their intentions very clear as demonstrated by the following statements: "Pursuing international tax evasion is a priority area for IRS Criminal Investigation, and we will continue to follow the money here in the United States and around the world," said IRS Commissioner Koskinen in response to the 2014 Credit Suisse guilty plea of conspiracy to aid and assist U.S. taxpayers in filing false tax returns. The commissioner further stated, "I want to commend the special agents in IRS Criminal Investigation for all of their hard work in this area and the close cooperation with the Department of Justice. Today's guilty plea is another important milestone in ongoing law enforcement efforts to investigate the use of offshore accounts to evade taxes. People should no longer feel comfortable hiding their assets and income from the IRS."

## Bitcoin AML, BSA and FATCA Quicksand Takeaway

Bitcoin has been hailed for being completely anonymous even though it's pseudonymous at best, all of which seems antithesis to regulatory regimes. Individuals can use myriad web platforms, altcoins, books and other tricks to fly under the radar and maintain anonymity, yet all this requires a lot of work. The choice for privacy and anonymity should not be used as a strategy for masking illegal behavior, regardless of philosophical beliefs. Businesses, on the other hand, have a duty to act in good faith, present a positive public image and offer as much transparency as possible.

A significant amount of resources are focused on anti-money laundering regulations on a global basis, including member-country participation in the inter-national standards set forth by the Financial Action Task Force (FATF). Money laundering and financing of terrorism have always taken place and will continue to take place by bad actors regardless of financial systems, bitcoin or otherwise, thus adding another unfortunate expense to the cost of doing business. Hopefully, the promise of the bitcoin protocol will somehow lead to a decentralization and elimination of criminal activity. In the meantime, these types of regulations have to strike a balance without stifling innovation and capital investment. Bitcoin is already a good self-regulatory system and should be embraced to create an even better one.

These regulations are the most extreme form of compliance created to deter offshore shenanigans. Fortunately, there are several voluntary disclosure programs available to get back into compliance yet the window for these programs doesn't remain open forever. The penalties for voluntary disclosure vary, but the cost of avoidance and getting caught is far more painful.

If bitcoin is everywhere and nowhere at the same time, then who has custody and control of bitcoin in a multisig scheme when key holders reside in multiple countries? Generally, in multisig no single party can move funds or has sole custody of funds while the group of signers that comes together for one transaction may be different than the next, in a 4/7 multisig scheme for example. Would bitcoins be considered reportable if a foreign financial institution happens to hold a multisig key? This is a classic case where technology jumps way ahead of the understanding of the technology, leaving both businesses and individuals in no man's land. In other words, bitcoiners will gladly tell you no single party has custody but regulators may come to the opposite conclusion.

The more crypto-investments, cryptocurrencies and related value appreciation is managed by an individual or business, the more complicated the compliance exercise. There are no bitcoin precedents to draw guidance from; thus, conservatism is probably the best approach. Bear in mind, the smaller the required filing the more painful the penalty for non-compliance. The cost of figuring out whether to file and the risk of not filing is so high, it's imperative to get the right advice and be able to sleep at night. Foreign custody considerations under BSA and FATCA are likely too complex to navigate on your own and investments in bitcoin-related businesses and outright investments in bitcoin and crypto assets can make for a tricky obstacle course. The pioneering risk of becoming a precedent for what not to do is probably not worth bearing. As always consult your advisor regarding individual and business circumstances. If you are concerned about past or future compliance, please contact us at BestBitcoinBookEver.com to get pointed in the right direction.

# Bitcoin Crowdfunding & The SEC

## The SEC and Crypto Crowdfunding

Additional regulatory considerations include the Securities and Exchange Commission (SEC), regardless of whether a project originates in the United States. The JOBS Act of 2012 attempted to usher in a new and easier way for both new companies and small investors to engage in successful crowdfunding. Previously, the standards for startup investing were time and capital intensive for a new business and prohibitive for investors unless they met the accredited investor status. Crowdfunding projects are generally global in nature and any non-U.S. based project will likely raise funds from a U.S. person while falling under the SEC rules. As highlighted in the chapter "Beyond the Coin," many bitcoin 2.0 projects have used some variation of crowdfunding with a corresponding project, an appcoin or altcoin, to facilitate fund raising.

The SEC finally issued proposed crowdfunding rules in late 2013 leaving many bitcoin-related projects in no-man's land with no finals rules to live by. The proposed rules are no surprise, including disclosures such as the identity of certain owners of the company, risks of the investment, use of funds, nature of the business and company financial information because they are similar to disclosures required by registering securities under other SEC rules. The real surprise is why it takes years to issue final guidelines for an ACT that was meant to stimulate business activity instead sidelining many projects from a lack of clarity. [188]

## Crowdfunding Fireworks

In March 2015, the SEC issues final regulations expanding the exemption of Regulation A for smaller issuers of securities bringing much anticipated clarity to crowdfunding as created in the JOBS Act. Companies can now file a mini-registration statement with the SEC and sell securities to ordinary people over the Internet. [189]

Start-ups will still need audited financial statements, ongoing SEC reporting and legal advice but the biggest benefit is the removal of steep exclusionary qualification rules reserved for accredited investors so almost anyone can participate who would otherwise be watching from the sideline. Careful private solicitation to a select group of investors has been transformed into general public solicitation to anyone.

This is not a total slam-dunk because entrepreneurs still need the same degree of legal advice to avoid stepping into quicksand. Small companies can raise capital in two tiers of $20MM and $50MM within a 12-month period with certain restrictions. Investors are limited to investing no more than the greater of 10% of their net worth or income. However, investors can self-certify thus avoiding a costly verification process for the start-up. United States and Canada-based business entities qualify under these rules. [190]

## The Wider Net

A larger issue arises from understanding how a bitcoin 2.0 crowdfunding project may fall within the general definition of a security. [191] The SEC casts a wide net concerning the general issuance and regulation of securities within the following framework:

1) An investment of money
2) In a common enterprise
3) With the expectation of profits
4) Based solely on the efforts of a third party

The distinguishing feature of these projects is the issuance of a project token such as an appcoin or an altcoin purchased with bitcoin. For example, an appcoin like Storjcoin X is issued in conjunction with a  decentralized file-sharing service, Storj, allowing users to both receive coins and use coins for renting unused hard drive space and storing files, respectively. An appcoin is not an investment in the company or project and does not represent any ownership. The coin can be bought and sold freely on crypto exchanges with its own market value completely independent of the company's value and ownership. This unique crypto scenario may NOT appear to be an investment of money in a common enterprise, but the SEC could interpret the general framework to encompass these types of projects. SEC Chair Mary Jo White, wrote, "Whether a virtual currency is a security under the federal securities laws, and therefore subject to our regulation, is dependent on the particular facts and circumstances at issue." Meanwhile, a typical appcoin participation disclosure goes something like this, "The software sale will NOT provide you with a 'security' or 'equity' stake in this project. The digital token is only useful for accessing the software after its development is complete." [192]

## Love Letters

The SEC supposedly sent out several letters to bitcoin companies and bitcoin-related projects in the fall of 2014 seeking information about crowdfunding activities related to the possible issuance of unregistered securities. [193] Some crypto platforms are designed to easily allow users to set up crowdfunding campaigns and issue coins. Project teams are warned to seek legal counsel and use these platforms at their own risk. In many cases startups seek proper legal counsel or reside in a more digital currency-friendly country while others bypass the due diligence stage and start crowdfunding. Securities issuance is a slippery slope, highly regulated due to the inherent risk of fraud arising from the investor's inability to resist the temptation of impossible returns. The SEC's current and future inquiry should be no surprise but will hopefully lead to a better understanding of the technology and position on the matter without stifling innovation.

## CFTC Cousin

The Commodities Futures Trading Commission (CFTC) is like a cousin to the SEC, regulating commodities broadly defined to include more complex financial products, including derivatives. Wherever the SEC leaves off regarding bitcoin the CFTC will likely regulate. For example, TeraExchange received approval for a bitcoin derivative in September 2014. Other derivatives platforms like BTC.sx and BitMEX, based in London and Hong Kong, respectively, may have CFTC considerations in addition to their own native regulation. CFTC Chair Timothy Massad, stated, "While the CFTC does not have policies and procedures specific to virtual currencies like bitcoin, the agency's authority extends to futures and swaps contracts in any commodity...derivative contracts based on a virtual currency represent one area within our responsibility."[194]

## Bitcoin Crowdfunding & The SEC Takeaway

Regulators of financial instruments including the SEC and CFTC have broad definitions of securities and commodities, which allows them the freedom to cast a wide net for applying existing rules to emerging technologies like bitcoin. The realm of the CFTC includes any instrument involving futures and swaps therefore virtual currency derivatives appear to be covered by the existing regulatory framework.

Defining appcoins and related crowdfunding as a form of security or equity is open for debate and more clarity is likely to unfold over a period of years through precedents. Any rules stimulating innovation by allowing a low-cost, low regulatory intensive playing field will be welcome by entrepreneurs and investors alike. The JOBS Act crowdfunding clarity will cascade into massive blockchain innovation with projects featured on crowdfunding platforms like Koinify and Swarm that specialize in crypto-based projects while using bitcoin technology for project accountability.

# Bitcoin Regulatory Zigzagging

To regulate or not to regulate, that is the question. Every government around the world has had or will have the debate about whether or not bitcoin should be regulated and how it should be regulated. It's a classic game of attempting to fit the square peg of new technology that's rewriting the rules into a round hole of old model legacy rules. Bitcoin's new paradigm requires a new look at how we've been doing things the same way the Internet went through the regulatory gauntlet. Some regulatory responses will inevitably change over time as adoption accelerates and the technology is better understood.

## Regulatory Zigzagging

Singapore's IRAS taxing authority quickly issued clear guidelines for taxation of bitcoin while the IRS was much slower in issuing guidance. The United States FinCEN and Canada's FinTRAC issued money service business guidelines even though Canada was hands off for a long time. [195] The U.S. Federal Reserve has clearly stated that it has no authority to regulate bitcoin while U.S. Congress showed a positive sentiment towards the technology.

Surprisingly, Japan said it would not regulate bitcoin during hearings prompted by the infamous bankruptcy of Japan-based Mt. Gox. Meanwhile, China's central bank, PBOC, came down with the hammer on bitcoin, banning banks and third-party payment providers from doing business with bitcoin exchanges and related businesses. Their bank accounts were shut down even though the PBOC governor declared, "It's out of the question to ban bitcoin."[196]

## Imposed Upon or Self-Imposed

Regulation is either imposed by a government entity or self-imposed by groups of people with mutual interests. In other words, either the government provides regulation or a group provides its own regulation called a self-regulatory organization (SRO), or there may be some combination of the two. If a community fails to regulate itself then governments typically step in and take over the regulation. For example, the accounting profession requires Certified Public Accountants (CPAs) to be state-licensed in the U.S. to regulate ethical behavior and dole out punishments for violators. Aside from this government imposed regulation, a majority of the profession regulates itself through multiple organizations, such as the Institute of Management Accountants (IMA), the American Institute of Certified Public Accountants (AICPA), International Auditing and Assurance Standards Board (IAASB), International Accounting Standards Board (IASB) and the Financial Accounting Standards Board (FASB) to name a few. Then Enron happened and the U.S. Congress passed the Sarbanes Oxley Act in 2002. For the first time in history, auditors of public companies were now subject to external and independent oversight by the newly created Public Company Accounting Oversight Board (PCAOB). The auditing industry pushed the bounds of integrity at the cost of having to give up some self-regulation.

## Bitcoin is Capable

Bitcoin is regulated by a consensus algorithm, which discourages cheating by requiring agreement from a majority of participants, the network nodes and miners. The bitcoin network is decentralized and no single person or group of people has supreme power to change the rules, steal bitcoin or shut down the network. This seems counterintuitive and a little difficult to grasp when everyone is conditioned to multiple, old world centralized models. Bitcoin is the perfect example of built-in self-regulation that could operate without oversight boards or government imposed regulations and it has a seven-year, battle tested track record and counting. Bitcoin has end points within existing regulated frameworks thus bitcoin has an element of regulation by default through the process of entanglement.

## Fifty-One Percent

The concept of the infamous 51% attack refers to one person or group of people who could theoretically control a majority of network computing power and therefore control the network. Unlike many other models where fraud or some other manipulation is only discovered at the implosion point, an accumulation of 51% computing power would be known by the entire network almost instantly. [197]

Further, if someone started a 51% attack, the attacker would be simultaneously sabotaging himself and possibly impacting the value of his own bitcoin and mining investment while blacklisting himself as a miner. Miners would be exposing themselves to reputation risk with a huge potential economic loss. The attacker can potentially rewrite a couple blocks worth of blockchain history thereby orphaning previously confirmed blocks while transactions during that time get cancelled. Other people's bitcoins can't be stolen, redirected or spent in a 51% attack making the cost of an attack far greater than the benefit. [198] It's more lucrative for a bad actor with malicious intent to steal private keys and fraudulently obtain bitcoin than to engage in a 51% attack.

## Regulatory Failure

What do you think of when somebody says "2008"? The Great Recession, the financial crisis of 2008, financial institution implosions and mortgage foreclosures? It's hard to think of anything else considering the impact is still lingering for many people around the world. How did this happen if regulations provided the right framework for regulators to do their job effectively? Was it the result of obsessive risk-taking or a fraud of epic proportions? The final report of the Financial Crisis Inquiry Commission used the word "fraud" 157 times, concluding there was a "systematic breakdown with signs of fraud everywhere to be seen." In either case, most Americans believe that nothing's really changed while 44% of the population think there shouldn't have been a bailout and 53% don't think enough was done to prosecute bankers. [199, 200]

The worse crime is not doling out enough punishment to show who's in charge, effectively giving out the "too big to fail" handbook of rule breaking, which turns bad behavior into a cost-benefit exercise. "Too big to fail is a phenomenon that is definitely not acceptable," says Hank Paulson, former U.S. Treasury Secretary during the Great Recession, who goes on to clarify, "I get asked all the time, what's the likelihood of another financial crisis? And I begin by saying it's a certainty. As long as we have markets, as long as we have banks, no matter what the regulatory system is, there will be flawed government policies. Those policies will create bubbles. They will manifest themselves in a financial system no matter how it's structured and how it's regulated." [201]

## How Deep is the Capture?

Regulatory capture is a phenomenon whereby regulators who are tasked with overseeing groups or industries advance the interests of these groups instead of serving the public interest. George Stigler developed this theory in a 1971 whitepaper called "The Theory of Economic Regulations" in which he asked, "Why does an industry solicit the coercive powers of the state rather than its cash?... Indeed the problem of regulation is the problem of discovering when and why an industry is able to use the state for its purposes." [202]

Subtle erosions of power and control happen over time in numerous ways. Lobbying and political donations have turned into one of the highest returns on investment for big and powerful players who exploit regulators' weak punishments and lack of resources. In his report, Stigler further stated, "The industry which seeks regulation must be prepared to pay with the two things a party needs: votes and resources." Does this sound like it applies to 2008? The deepcapture.com team, which exposes how regulators have been "captured" by the very industries they're supposed to oversee, asserts the phenomenon is pervasive and control extends beyond regulators to law enforcement, national media, elected officials and respected intellectuals. The capture goes way "deep", as it were. The control can be so subtle that the captured don't realize they've been captured and the capturers don't realize they are advancing their own interests outside the rules of engagement. For example, a regulator overseeing a hedge fund may have the promise of one day getting hired by the fund with a compensation upside 5 to 10 times greater than the regulator's current salary, which creates an inherent conflict of interest. If a regulator maintains full integrity by coming down with the hammer if and when necessary, the promise of the glorious salary could be jeopardized. On the other hand, walking the line and going soft may ensure the inevitable job offer. Further, there are plenty of hard-working folks with high integrity in all of these areas, but conflicts of interest are the temptations ultimately leading to integrity breakdowns and fraud.

## Deep Capture and Fraud Explained

There's a scientific explanation for the failure of regulation and pervasiveness of fraud. Edwin Sutherland, Donald Cressey and Steve Albrecht all deserve credit for contributing research to the three intersecting elements of the now famous "fraud triangle" which explains the recipe for fraud. Essentially, humans want to trust people but a quick study of the fraud triangle reveals why trust is the worst internal control of all time—and why this failed inclination may well explain 2008 as well as deep capture.

Sutherland developed the "differential association theory" explaining why people commit crimes. Cressey is known as the "father of the triangle elements" and Albrecht coined the term "fraud triangle." Differential association theory concludes that criminal behavior is learned through the process of communication and leading by example, including the techniques for committing crimes, and the motives and attitudes of the perpetrators. Fraudulent behavior is inherited by associating with people in a criminal environment.

"Criminal behavior is learned and will occur when perceived rewards for criminal behavior exceed the rewards for lawful behavior," says Albrecht of Sutherland's insight. [203]

Cressey formulated his hypothesis by stating, "Trusted persons become trust violators when they conceive of themselves as having a financial problem which is non-shareable, are aware this problem can be secretly resolved by violation of the position of financial trust, and are able to apply to their own conduct in that situation verbalizations which enable them to adjust their conceptions of themselves as trusted persons with their conceptions of themselves as users of the entrusted funds or property." [204]

Albrecht elaborates in a 1991 journal article, "Research has shown that individuals commit fraud when a combination of three factors exist: perceived pressure, perceived opportunity to commit and conceal, and a way to rationalize the behavior as acceptable. These three factors combine to create the 'fraud triangle.' The fraud triangle is very much like the 'fire triangle.' In order to have a fire, three conditions must exist: there must be oxygen, heat and fuel. If any one of these is removed there will be no fire. Likewise with fraud: if either the pressure, opportunity or rationalization is removed, fraud does not occur." [205]

People commit acts of fraud *against* a company or on *behalf* of a company. Without the proper internal controls or checks and balances, there's a sea of opportunity for exploitation in either direction.

Employees and subcontractors often have serious financial hardships and when enough pressure builds up, they may rationalize certain behaviors and take advantage of company weaknesses. Employees pull the fraud trigger by convincing themselves it's the right thing to do.

Or, pressure to meet earnings expectations from outside the organization combined with pressure from C-level executives to make the numbers work leads to rationalizing the behavior for organizational survival.

# The Fraud Triangle

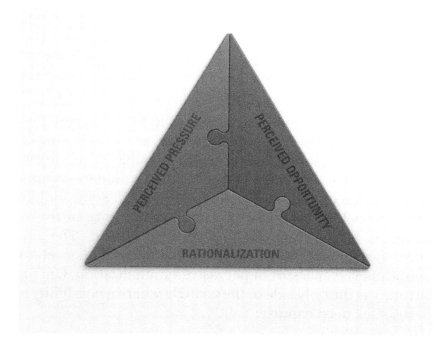

Image credit iStock/Thinkstock
© Association of Certified Fraud Examiners, Inc.

Incentive/pressure and rationalization are the two sides of the triangle hidden from the employer's view. Businesses only have control over the opportunity side of the triangle therefore a one-dimensional influence exists for controlling fraud. If trust were relied on with no other internal controls, fraud would be the number one customer of every business.

Trust, humans and money do not mix.

## Deep Compromise Explains More Than Fraud

Albrecht further decrees, "As I've worked with fraud triangles and red flags over my career as a researcher, expert witness, consultant and professor, I've come to realize that we can use the fraud triangle to explain more than just fraud. In fact, I often now refer to it as the compromise triangle. Whether it's fraud or any other type of compromise, the same three elements are always present." [206]

In the deep capture scenario, exploited opportunities are easily rationalized. However, the incentive/pressure is replaced by greed, a let's-make-as-much-money-as-possible-at-whatever-cost kind of attitude, where one person or a few colluders committing fraud is replaced by organizations and industries. Some individuals in the organizations may not be consciously aware of the subtle shenanigans because it's all they've ever known. The erosion of integrity expands outward from the individual level to the organizational level, a sort of pervasive rationalization. Once again opportunity is the only side of the triangle where a possibility exists to thwart such deep capture.

Greed and rationalization are uncontrollable human behaviors that will continue in perpetuity. So how can the opportunity be eliminated when bad actors control the opportunity?

## Crypto Regulation and The Global Premium

Finally, a beautiful thing called bitcoin has arrived. It's something no one has control of, no one can cheat, and it's ruled by a self-regulating algorithm that eliminates opportunity from the equation. The blockchain, the bitcoin public ledger, cannot be altered, which alone provides a previously unavailable, infallible transparency. If this technology were expanded to include all financial instruments and legacy organizations then the shenanigans of 2008 could be a thing of the past. However, it deserves a hands-off approach so it can thrive and demonstrate what's possible to the world.

Terrorism, mafia-related activities and other white-collar crimes are a global pandemic adding even more financial cost to the already outrageous $3.7 trillion of the estimated cost of global occupational fraud and abuse in 2014. [207] It all adds up to a gigantic premium on all goods and services purchased by anyone anywhere in the world as an individual or business. This is an unacceptable, invisible tax addressed by regulations from FinCEN, FinTRAC, FATF, OFAC and similar organizations. This behavior can't be left unchecked and the current model—status quo at best—is thirsty for a new way to fight fraud. If the current regulatory schemes are so great, why isn't fraud going down? How is the traditional, anti-money laundering, information-gathering exercise, which is prone to the same attacks as credit card breaches, going to lead us into the 21st century? The traditional data collected to identify individuals is based on a set of metrics that is losing value in our expanding digital universe.

There is no doubt Bitcoin, the technology, can solve these issues. If Bitcoin can transform banking into a nearly instantaneous, peer-to-peer transfer of value at almost no cost, it becomes obvious that Bitcoin could do the same thing to AML and KYL compliance. Bitcoin plugs into credit card chaos, money transfer madness and the banking burnout bonanza to exchange fiat currency into bitcoin and vice versa. Anti-money laundering regulations are applied consistently at the point where bitcoin connects with legacy systems. These types of regulations are the best they can be for the systems in which they operate, but it's simply time for a new system.

## Taxation and Indirect Regulation

Bitcoin is already regulated indirectly based on the jurisdiction where an individual resides or the jurisdiction where a corporation or similar business structure is formed. In addition, a business may be formed in one country and conduct business B2B or B2C in another country requiring it to comply with those laws. It basically boils down to a nexus issue similar to figuring out where a sale took place, which can obviously be challenging in the online world where the entire business, including its information products, could exist entirely in cyberspace. Determining where a sale took place, especially when it comes to the delivery of physical goods, seems simple in theory but it can be very complicated. For example, in the

United States each state has its own regulations regarding nexus that may be in conflict with one another.

One of the primary reasons for determining nexus is to figure out what tax to pay and whom to pay it to. Transacting business in bitcoin and other cryptocurrencies creates crypto-nexus, a situation for considering both the medium in which the sale was transacted and where the sale took place. Both components may be necessary to determine compliance with laws and regulations including multiple tax considerations. Substituting one medium of exchange for another using the same transaction will generally be subject to the same tax liability. In other words, bitcoin and cryptocurrencies are not a "free pass" for avoiding taxes, regardless of any anonymity component.

## Bitcoin Regulatory Zigzagging Takeaway

The love-hate bitcoin regulatory debate will continue for many years. The real focus should be on eliminating deep capture and fraud of epic proportions instead of trying to figure how to stuff Bitcoin into existing regulatory schemes. The current financial system is broken and the agencies designed to keep them in check are broken. Every individual and business pays a 5% premium on the hidden cost of fraud, yet it could be closer to 25% considering that frauds is invisibly living inside a majority of the frameworks we are supposed to trust. In some countries, fraud, corruption and abuse are standard business practice. Regulations to circumvent fraud, such as the anti-money laundering regulations applied to many bitcoin exchanges and their connection point with existing financial systems, add costs to the system. A few bad actors burden the rest of us with inconveniences such as having bitcoin exchange and traditional bank accounts shut down, transactions scrutinized and a feeling of being constantly watched. Some bitcoin exchanges offer low transaction amounts with minimum identity verification and higher transaction amounts when more information is provided.

The Bitcoin community will continue to innovate and self-regulate at a pace that can't be matched by regulators. Every system or organization has the inherent right to self-regulate, continues to earn this right by demonstrating its ability to do so, and thereby keeps this right until demonstrating it's not capable. Bitcoin has earned the right to self-regulation and deserves the freedom to breathe. The self-regulatory nature of bitcoin and the blockchain is superior to almost every existing system; thus, it is only logical that bitcoin technology will eventually weave its way into and transform existing regulatory systems. Regulations attempting to control the self-regulatory nature of bitcoin should not be done in haste and may end up being a waste of resources. The bitcoin protocol will eventually change the way everything gets regulated by its inherent ability to decentralize through algorithmic governance.

Bitcoin has received a lot of love for the possibility of operating freely and independently of current financial systems: in a utopian world with no regulation, no taxation and complete anonymity. However, every paradigm in the entire world would have to change to make this possible. In the meantime, individuals can choose to take the completely anonymous path, but businesses hold themselves out to the public with a duty to maintain integrity and provide high levels of transparency. In the same way that people are interdependent and generally can't function 100% independently of society, bitcoin has interdependency with the rest of the world. The benefits from the power of choice and the gravity of decentralization will far outweigh the burden of bitcoin regulations.

# Practical Bitcoin Business Tools

Hopefully your business already accepts bitcoin by now or you've chosen to start accepting bitcoin. As previously mentioned, most bitcoin payment processors have an option to cash out bitcoin sales into fiat currency and hold 100% of bitcoins or some combination of the two, such as 50% fiat and 50% bitcoins. The value of bitcoin comes from being able to use and spend it on unique, Bitcoin-based business models that only transact in bitcoin. Lending your bitcoins and making money, borrowing bitcoins, paying bills in bitcoin to vendors who don't accept bitcoin, time stamping documents, buying goods at a huge discount, privately storing files, and creating business transactions with a trustless escrow agent, are among the practical tools available with bitcoin. Let's examine a few in more detail.

## Lend and Borrow Bitcoins

BTCjam.com is a global, peer-to-peer lending network with solid returns for investors and low fees for borrowers, all made possible by bitcoin. The impressive venture capital investors listed on the site brings credibility to the platform. Lenders can invest directly in loans or create an automated investing plan, yet success is based on diversity of invested loans. Borrowers set the desired loan amount, interest rate and the amount of time to repay the loan with the ability to promote the listing to family and friends. Borrowers can choose to get verified and supply more information to lower borrowing costs. BTCjam uses a proprietary global credit scoring system using hundreds of data points, including social media accounts and a peer-to-peer reputation system resulting in a 90% repayment rate. Bitcoins are automatically released to the borrower after the lender chooses a loan for investment or is automatically matched with a loan. When borrowers successfully repay a loan as promised, their rating goes up and their borrowing cost goes down in the cycle of continuing credibility. [208]

## Anonymous Escrow

BTCrow.com, the original bitcoin escrow service, only requires an email and bitcoin to use the platform. In this classic model, two parties unfamiliar with each other can confidently exchange anything of value with a quasi-guarantee kept in check by a third party who temporarily holds funds until the transaction completes. This is similar to traditional escrow services; however, bitcoin eliminates legacy waiting and wondering for funds because they become immediately available when all parties sign off. Buyers or sellers can initiate a trade while the buyer always puts up the bitcoins held by BTCrow in escrow. The seller sends the goods to the buyer who has five days, or longer as agreed, to confirm receipt and sufficiency. BTCrow releases the bitcoins to the seller upon buyer confirmation and everyone loves bitcoin more than they did before the transaction. This is a no-frills basic service, but it comes with a $500 USD guarantee for any losses arising by fault of the platform. [209]

## Escrow-less Trust Platform

Bitrated.com is a reputation management system providing consumer protection for the bitcoin ecosystem. It's a self-described bitcoin trust platform while the underlying service enables peer-to-peer trade of goods and services using multi-signature smart contracts. The buyer creates a contract called a trade, selects an arbiter called a trust agent, and invites the seller to accept the terms of the trade. When the seller accepts the terms, the buyer sends bitcoins to the multisig address, verifiable by the seller before sending the goods. The bitcoin goes into temporary lock down until the buyer and seller agree the trade is complete; thus, meeting the sign-off required in a typical 2 of 3 multisig scheme. If the buyer and seller don't agree, then the two sign-offs are comprised of the trust agent and either the buyer or seller, depending on the trust agent's dispute decision. The beauty of Bitcoin is demonstrated here with the power of escrow, but without a third-party escrow agent who by definition has possession and control of funds. This contrasts with the BTCrow.com service, which is more similar to a third-party escrow service.

## Leveraging Reputation

The reputation model leverages trust by weaving together users' existing social media profiles, reviews of trades and their web of trust into a reputation score. The web of trust is a peer-to-peer vouching system where one person can write a description about how they know and trust another person. The trust of one person can be connected to the trust of another and so on, creating a basis that other people can rely on when choosing to do business with an unknown party. Bitrated users with good reputations can offer arbiter services for a fee since every trade on the platform requires a trust agent. Bitrated is also an excellent place to gauge someone's reputation for prospective business transactions, even for those conducted outside of the platform. Therefore, it serves as both a platform for trustless multisig transactions with a trust agent and an independent source for reputations. [210]

## Pay Any Bill

BillPayForCoins.com is an easy way to pay any bill with bitcoin in the United States to any vendor who doesn't accept bitcoin. Set up a vendor to pay or select one from the recognized vendor list, choose the amount of the payment in US dollars and send bitcoins as instructed via QR code, or copy and paste the bitcoin address. Payments up to $9,000 can be made with a small 1.99% service fee and a maximum cap of $75. All Bitcoin, Litecoin and Dogecoin payments are handled by payment processor, GoCoin, and delivered to the vendor in U.S. dollars within 5 days. LivingroomOfSatoshi. com can be used in Australia and Bitwa.la can be used for any Eurozone country to pay bills the same way. BillPayForCoins also has an international debit card and bitcoin text messaging service available in multiple countries. You can buy, sell and send bitcoins through the texting service as well as transfer bitcoins to and from the debit card, making this quite a versatile platform. [211]

## Universal eCommerce

Bitcoinshop.us, an ecommerce platform with hundreds of thousands of products for sale and growing, is like an Amazon for bitcoin shoppers. With the ticker symbol BTCS, Bitcoin Shop is one of the first publicly traded, bitcoin-based companies. It uses an intelligent shopping engine to deliver customers the best price on products. When you click on a product, for example, two or more choices appear for vendors like Best Buy and Home Depot with prices in bitcoin. Each vendor may or may not have a 3% processing fee while a total best price is presented to the customer. Bitcoin Shop is morphing into a universal digital currency platform by adding features, including digital currency wallets, mining, and bitcoin ATMs to existing ecommerce services as one point of access to store, earn, buy and spend bitcoins. Businesses should consider fixed asset purchases using this platform. Alternatively, spendabit. co is simple search tool like a browser or search engine where you can "find more than 2.5 million things you buy with bitcoin." In addition the spendabit merchant suite allows merchants to sign up and become searchable on the platform. This is yet another place where you should get your business listed. [212]

## Compelling Use Case

Purse.io one of the best reasons to start using bitcoin. Users can buy stuff from Amazon at up to a 20% discount, and sometimes more. The average person in the U.S. spends $1,500 per year at Amazon resulting in a potential $375 savings. Businesses with thousands in annual Amazon purchases can save even more. Simply add items to your Amazon wish list, link it to a purse account and make purchases with bitcoins while choosing your desired discount. Purse can also be used to buy bitcoins with debit and credit cards, purchase Amazon gift cards and address Amazon payments balances.

The magic happens when the people who want to buy bitcoins browse and select an Amazon item already purchased by another user. For example, Jill wants to buy a Joby iPhone tripod to make videos for her business. She pays for it with bitcoin from her wish list in Purse and chooses a 20% discount. Sam wants to buy bitcoin with a debit card and finds the Joby tripod listed at an acceptable bitcoin price premium. He buys the tripod, Amazon ships it to Jill and Sam gets the bitcoins that Jill used to buy the tripod. People are willing to pay a premium for bitcoins because of convenience and speed or a lack of other available options in a particular country. The platform includes a rating and reputation scoring system. Find out for yourself and start saving today. [213]

## Blow Your Mind File Storage

Storj.io is one of the world's first blockchain-based file sharing apps that runs on top of the counterparty platform. It's a classic use case for employing otherwise unused computing power on millions of computers, creating the possibility for the one of the largest peer-to-peer file storing services. Users can simultaneously earn money by sharing their unused hard drive space in a community cloud while renting space to store their own files at 10 to 100 times less than the cost of traditional file sharing models.

Privacy and security are the biggest benefit because unlike centralized models, Storj-based files are stored in little pieces not susceptible to hacking or other prying eyes. The platform uses a token called Storjcoin X to facilitate both the earning and usage of file sharing. Two simple interface-friendly apps handle both sides of the equation. Storjcoin X, SJCX, can also be bought and sold through crypto exchanges allowing users to choose how they want to support and participate on the Storj platform. [214, 215]

## Cover Your Ass (CYA)

Proofofexistence.com is a great alternative use example of the blockchain. This simple yet highly valuable tool allows businesses and individuals to get a time-stamped cryptographic proof on any document where proof of creation and ownership is very important. Example use cases are copyrights, inventions, software code, other intellectual property, contracts, bylaws, operating agreements, wills, directives and more.

Simply upload or drag-and-drop files, pay a small fee in bitcoin and get a time-stamped receipt referencing the document through a cryptographic hash embedded in the blockchain. The document is not uploaded to the blockchain and therefore not publicly viewable. If the document is later changed in any way, the cryptographic proof will fail while any disputes of ownership can be settled by verifying the timestamp. We used this practical bitcoin business tool for time stamping the book manuscript before submitting it to the publisher. Take proof of existence for a test drive by choosing a will or other important and practical business document for time stamping. You'll see the power of the blockchain beyond bitcoin as a digital currency. In addition, Block Notary is a handy smart phone app that provides the same value by snapping a picture of a document and time stamping it with bitcoin.

## A Successfully Hashed Document

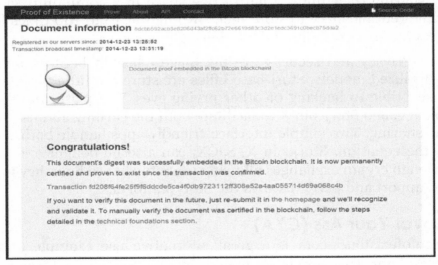

Image courtesy of proofofexistence.com

## A Giant Solution

Factom.org is a scalable data layer for the blockchain changing how businesses manage enterprise-level recordkeeping. It's a developer's toolbox allowing existing business applications to communicate via the Factom API to create an immutable document trail. Proofofexistence.com is a simple tool for hashing or time stamping single documents into the blockchain, whereas Factum is a system for time stamping and tracking thousands of interrelated documents into single bitcoin blockchain hash with auditing capabilities. Factom is like a document management lifecycle triple play, including proof of publication, a timestamp proving a document existed, proof of process (proving a new document is linked to an existing document), and finally proof of audit, proving changes to a document. Factom's native currency, called "Factoids," and related entry credits, are used to hash document sets while the protocol simultaneously rewards Factoids to the Factom and Audit servers for securing the Factum network.

Factom's use case examples include the 2008 U.S. mortgage crisis and multi-billion dollar fines slapped on Bank of America, JPMorgan Chase and Citi, resulting from poorly managed, complex sets of related mortgage documents. Bank of America acquired Countrywide, inheriting a giant unknown liability in the form of troubled assets. A Factom audit trail would have provided a document review not previously possible, with speed, reliability and cost savings. This would equate to the highest return on investment relative to billion dollar fines avoided.

Factom is partnering with the Honduras government to create a land title registry in a country with a long history of land rights abuse. A corrupt land title transfer could strip property rights from a family overnight and leave them penniless. A permanent, unalterable Factom solution will end this disgraceful fraud perpetrated by multiple corrupt actors around the world. [216]

## Universal Debit Cards

The e-coin.io universal debit card can be used anywhere Visa and MasterCard are accepted. Cardholders can fund the card with fiat money, spend with bitcoin and withdraw cash at an ATM. The card can be funded by bank wire, PayPal or fiat debit card. You can get a plastic card or use it virtually to buy, sell, use, store and manage bitcoin all with a mobile app. As of 2015 the e-coin debit card is available in over a hundred countries in USD, Euros and GBP versions with multiple fiat currencies on the way. It will eventually be available to US customers, when e-coin overcomes the burdensome US regulatory scheme. The physical card can be purchased for a one-time fee while monthly fees and bitcoin conversion fees apply which is standard for bitcoin debit cards. E-coin funds are secured with BitGo multisig technology and insured by a premier global insurance company. E-coin is a hybrid innovation providing a convenient way to spend bitcoins using existing old rail card networks.

Wagecan.com is a Taiwan based interest bearing debit card service for spending bitcoins anywhere MasterCard is accepted. Send bitcoins to your online wallet, load the card and you're ready to spend or withdraw cash at an ATM. Anyone in the world can send bitcoins to the bitcoin address associated with the debit card for easy replenishment. Wagecan pays .011% daily interest on bitcoin balances by arbitrage between bitcoin exchanges. This service is the equivalent of an online hot wallet, therefore use it with discretion. The card is also available to U.S. residents.

## Practical Bitcoin Business Tools Takeaway

Things not previously possible with fiat currency are now only possible using bitcoin. Therefore, a good strategy should include holding some bitcoin to realize these new business benefits. Saving up to 25% on Amazon purchases is reason enough to hold bitcoin and keep it in the ecosystem. You can also lend otherwise idle bitcoin and get double-digit returns with a 90% confidence rate. Borrowers can reap the opposite benefit with peer-to-peer lending. Eliminate escrow agent risk using multisig Bitcoin technology, which was non-existent in the days before bitcoin. Increase privacy and security by decentralizing document file storage while proving the existence of documents and related changes. For example, if centralized, Dropbox-like services were hacked, proprietary business information could be stolen, altered or deleted. Implementing the aforementioned tools can significantly reduce information management risk. Head over to BestBitcoinBookEver. com/bonus to stay updated on new business tools and platform features.

As with all platforms, do your due diligence. Remember that multiple choices are available to match your risk appetite and you can always test the waters before diving in. These are just some of the benefits available in this new realm of innovation. In the next chapter, Beyond the Coin, we'll examine additional technology developments, platforms and tools that are opening up potentially broader applications for the next 20 years and beyond.

# Beyond the Coin

## Light Speed

The bitcoin universe is evolving so quickly that new concepts and platforms are being written about on a daily basis. The importance of these developments can't be overlooked relative to the future positive impact they will have on your business.

There are hundreds of altcoins with a unique variation of the bitcoin protocol, or in some cases an entirely new platform. The possibilities and the opportunities for using the bitcoin protocol go way beyond its disruptive potential as a digital currency. Innovators are pioneering new languages, libraries and platforms usable in a variety of industries for creating new business models that work in tandem with the blockchain. Versatility allows other models to be stacked on top of and work in conjunction with Bitcoin. For example, several platforms highlighted below are asset exchanges supporting the transfer of hundreds and soon to be thousands of digital assets between peers including altcoins or a new token you create with your company name. A digital asset can be a coin representing a physical asset, a token with a built-in contract and numerous other yet-to-be-thought-of use cases.

Most of these models are open source experiments challenging the centralized, status quo paradigm within governments and industries. No one needs permission to innovate, thus giving rise to a tidal wave of creative development before bitcoin itself has become widely adopted. Developers and others are often passionately contributing, without compensation, or without knowing how or when they may get compensated.

## The Next Layer

Omnilayer.org was one of the first bitcoin 2.0 projects providing an open source, fully decentralized asset creation platform to extend bitcoin capabilities for creating crypto exchanges, decentralized applications, wallet services and smart tokens. Many notable companies and projects have been created using the Omni Layer such as MaidSafe, GoCoin, Poloniex, MasterXchange, Holy Transaction, Factum and more. Mastercoin, the original name of the platform, is the native currency of the protocol, which can be bought and sold on exchanges including the masterxchange.com. Digital tokens such as APIcoin, Mastercoin, Dash, Counterparty-based tokens and Coloredcoins can be bought on this exchange. A fixed amount of Mastercoins were issued during August 2013 in exchange for bitcoins in order to fund the development of the protocol, therefore no more Mastercoins will ever be created. [217]

Omniwallet.org, a free user-controlled wallet created by the Omni project, is setup with a simple password and no account registration. The wallet stores multiple tokens including some of the ones just mentioned, thus eliminating the need to have a different wallet for each token. Mastercoin tokens are digitally signed transactions representing a contract for property rights similar to other platforms with token issuance. Tokens can be created for crowdsale funding of products or services while giving access to a song, file or some other right in addition to being tradable on an exchange and storable in an omniwallet.

## Decentralized Internet

In April 2014 MaidSafe.net, a decentralized Internet project, used the Omni Layer for a bitcoin 2.0 crowdsale by issuing Safecoin resulting in a $7M raise in just five hours.[218] MaidSafe allows individual users called "farmers" to contribute their unused computing power, file storage and bandwidth to create a decentralized Internet of sorts where no single party controls information, including files spread out over the network. This is the ultimate in security, privacy and freedom and the opposite of the centralized server model. MaidSafe founder, David Irvine, had the epiphany that the central server model exists nowhere in nature and therefore can't be an efficient model. [219]

Services similar to Facebook, Dropbox, Google and Twitter can be built on MaidSafe with no infrastructure cost or barrier to entry. Hundreds of developers, called "builders," immediately jumped in to kick start the innovation. Both farmers and builders are automatically compensated with Safecoin based on their contribution and user adoption. This brilliant, win-win model will deliver a more secure Internet option and other services at a fraction of the cost.

## No More Middleman

Counterparty.io is a free, open source, peer-to-peer financial and exchange protocol built on bitcoin, which allows users to exchange assets, create project tokens or start a crowd sale where profits or coin distributions can be automatically distributed to token holders or partners using its native currency, called XCP. A trustless escrow service enables trading of assets without broker fees, exchange fees or middlemen thereby eliminating counterparty risk and hence the name of the platform. It's a cost elimination, verifiable transaction and risk reduction platform including "bug bounty" rewards for maintaining open source quality. The Counterparty founders avoided a self-serving, crowd funding launch of the XCP currency using an innovative, "proof of burn" model, where bitcoins were sent to an unspendable address and only XCP came out. Co-founder, Robby Dermody, said, "It was a very unconventional kind of release but we wanted to have a fair release and prove that you could do a lot with a little. It forces you to make solid decisions." [220]

During January of 2014, participants sent 2,100 bitcoins were sent to an un-spendable bitcoin address and XCP coins were born, creating a fair, decentralized and equal financial opportunity for both the developers and everyone else. There were no special distributions for developers, so if you wanted to get in you had to burn bitcoin unlike other digital currency launches where the founders and developers sometimes make self-serving distributions.

Anyone can easily create a free webwallet at counterwallet.io with a client-side, 12-word, encrypted passphrase. It has a clean, simple, intuitive interface where users can create multiple bitcoin addresses to store any counterparty-based platform tokens. For example, XCP, bitcoins, Storj Coin, Folding Coin and LTB Coin can all be stored together by sending them to the same counterwallet bitcoin address. A new token can also be created in minutes by filling in a few fields as shown below. Users are fully in control of their crypto assets and therefore passphrases should be handled carefully. Participation in other altcoins and crowdfunding campaigns often require bitcoins to be sent from a wallet like counterwallet and not an exchange, otherwise the new coins will not get distributed to your wallet. [221, 222]

## Counterwallet Token Creation

Image courtesy of Counterparty

For example, Swarm.fund is a new-model crowdfunding and crypto equity platform using the Counterparty protocol. It empowers project supporters by allowing them to reap the rewards of a project's success beyond just getting a new product or book. The famous, record-breaking, Kickstarter project, Oculus Rift, raised $2.5 million dollars for a virtual headset project that was later sold to Facebook for $2 billion while returning nothing to the Kickstarter supporters other than a headset. [223] If this project had been set up on Swarm, all of the supporters would be shareholders of sorts, potentially reaping some of the gains. Every Swarm project issues its own coin to crowdfunding supporters who can hold the coin for long-term benefits or sell the coin at any time. Swarm coin returns the platform's profits to its coin holders allowing anyone to simultaneously benefit from the success of both individual projects and the Swarm platform as a whole. [224] The Swarm coin can also be bought or sold on crypto exchanges. Counterparty created a useful tool on top of bitcoin and Swarm created a disruptive, crowdfunding model with Counterparty.

## From the Inside Out

T0, pronounced tee-zero, is a U.S. blockchain based securities trading platform where the trade is the settlement. Nanosecond trades followed by 3 days for settlement will be a thing of the past hence the name T0. The new service led by Patrick Byrne of Overstock, will be a robust, parallel stock market alongside Wall Street and other traditional worldwide exchanges. T0's approach includes navigating the waters of the U.S. Securities and Exchange Commission and other regulatory frameworks, effecting change from the inside out en route to replacing the old model with the new and creating a choice for businesses and individuals. People who buy securities on the crypto security stock exchange will directly own that security with indisputable public proof of the ownership tied into the bitcoin blockchain. No third parties and no layers of mystery exist in the new model. [225] Patrick Byrne said it like this, "Cryptotechnology can do for the capital markets what the Internet has done for consumers." [226]

# What's Next?

NXT.org, pronounced next, is a second-generation cryptocurrency built from scratch with an entirely different protocol than bitcoin. It's a decentralized network owned by no one and "developed to allow a sustainable, fair and versatile platform that would benefit everyone," declares the NXT community. It uses a 100% proof of stake model, securing the network by rewarding transaction fees to people who own and hold NXT tokens in the NXT wallet client. NXT has faster one-minute transaction confirmations from a transparent forging algorithm that pre-determines which stakeholder's node confirms the next transaction. This is a stark contrast to the heavy-lifting, proof-of-work computing power required to secure the bitcoin network, where miners compete to solve a block on a 10-minute average.

NXT tokens can be used to buy smart contracts with a revenue sharing component. The Secure Asset Exchange (secureae.com) is an NXT-based decentralized, peer-to-peer platform for creating and trading smart contracts and other crypto assets. A smart contract in this context is a binding agreement enforced by technology from verified data. For example, the ABC cryptocurrency news website offers gross revenue sharing paid from affiliate and ad revenue. The ABC tokens automatically return the revenue share as additional tokens based on the programming in the smart contract. This is another method for raising business capital by offering returns on verifiable revenue streams. Smart contracts are only limited by imagination and can be created by anyone. Buyers should beware and use the same degree of due diligence with any other asset consideration. [227]

# A New Crypto Consensus

BitShares.org is a new, decentralized consensus model built from the ground up as a bitcoin alternative, which uses delegated proof of state, a hybrid of sorts between bitcoin's proof of work and NXT's proof of stake algorithms. Owners of the platform's native currency, called BitShares (BTS), are entitled to pro rata voting rights to elect delegates who secure the network. Stakeholders who become one of 101 delegates take turns signing transaction blocks while getting rewarded from transactions fees. This middle ground model of trust is a technological democracy where anyone who owns BTS can vote for or against delegates in an effort to keep the consensus in check. [228]

BitShares 1.0 started as a technology that empowered the creation of decentralized autonomous companies (DACs), which is like a set of automated, software-based business rules with an unmanned board of directors. Industries like music, publishing and insurance are ripe for this kind of transformation and middleman disruption. For example, The BitShares Music Blockchain is a new DAC focusing on the world of digital music. Peer Tracks rests on top of the music DAC allowing artists and fans to interact through its user-friendly website. Notes are the tokens of the music blockchain facilitating the interactions and the distribution of artists' profits. This game-changer puts power back in the hands of the artists in a world where everyone other than the artist makes all the money.

BitShares 2.0's industrial-grade, financial, smart contract platform is blazing a new path in crypto innovation. The platform boasts processing capacity of over 100,000 transactions per second with the speed of NASDAQ and scalability beyond the VISA network. You can create named accounts for payment addresses using your company name similar to selecting a domain name and without having to use a string of characters like bitcoin addresses. Named accounts can be transferred to another party making them valuable in their own right. Bitshares 2.0 also solves the recurring and subscription payments challenge in bitcoin. It uses smart contracts to set up flexible withdraw permissions, including start date, end date, withdraw limit and the number of withdraws. [229]

Additional features include the following.

- Institutional-grade, decentralized exchange
- Price-stable cryptocurrencies
- Stakeholder-approved project funding
- Regulation compatible, user-issued tokens
- Dynamic account permissions

## A Token-less Mining Free Platform

Opentransactions.org is a free open source commercial grade software toolkit developed by a worldwide community of volunteers. It's a financial cryptography library for creating multiple financial instruments using the same familiar terms used by financial institutions for ease of use and understanding. For example, vouchers are like cashier's checks. Checks are deducted when claimed by recipients while invoices, deposits, transfers, securities, market orders and limit orders have the same function as their commonly understood definitions. Smart contracts are created using the Ricardian Contract model, a combination human readable and automatic executable software contract for maximum versatility. In addition, it also employs an untraceable cash feature using blind signatures for transaction anonymity.

The protocol works on a federated network of servers similar to the Internet. In this case, each server acts as a third-party witness by signing every transaction or contract. This triple-signed receipts method even works on untrusted servers because the servers cannot alter contracts in any way. Only the sender and receiver can make changes or execute the agreement. Anyone can operate an Open Transaction (OT) notary server to compete for transaction signing fees all made possible by a lightweight system only requiring the previously signed receipt to verify the current one instead of using an entire back-to-the-beginning transaction history. [230]

The OT approach doesn't include its own coin, mining, pre-mining distributions or crowd sales. OT developer, Chris Odem, says "Whenever you make a system that uses an appcoin, there's going to be some comparable system in the near future that doesn't have an appcoin that has the same functionality." For example, Monetas.net is launching the "financial inclusion revolution," a robust platform using the OT protocol to build consumer apps, merchant solutions and an enterprise platform for entrepreneurs to build new financial products and services. [231, 232]

## Ether, But Not the Surgical Kind

Ethereum.org is like a cryptocurrency with a built in programming language also creating next-generation applications that any programmer can develop. Users can secure and trade almost anything using contracts, the main building block of the Ethereum platform. Contracts are like mini programs containing memory, code and balances that use Ether, the internal currency of the platform, to represent the assets being exchanged. A contract could be written as an internal control for a business policy requiring two approvers for payments over 4 BTC or three approvers including one C-level person for payments over 25 BTC. This is an example of conditional approvals with more flexibility than traditional multi-sig wallets. Ethereum completed a much-anticipated crowdsale of Ether in September 2014 raising $14M in bitcoin while becoming one of the most successful crowdsales in bitcoin 2.0 history. The team included numerous developers who worked for months without compensation way before the crowdsale produced funding for the project. [233]

## Exchanging Any Unit of Value

Ripple.com is a combination currency exchange, payment system and remittance network built on an open source consensus ledger using a native currency called Ripple (XRP). It's like the digital version of the informal Hawala value transfer system of mutually trusting brokers. The Hawala system, used in the Middle East and Africa, operates outside of traditional banking allowing two people to exchange different currencies in different countries using a pair of trusted brokers who charge very low transaction fees. Ripple enables users to send anything of value including fiat currency, digital currencies, commodities, mobile minutes and more to be received as a different currency on the other end. It boasts nearly free, lightning fast, ten-second transactions of any size anywhere in the world. Ripple's path-finding algorithm matches up two parties and eliminates exchange rate risk where party A can transact in bitcoin and party B can transact in yen without losing value on the conversion of one currency to another. Fidor Bank successfully implemented the Ripple Protocol to offer customers instant international money transfers. Anyone can become a market and earn transaction fees by supplying liquidity to the Ripple network.[234]

## Slashing Millions

Tradle.io offers banks a KYC network on blockchain to reduce the amount of know-your-customer due diligence checks while giving bank customers co-ownership of their verified identity, which they can use with other network participants. Tradle's subscription app helps reduce the 10% to 20% cost of bank staff working on redundant compliance and regulatory issues. The app is like the Instagram for KYC creating a natural user experience for the tech-savvy and millennials alike. Tradle Founder, Gene Vayngrib, says, "The auditing of the bank by the regulators in such a way preserves privacy as much as possible. The regulator could get information about suspicious transactions without banks sharing a lot of raw, private data with them."

For example, Jill visits her bank website, clicks on a link to download the Tradle TiM (Trust in Motion) app and snaps pictures of her passport, license and so forth, while chatting with the bank representative. The verifications are automatically digitally signed, encrypted and time stamped via any blockchain. Identity re-validation is automatic and new documents can be added to strengthen a customer's identity profile. Banks can slash millions in compliance costs by accepting full or partial verifications performed by another bank. Meanwhile, Jill is fully in control of her identity by requesting and authorizing the re-validation between banks with the TiM app on her smart phone. Tradle eliminates redundant identity information silos by transforming the costly practice into a universally accessible, blockchain-based model where customers have control and co-ownership of their identities. [235]

## Old Model Transformed

Sericatrading.com is a trading platform for gold, silver and bitcoins with a blockchain-based proof of custody. When users buy gold with bitcoin, they can verify ownership on the blockchain with a corresponding digital token representing the actual gold held in physical custody by a third party. The token can be redeemed for physical delivery of the gold, traded for other precious metals or traded for bitcoin and back into gold tokens as a profit and hedging strategy. Blockchain transactions provide the highest level of undisputable proof available today, which reduces the risk of holding a physical asset with a third-party platform and a third-party custodian. [236] In a world of deep capture and having to wonder who really owns an asset, Serica has come to save the day.

## Crypto Permaculture

Permacredits.org is both a platform and a currency combining permaculture with bitcoin technology in a way that's never been done before. It's a great example of adaptive use technology beyond the coin in the same way the Internet gave birth to new platforms and new ways of doing things. Permaculture is a philosophy of working with nature to develop regenerative, sustainable ecological projects. Permacredits creates a global membership of eco resorts, sustainable living spaces, retreat centers and permaculture farms focused on a profits-people-planet, triple-bottom-line approach.

Anyone can submit a permaculture project or buy permacredits for global membership and participation. Permacredits holders use their tokens to vote on projects while automatically receiving project profits distributed as additional tokens. Projects get funded in permacredits after a round of voting and approval by a review council. The tokens can be used to pay employees and vendors, receive payments from customers, or may be exchanged for bitcoin or fiat money. For example, someone in Chile can support a project in China by buying permacredits and voting on the project. Users are not investing in specific projects but they can vote on every project while benefiting from global profits of all projects. The currency aspect of permacredits provides a universal exchange of value so the world can come together on a local level. [237]

## Let's Talk Bitcoin (LTB)

The LTB network provides free, best-of-class, up-to-date information on everything happening in the bitcoin ecosystem. It started as one podcast in April 2013 and quickly expanded into a network of podcasts as well as articles from contributing writers and forums for connecting listeners who can make comments on content or just start new threads. The flagship podcast, Let's Talk Bitcoin, is a twice-weekly show about the ideas, people and projects building the digital economy and the future of money. Says Adam B. Levine, LTB founder, "We are just obsessed companions walking the road towards a more peer-to-peer future."

Let's Talk Bitcoin pioneered LTBcoin, leveraging the bitcoin protocol using previously mentioned Counterparty to connect the platform with its audience by giving out tokens to everyone who participates. The LTBcoins are rewards distributed to the people who listen and read, contribute articles, create podcasts and contribute to platform development. Anyone who received LTBcoin can trade it for goods and services with anyone willing to accept it. Advertising slots on the Let's Talk Bitcoin podcast have to be purchased with LTBcoin, thereby motivating interested advertisers to participate and obtain the coin. The coins make it more fun to participate in something already providing tremendous listener value.

The LTB platform is open source and transparent including a web page dedicated to disclosing the total coins to be distributed, the coin allocation and distribution timeline. It's truly a great experiment in something that's never been done before as it continues to create new ways to reward participants. This is one of the best sources for learning about bitcoin and cryptocurrencies while earning digital tokens in a fun and easy way. Create an account today at letstalkbitcoin.com.

# For the Good of Science

Foldingcoin.net is a project assembling the idle computing power volunteered by participants to simulate protein folding for research and advances in medicine. Essentially, the research requires massive amounts of calculation to find cures for diseases such as ALS, Parkinson's, Alzheimer's and various cancers, so users are invited to donate computing power to accelerate the process. Volunteers simply download folding client software, which automatically receives and sends protein folding instructions and results. Folding Coin tokens are distributed daily into counterparty wallets with a pro rata calculation based on computing power. Bitcoin technology makes folding coin rewards possible considering similar projects were previously unable to reward volunteers. It also allows people to contribute by purchasing Folding Coin (FDLC) from an exchange without having to supply computing power. FDLC uses may include computer gaming credits as well as other future use cases.

## Beyond the Coin Takeaway

Hopefully this journey beyond the coin has provided a glimpse into the future where every business and industry has a mutually beneficial blockchain-based transformation. The new business future has simplified processes, provides better business tools, uses fewer resources, adds value and slashes costs, removes fraud from the equation and affords perfect scalability for everyone from the microbusiness to the Fortune 500. In the words of Tim Ferris, author of The 4-Hour Workweek, "Never delegate what you can automate and never automate what you can eliminate." These new technologies are the beginning of an automation, elimination and transparency revolution, as highlighted by the Decentralized Autonomous Companies concept.

The time has come to remove the reliance on trust through decentralization, swapping higher returns and more risk for higher returns and less risk. Trust approaches elimination in the blockchain model while transparency skyrockets with a single version of the truth, allowing people to trade digital assets with almost no fees. Finally, people all over the world have a previously unavailable choice over typical fraud-laden business and bureaucratic models. In the old business model you're left wondering what vendors are doing with deposit money, and whether a customer is going to pay or whether you can trust your financial institution. We've become conditioned to business anxiety left unchecked in a world of no alternatives. In the new model, peace of mind will become commonplace because we'll be able to program money and contracts without having to wait and wonder.

# Bitcoin Additional Resources

Bitcoin and digital currencies are an art, the craft of which requires continuing education the same as in life and business. The following resources are invaluable for continuing your journey into this era of innovation. Whether you are a business executive, entrepreneur or professional, once-in-a-lifetime opportunities abound for those willing to seek and understand what this new technology, Bitcoin, has to offer. Add these resources to your crypto toolbox by setting them up in a password manager like Last Pass or by saving them as favorites in your browser for platforms without an account setup.

## Publications

The Ultimate Bitcoin Business Guide: Your ongoing resource for continuing your Bitcoin and digital currency journey with companion site, BestBitcoinBookEver.com.

Mastering Bitcoin: A book primarily written for developers and a must-have on everyone's bookshelf.

Anonymous Bitcoin: A guide on best practices for buying and using bitcoin anonymously.

The Bitcoin Comic: This graphic novel uses a comic book style to communicate Bitcoin in an entertaining way.

The Age of Cryptocurrency: The title speaks for itself.

The Bitcoin Big Bang: Another great angle on the digital currency revolution.

Digital Gold: An inside story of the people reinventing money.

The Great Credit Contraction: An inside look at the illusions of fiat currency.

yBitcoin Magazine: The Future of Money: A free, high-quality coffee table magazine with educational articles focused on people who are beginning their Bitcoin journey.

Bitcoin Magazine: The original magazine created with a technical focus on Bitcoin.

## Organizations

Digital Currency Council: The association of professionals in the digital currency economy especially attorneys, financial advisors and CPAs. It's also a place to get trained, get certified and get connected as a leader in advising clients about digital currency and a place to get new business from people looking for expert advisors.

Crypto Consortium: An organization of industry leaders developing a CryptoCurrency Security Standard to standardize techniques and methodologies for business best practices and end-user due diligence decisions about using a cryptocurrency platform. They also developed certifications for trusted professionals in trustless technologies for both professionals and developers.

University of Nicosia: The world's first university offering a master's degree in digital currency with certificates hashed into the blockchain. They also have a free Introduction to Digital Currencies course, the first course of the master's program.

College Cryptocurrency Network: A network of hundreds of Bitcoin clubs from universities around the world focused on education and advocacy. All undergrad to PhD university students interested in cryptocurrency should get connected and take advantage of resources and opportunities.

Global Bitcoin Alliance: A global connector whose mission is to promote growth of Bitcoin communities worldwide by sharing knowledge and resources and by connecting local, regional and national organizations. The member organizations are responsible for their activities while the GBA represents the communities on a global level.

Coin Center: A research and advocacy group focused on public policy issues whose mission it to promote a regulatory climate that preserves the freedom to innovate. They publish research from respected academics and experts to educate and influence policymakers for sound public policy.

Digital Chamber of Commerce: An authoritative industry representative in Washington, DC, whose mission is to promote the acceptance of digital currencies and digital assets to government and the public. They respond to press releases and explain the value of digital assets to inquiring government officials.

## News sites

coindesk.com
cryptocoinsnews.com
cointelegraph.com
bitcoinist.net

## Cryptocurrency market information websites

coinmarketcap.com
coincap.io
bitcoincharts.com
worldcoinindex.com
cryptocoinrank.com
cryptocoincharts.info

## Blockchain explorers and related data sites

blockchain.info
blockr.io
blockscan.com
blockinfo.org
blockcypher.com

## Bitcoin and crypto data analytics sites

bravenewcoin.com
coinometrics.com
coinalytics.co

# Bitclusion: Wrapping it Up

## The New Paradigm

I hope you enjoyed The Ultimate Bitcoin Business Guide and the journey into bitcoin's new financial paradigm as a trustless system, a public transaction ledger, controlled by no one, with no third-party banks, no central banks, no long-term inflation, no crazy bank and credit cards fees, no bank withdraws or bank account closures without your permission, and the ability to send bitcoins nearly instantaneously to anyone anywhere in the world from the comfort of your own home or office. Your business can't afford to wait another day and now is the time to get into action. If you said to yourself, "I wish I knew then what I know now about the Internet" now you can say, "I'm glad I found out about bitcoin in the early days." Adopting bitcoin is also about turning on your bitcoin radar and becoming aware of the current and future transformation in every way that business is conducted.

Bitcoin will transform money the way the Internet transformed information and commerce—and that's just the beginning, as newly created business models and services take us into the cyber stratosphere. It will magnify the adapt-or-die global game of business, creating more organizational transformation and more extinction than any other time in history. We're at the beginning of a spectacular new renaissance revealed by the endless possibilities of Bitcoin. The contributions of the great Renaissance masters and thinkers from 500 years ago still influence us today just like Bitcoin technology will influence this century and beyond.

## Bitcoins and Risk

The law of bitcoin risk management says that security and convenience are inversely related, therefore the more secure a system the less convenient it is, and conversely, the more convenient a system the less secure it is. Innovation is rapidly flipping the inverse relationship so users can have both security and convenience. Even though the gap is closing, the law is still the golden rule of the road on the bitcoin highway. Bitcoin grants special powers in the form of 100% responsibility including custody and authority for your business finances. This gift requires patience and strategy while navigating your way to crypto success.

## The Value of Peace of Mind

Increasing revenue, decreasing expenses, having full control, reducing fraud, corruption and abuse, employing 21st century internal controls, getting higher returns with less risk, and having a financial choice are some of the more obvious, attention-getting benefits of adopting bitcoin. Most of its value, however, comes from the often-overlooked benefits. In business and in life, the high cost of frustration is discounted and the benefit of peace of mind is undervalued. Both of these are subjective transactions typically not accounted for like the purchase of goods and services. Bitcoin is a Credit Card Chaos, Money Transfer Madness and Banking Burnout Bonanza frustration eliminator in the lives of individuals and businesses while simultaneously transforming industries, nations and the global economy, the benefits of which cycle back into peace of mind. Peace of mind is the most valuable, never-accounted-for asset and something you can't buy because it's earned through your own awareness.

## Bitcoin Trifecta

Bitcoin combines a digital currency, a network and a protocol into one self-contained trifecta. The value goes far beyond the digital currency by aligning incentives within a single decentralized system—beautiful in its simplicity—where participants can come and go as they please. Bitcoin's store of value and medium of exchange attributes of money are locked together in a perfect dance with a brand new attribute called programmable money. For the first time in history we can turn money into data, program it and do things that have never been done before. These new things will drive the new renaissance for generations to come. The patchwork of old rail models, centralized authorities, deep capture, competing interests and unnecessary, head-spinning complexity within our current money systems is the opposite of everything Bitcoin. The passage of time will write the final whitepaper on the value of the Bitcoin Trifecta.

## The Bitcoin Trophy

Whether or not bitcoin maintains its digital currency dominance or gets superseded by another innovative platform, its influence will land it in the Cryptocurrency Hall of Fame and just like the Super Bowl's Lombardi Trophy, the Cryptocurrency Championship's coveted award will be named the Bitcoin Trophy. Vince Lombardi's legacy for football and leadership is as alive and well today as it was 50 years ago. Bitcoin will be alive and well in the future as every cryptographic-based, bitcoin-inspired system that we operate from pays homage to bitcoin and Satoshi Nakamoto. This is the beginning of a transformation, the final outcome of which is hard to predict the same way that truth is stranger than the best fiction. Johnston's Law states, anything that can be decentralized will be decentralized and the world won't look anything like it does now in another generation.

## It's a Rising Sun

The earth and our global community are in need of a higher intelligence to avoid our current collision course with self-destruction. Bitcoin has given us a glimpse into what's possible for harmoniously aligning incentives and balancing the benefits for all stakeholders in a given system. The beautiful balancing act of Bitcoin starts to eliminate those negative human traits such as greed, deception, manipulation, wastefulness, indulgence and corruption exploited for the benefit of self-interest instead of abundance for all. Those human traits simply get in the way of a sustainable, universal and fair allocation of all resources.

During the Constitutional Convention of 1787, Benjamin Franklin stared at the sun carved on the top of George Washington's chair and with the young nation hanging in the balance wondered whether or not the Founding Fathers could agree on its direction, famously commenting, "I have often in the course of the session, and the vicissitudes of my hopes and fears as to its issue, looked at that behind the president without being able to tell whether it was rising or setting. But now at length I have the happiness to know that it is a rising and not a setting sun." [238, 239]

Bitcoin not only holds the promise for the future of money but the promise for the future of humankind. I share Franklin's sentiment, in the context of bitcoin's boding for the human race, and say that I, too, have the happiness to know—we are facing a rising sun.

## By the Inch It's a Cinch

It's an exciting time to be alive in the age of the Internet and smart phones and even more exhilarating to live in the age of bitcoin and cryptocurrency. We took on understanding bitcoin by understanding its opposite, looked at compliance and regulation, taxes, accounting, digital identity management, exchanges, bitcoin wallets and safekeeping, social networks and many other parts of the ecosystem. Congratulations on completing an important part of your bitcoin business journey! Now it's time to implement and benefit from the nuggets in this book. As I like to quote Stephen Covey, "By the inch it's a cinch and by the yard it's hard." [240] The easiest way to master bitcoin is to learn and experiment every day.

I hope this book has inspired and imbued you with confidence to get your business into action. Sign up and start using the platforms, as experience is the best teacher. Bitcoin is a rapidly changing space and although many more milestones will be achieved and sound bites shared after this book, I attempted to paint a picture about why the old model is ripe for transformation and why the new model should be embraced. The end of this book is not the end of your journey with The Ultimate Bitcoin Business Guide. The companion site is coming to help with the rest of your journey including updates, best practices, tools, platforms, education and more. Head over to BestBitcoinBookEver.com/bonus right now to claim your bonuses, stay on course and stay connected.

Live long and prosper. Kirk out.

# About the Author

Kirk Phillips, aka the TheBitcoinCPA, is an entrepreneur, Certified Public Accountant (CPA) and a self-taught woodworker—an artist in all areas of life. He brings the same attention to detail necessary for creating finely crafted furniture into the business world. He is passionate about technology, business processes, fraud prevention, time management, learning and peace of mind.

Kirk discovered Bitcoin at the end of 2013 when a friend asked for advice, saying, "My husband and I want to invest $800 in a computer to mine bitcoin and make some money. What do you think?" to which he responded, "I don't know anything about Bitcoin, I'll have to get back to you." This simple inquiry led him down the Bitcoin Rabbit Hole, an experience described by many Bitcoiners, and ultimately gave birth to *The Ultimate Bitcoin Business Guide*.

The Bitcoin journey has magnified Kirk's commitment to helping business get done with greater ease and transparency at all levels. Kirk brings more than 15 years' experience working in public accounting while also working in private industry and with business owners and individuals. He has launched multiple businesses, including invizibiz.biz a virtual accounting and back office subscription service.

Because of his desire for continuous learning and development (and a slightly obsessive approach to everything that interests him), Kirk became DCC Certified with the Digital Currency Council and also earned the Certified Bitcoin Professional (CBP) designation issued by C4, the Crypto Currency Certification Consortium. He earned a Certificate of Completion from the University of Nicosia, Introduction to Digital Currencies MOOC Course. He has also authored several articles about Bitcoin.

Kirk holds additional designations as a Certified in Financial

Management (CFM) Certified Management Accountant, CMA Certified Fraud Examiner (CFE) and a Charted Global Management Accountant (CGMA).

Kirk has immersed himself in bitcoin and is currently one of only a handful of qualified CPA strategic advisors in the bitcoin and cryptocurrency space. He weaves risk management into business process outsourcing and also provides crypto business consulting and education. You can contact Kirk at TheBitcoinCPA@gmail.com or on twitter @TheBitcoinCPA.

# Works Cited

1. Evolution of a Profession. AICPA TV. AICPA, 7 June 2012.
2. Backstory: Early Accounting. AICPA TV. AICPA, 25 May 2012.
3. Nahnybida, Simon. "Getting Ready for Mass Adoption Presentation." Proc. of Inside Bitcoins NYC, April 7, 2014.
4. A letter to John Taylor, May 1816, Thomas Jefferson Quote, Monticello.org.
5. First Bank and Second Bank of the United States, wiki
6. President Jackson's Veto Message Regarding the Bank of the United States (1832). Print.
7. The Progressive Covenant With The People, August 1912. Theodore Roosevelt, authentichistory.com
8. A letter to Edward Mandell House, November 1933, Franklin D. Roosevelt, themoneymasters.com
9. "What Is the Fed: History." Federal Reserve Bank San Francisco. Web. 18 May 2014.
10. Causes of the Bank Suspensions in the Panic of 1893, Mark Carlson, Federal Reserve Board, unknown year
11. The Panic of 1893.
12. Kavoussi, Bonnie. The Panic of 1907: A Human-Caused Crisis, or a Thunderstorm? (n.d.): n. pag. Web.
13. Peeler, Kelly. The Rise and Fall of J.Pierpont Morgan: The Shift in John Pierpont Morgan's Public Image From the Bailout of the Moore & Schley Brokerage House in 1907 to the Pujo Hearings in 1913 1 (n.d.): n. pag. Web.
14. Chen, Lucy. Banking Reform in a Hostile Climate: Paul M. Warburg and the National Citizens' League (2010): n. pag. Web.
15. "History of the Federal Reserve." Federal Reserve Education. Web. 18 May 2014.
16. Lindbergh, Charles. United States. Congressional Record. Cong. Rept. Vol. Vol. 51. N.p.: n.p., December 1913. Print.
17. "What Is the Purpose of the Federal Reserve System?" Federal Reserve Bank. Web. 18 May 2014.
18. "Is the Fed Audited?" Federal Reserve Bank of St. Louis. Web. 18 May 2014.
19. "Is the Federal Reserve Accountable to Anyone?" Federal Reserve Bank. Web. 18 May 2014.
20. "Audit the Federal Reserve." Ronpaul.com. Web. 18 May 2014.
21. Miller, John. "The Federal Reserve Transparency Act Deserves Vote." Motleyfool.com. 1 Nov. 2013.
22. "TARP Programs." TARP Programs. N.p., n.d. Web. 28 Feb. 2015.
23. Federal Regulation of Financial Markets. 23 Oct. 2008. Web. 28 Feb. 2015.
24. "Money For Nothing: Inside the Federal Reserve." Money For Nothing: Inside the Federal Reserve. N.p., n.d. Web. 28 Feb. 2015.
25. "EB93 – Simon Dixon: How Bank To The Future Is Rethinking Finance." Audio blog post. Epicenter Bitcoin. N.p., 24 Aug. 2015. Web.
26. "Visa Inc." Wikipedia. Wikimedia Foundation, n.d. Web. 28 Feb. 2015.
27. "MasterCard." Wikipedia. Wikimedia Foundation, n.d. Web. 28 Feb. 2015.
28. "3 Major U.S. Banks Sued for Colluding on ATM Fees." Insidecounsel.com. 11 Oct. 2011.

29. "Interview with Aaron Williams, Bitcoin AML & KYC Compliance and 10-year Payments Industry Veteran." Telephone interview. 15 May 20.
30. "MasterCard Interchange Rates & Fees." MasterCard. Web. 18 May 2014.
31. "Average Credit Card Processing Fees." Credit Card Processing Insider. Web. 18 May 2014.
32. "What You Need to Know About Credit Card Processing." Web log post. NYtimes.com, 25 Mar. 2013. Web.
33. "EB87 – John McDonnell: How Bitcoin Will Win Online Payments." Audio blog post. Epicenter Bitcoin. N.p., 13 July 2015. Web. 18 July 2015.
34. "Interchange Rates | MasterCard®." Interchange Rates | MasterCard®. N.p., n.d. Web. 12 June 2015.
35. "Bitcoin Merchant On-Ramp." "Inside Bitcoins | Conference and Expo for Virtual Currency and Cryptocurrency." April 7-8, 2014.
36. "Interview with Ashok Misra." E-mail interview. 10 Mar. 2015.
37. Nahnybida, Simon. "Bitcoin: Getting Ready for Mass Adoption." Proc. of Inside Bitcoins, NYC April 7-8. N.p.: n.p., 2014. N. pag. Print.
38. "Interview with Rony Garcia, Foreign Worker, on Foreign Remittances to Guatemala and California." Personal interview. 13 Mar. 2015.
39. Ratha, Dilip. "Finance & Development." Remittances: Funds for the Folks Back Home. International Monetary Fund, n.d. Web. 22 Mar. 2015.
40. "SWIFT The Global Provider of Secure Financial Messaging Services." SWIFT – The Global Provider of Secure Financial Messaging Services. N.p., n.d. Web. 07 Feb. 2015.
41. "European Automated Clearing House Association." European Automated Clearing House Association. N.p., n.d. Web. 07 Feb. 2015.
42. CHIPS. N.p., n.d. Web. 07 Feb. 2015.
43. "ACH Network: How It Works." ACH Network: How It Works. N.p., n.d. Web. 07 Feb. 2015. <https://www.nacha.org/ach-network>.
44. Bank of America Small Business Resources, Fees at a glance.
45. Crawford, Stephanie. "10 Sneaky Banking Fees - HowStuffWorks."HowStuffWorks. N.p., n.d. Web. 07 Feb. 2015.
46. Monga, Vipal. "U.S. Companies Cling to Writing Paper Checks." Editorial. WSJ n.d.: n. pag. WSJ. Web. 07 Feb. 2015.
47. Peterson, Andrea. "Hal Finney Received the First Bitcoin Transaction. Here's How He Describes It." The Washington Post, 03 Jan. 2014.
48. Digital Currency Council, Certification and Training Course. 10 Jan. 2015.
49. "What Is Bitcoin Mining, and Why Is It Necessary? • Coin Center." Coin Center. N.p., 15 Dec. 2014. Web. 12 June 2015.
50. "Interview with Dani Eder, Bitcoin Miner." Telephone interview. 20 May 2015.
51. University of Nicosia, Introduction to Digital Currencies Course. 22 Oct. 2014. Session#2: The Byzantine Generals' Problem.
52. "Why Is The Bitcoin BlockChain Important?" Points and Figures RSS. N.p., n.d. Web. 12 June 2015.
53. University of Nicosia, Introduction to Digital Currencies Course. 6 Nov. 2014. Session #4: Cryptocurrency and Central Banking.
54. "Lessons from Bitcoin: Push versus Pull." Richard Gendal Brown. N.p., 21 Oct. 2013. Web. 12 June 2015.
55. "State of Bitcoin 2015: Ecosystem Grows Despite Price Decline." CoinDesk.

com. N.p., 07 Jan. 2015. Web. 08 Feb. 2015.

56. Zeiler, David. "Venture Capitalists Are Investing in Bitcoin at the Fastest Pace to Date." Money Morning We Make Investing Profitable. N.p., 16 June 2014. Web. 08 Feb. 2015.

57. Wong, Joon. "Bitcoin VC Investment This Year Already 30% Higher Than 2013's Total." CoinDesk RSS. N.p., 05 June 2014. Web. 08 Feb. 2015.

58. State of Bitcoin Q1 2015. Slide Presentation. CoinDesk, 10 Apr. 2015. Web. 13 June 2015.

59. Schubarth, Cromwell. "Palo Alto Bitcoin 'vault' Xapo Raises $20M from Benchmark, Others - Silicon Valley Business Journal." Silicon Valley Business Journal. N.p., 14 Mar. 2014. Web. 08 Feb. 2015.

60. Kharif, Olga. "Bitcoin Startup Xapo Sets $40 Million Fundraising Record."Bloomberg.com. Bloomberg, 8 July 2014. Web. 08 Feb. 2015.

61. Dougherty, Carter. "Bitcoin Startup Circle Secures $17 Million Venture Financing."Bloomberg.com. Bloomberg, 26 Mar. 2014. Web. 08 Feb. 2015.

62. Casey, Michael. "Bitcoin Processor Raises $30 Million." WSJ. N.p., 13 May 2014. Web. 08 Feb. 2015.

63. BitFury Raises $20 Million, Solidifying Its Lead in Bitcoin Infrastructure. Venturebeat.com, 30 May 2014. Web.

64. Boring, Perianne. "BitGo Raises $12Mil, Draws Attention of Institutional Investors."Forbes. Forbes Magazine, 6 June 2014. Web. 08 Feb. 2015.

65. Kharif, Olga. "VC Tim Draper Wins Entire Cache in Bitcoin Auction." Bloomberg.com. Bloomberg, 2 July 2014. Web. 08 Feb. 2015.

66. Ember, Sydney. "Blockchain Is Latest Bitcoin Start-Up to Lure Big Investment."NYTimes.com. N.p., 6 Oct. 2014. Web.

67. "Coinbase Raises $75 Million in Largest-ever VC round for Bitcoin company." Fortune Coinbase Raises 75 Million in Largest Ever VC Round for Bitcoin Company Comments. N.p., 20 Jan. 2015. Web. 12 June 2015.

68. "Bitcoin Startup 21 Announces $116 Million All-Star Backing." CoinDesk RSS. N.p., 10 Mar. 2015. Web. 12 June 2015.

69. CoinDesk State of Bitcoin 2014. Rep. N.p.: CoinDesk, 2014. Print.

70. "Bitcoin Hashrate Distribution." Blockchain.info. N.p., n.d. Web. 8 Feb. 2015. <https://blockchain.info/pools>.

71. Calouro, Eric. "Ghash.io Mining Pool Has Mined $250 Million in Bitcoin in One Year."NEWSBTC. N.p., 04 Aug. 2014. Web. 08 Feb. 2015.

72. Christensen, Neils. "2013: Year Of The Bitcoin." Forbes. Forbes Magazine, 10 Dec. 2013. Web. 07 Feb. 2015.

73. CoinDesk State of Bitcoin 2014. Rep. N.p.: CoinDesk, 2014. Print.

74. Liu, Alec. "Turning Five: A Timeline of Bitcoin's Greatest Milestones." Motherboard. N.p., 5 Jan. 2014. Web. 08 Feb. 2015.

75. Ibid.

76. Moskowitz, David. "Singapore Tax Authorities (IRAS) Recognize Bitcoin and Gives Guidance." Coin Republic Bitcoin News Trading and Consulting. N.p., 8 Jan. 2014. Web. 08 Feb. 2015.

77. "Perkins Coie LLP." Perkins Coie. N.p., 22 Mar. 2013. Web. 08 Feb. 2015.

78. Song, Sophie. "The Rise And Fall Of Bitcoin In China: Central Bank Shuts Down All Chinese Bitcoin Exchanges." International Business Times. N.p., 27 Mar. 2014. Web. 08 Feb. 2015.

79. Duhaime, Christine. "Canada Implements World's First National Digital

Currency Law; Regulates New Financial Technology Transactions."
Duhaime Law. N.p., 22 June 2014. Web. 08 Feb. 2015.

80. "This Senate Hearing Is a Bitcoin Lovefest." Washington Post. The Washington Post, n.d. Web. 28 Feb. 2015.

81. "Japan's Ruling Party Says Won't Regulate Bitcoin for Now." Reuters. Thomson Reuters, 19 June 2014. Web. 28 Feb. 2015.

82. Wong, Joon Ian. "UK's Plans to Regulate Bitcoin Revealed in Treasury Report." CoinDesk RSS. N.p., 18 Mar. 2015. Web. 18 July 2015.

83. "How To Stop Bitcoin Banking; Give It A BitLicense In New York." Forbes. Forbes Magazine, n.d. Web. 28 Feb. 2015.

84. Roberts, Daniel. "Bitcoin Company Ditches New York, Blaming New Regulations." Fortune Bitcoin Company Ditches New York Blaming New Regulations Comments. N.p., 11 June 2015. Web. 18 July 2015.

85. "Speech." - June 3, 2015: NYDFS Announces Final BitLicense Framework for Regulating Digital Currency Firms. N.p., n.d. Web. 18 July 2015.

86. Van Valkenburgh, Peter. "Our Thoughts on the BitLicense: California Is Winning • Coin Center." Coin Center. N.p., 03 June 2015. Web. 18 July 2015.

87. Linshi, Jack. "California Lifts Ban on Bitcoin." Time. Time, 30 June 2014. Web. 08 Feb. 2015.

88. "Mazacoin First Crypto Currency Of Sovereign Nation." Igotbitcoin.com. N.p., n.d. Web.

89. "State of Bitcoin 2015: Ecosystem Grows Despite Price Decline." CoinDesk RSS. N.p., 07 Jan. 2015. Web. 28 Feb. 2015.

90. Cary, Nic. Bitcoin Stories from Across the Globe. Proc. of Inside Bitcoins, New York, NY. N.p., n.d. Web.

91. "Welcome to Blockchain" Bitcoin Block Explorer. N.p., n.d. Web. 28 Feb. 2015. <http://blockchain.info/>.

92. "Bitcoin Hash Rate." N.p., n.d. Web. 28 Feb. 2015.

93. "Bloomberg to List Bitcoin Prices, Offering Key Stamp of Approval." WSJ. N.p., n.d. Web. 28 Feb. 2015.

94. Chang, Jon M. "First Bitcoin ATM Installed in Vancouver Coffee Shop." ABC News. ABC News Network, 30 Oct. 2013. Web. 28 Feb. 2015.

95. "Bitcoin Has Died Nearly 100 Times - CryptoCoinsNews." CryptoCoinsNews. N.p., 07 June 2015. Web. 12 June 2015.

96. Gladwell, Malcolm. The Tipping Point: How Little Things Can Make a Big Difference. Boston: Little, Brown, 2000. Print.

97. "Speakers | Inside Bitcoins | Bitcoin News | Price | Bitcoin Conferences." Inside Bitcoins. N.p., n.d. Web. 07 Mar. 2015.

98. Rogers, Everett. Diffusion of Innovations. N.p.: Free, 1962. Print.

99. Allaire, Jeremy. "Keynote." Inside Bitcoins. NY, New York. 7 Apr. 2014. Address.

100. "Tipping Point: How the Regulatory Ecosystem Can Be Bitcoin-Friendly." On Bitcoin. N.p., 03 Feb. 2014. Web. 07 Mar. 2015.

101. "Metcalfe's Law." Princeton University. N.p., n.d. Web. 07 Mar. 2015.

102. "Smartphone Users Worldwide Will Total 1.75 Billion in 2014 - EMarketer." Smartphone Users Worldwide Will Total 1.75 Billion in 2014 - EMarketer. EMarketer, 16 Jan. 2014. Web. 26 Feb. 2015.

103. Bundrick, Hal M. "Investing in Bitcoin: Gauging the Fair Value and Future

Price of Bitcoin." Investing in Bitcoin: Gauging the Fair Value and Future Price of Bitcoin. N.p., 30 Sept. 2014. Web. 18 July 2015.

104. Rizzo, Pete. "Is $518 the Fair Price of Bitcoin?" CoinDesk RSS. N.p., 02 Mar. 2015. Web. 18 July 2015.

105. Rizzo, Pete. "Tim Draper: Bitcoin's Price Still Headed to $10k." CoinDesk RSS. N.p., 12 Sept. 2014. Web. 18 July 2015.

106. Lauria, Gil, and Aaron Turner. Wedbush Equity Research: Bitcoin Investment Trust (GBTC), Initiating with Outperform and $40 Price Target; Fuel for Promising Technology in Early Days of Disruption. Rep. N.p.: n.p., 2015. Print.

107. Selkis, Ryan. "The Easy Way To Measure Bitcoin's Fair Market Value: A Do-It-Yourself Guide." Investopedia. N.p., 09 May 2014. Web. 18 July 2015.

108. Gravengaard, Eric, and Matt Kolbe. What Is a Bitcoin Worth as a Transaction Mechanism? Whitepaper. N.p.: n.p., 2014. Print.

109. Woo, David, Vadim Iaralov, and Ian Gordon. Bitcoin: A First Assessment. Rep. N.p.: n.p., 2013. Print.

110. Ibid.

111. Ibid.

112. Ibid.

113. Winklevoss, Cameron. "What May Have Happened At Mt.Gox."Winklevoss Capital. N.p., n.d. Web. 14 Mar. 2015.

114. Decker, Christian, and Roger Wattenhofer. Bitcoin Transaction Malleability and Mt. Gox. Rep. N.p.: n.p., 2014. Print.

115. Takemoto, Yoshifumi, and Sophie Knight. "Mt. Gox Files for Bankruptcy, Hit with Lawsuit." Reuters. Thomson Reuters, 28 Feb. 2014. Web. 14 Mar. 2015.

116. "Joint Statement Regarding Mt. Gox." The Coinbase Blog. N.p., 24 Feb. 2014. Web. 14 Mar. 2015.

117. Farivar, Cyrus. "Feds say Bitcoin miner maker Butterfly Labs ran "systematic deception" [Updated]." Ars technica. 23 Sept. 2014. 14 Mar. 2015.

118. Jeffries, Adrianne. "FTC Shuts down Butterfly Labs, the Second-most Hated Company in Bitcoinland." The Verge. N.p., 23 Sept. 2014. Web. 14 Mar. 2015.

119. SEC Charges Texas Man With Running Bitcoin-Denominated Ponzi Scheme. SEC, 23 July 2013.

120. Cawrey, Daniel. "Bitcoin Ponzi Schemer Charged With Criminal Securities Fraud." CoinDesk RSS. N.p., 06 Nov. 2014. Web. 14 Mar. 2015.

121. Stempel, Jonathan. "Texan Charged in First Bitcoin Securities Fraud Ponzi Case." Reuters. Thomson Reuters, 06 Nov. 2014. Web. 14 Mar. 2015.

122. Spaven, Emily. "Neo & Bee CEO Breaks Silence on Alleged Bitcoin Fraud." CoinDesk RSS. N.p., 15 Apr. 2014. Web. 14 Mar. 2015.

123. Bissell, Kelly, and Hannah, Gordon. The Changing Landscape of Digital Identity Management. Rep. WSJ Risk & Compliance Journal, 5 Nov. 2013. Web. 21 Mar. 2015.

124. Earnest, Mark. "Authentication, Authorization and Identity Management." PSU Security Day. Speech, 2006.

125. Tsui, Will, and Al Gutierrez. "Digital Identity Management on the Internet." Web. 21 Mar. 2015.

126. LastPass.com

127. Boyer, Paul. "How I Lost Your BitPay Donations." Audio blog post. Mad Money Machine Season 2 Episode 8. N.p., 11 July 2014. Web. 22 Mar. 2015.
128. Ibid. Episode 9.
129. "Hacker Surrenders After Roger Ver Offers 37.6 BTC Arrest Bounty." CoinDesk RSS. N.p., 23 May 2014. Web. 22 Mar. 2015.
130. Southurst, John. "How Roger Ver Got Hacked, and How He Stopped It." CoinDesk RSS. N.p., 24 May 2014. Web. 22 Mar. 2015.
131. "Make It Costly to Be Big." Audio blog post. Let's Talk Bitcoin. N.p., 12 July 2014. Web. 22 Mar. 2015.
132. Wong, Joon Ian. "Phishing Scam Targets US Marshals Service Bitcoin Auction List." CoinDesk RSS. N.p., 04 July 2014. Web. 22 Mar. 2015.
133. Reiner, Alan. Best Practices for Using and Securing Bitcoins. Proc. of Inside Bitcoins, NYC April 7-8. N.p., n.d. Web. 22 Mar. 2015.
134. Kuzin, Taras. "Why Bitcoin Adoption Will Continue to Grow." Why Bitcoin Adoption Will Continue to Grow. N.p., n.d. Web. 22 Mar. 2015.
135. Hambar, Sibel. "Bitcoin Finance 2014 – Dublin Conference." Bitcoin Finance 2014 Dublin Conference. N.p., 25 June 2014. Web. 22 Mar. 2015.
136. Laliberte, Scott. "PCI Presentation." Proc. of Institute of Internal Auditors, Philadelphia Chapter, Spring Conference. N.p.: n.p., 2015. N. pag. Print.
137. "Help - Bitcoin." Bitcoin Help. TigerDirect.com, n.d. Web. 29 Mar. 2015.
138. Puey, Paul. "Bitcoins in the Beltway." Personal interview. 22 June 2014. Airbitz.co Founder
139. "TigerDirect Brings in $250,000 in Bitcoin Payments in Under One Day." NEWSBTC. N.p., 24 Jan. 2014. Web. 04 Apr. 2015.
140. Fiegerman, Seth. "Overstock Tops $1 Million in Sales Made With Bitcoin in 2 Months." Mashable.com. N.p., 4 Mar. 2014. Web. 04 Apr. 2015.
141. Walker, Ryan. Bitcoin, Transaction Fees and the Cost of Poor Quality. Slide Presentation. N.p., 2014. Web. 4 Apr. 2015.
142. Ro, Sam. "Here Are The Profit Margins For Every Sector In The S&P 500." Business Insider. Business Insider, Inc, 16 Aug. 2012. Web. 04 Apr. 2015.
143. Higgins, Stan. "ProTip App Proposes Bitcoin Solution for Content Monetization." CoinDesk RSS. N.p., 29 Mar. 2015. Web. 01 Aug. 2015.
144. Dotson, Kyt. "Bitcoin Paying Streamium Plans to Cut out the Middleman for Livestreaming." SiliconANGLE. N.p., 25 May 2015. Web. 01 Aug. 2015.
145. Cawrey, Daniel. "Bonafide Raises $850k to Build Reputation System for Bitcoin." CoinDesk RSS. N.p., 02 Feb. 2015. Web. 01 Aug. 2015.
146. Thompson, Gillian. "Introducing Passcards, Your Digital Identity." Onename Blog. N.p., 11 May 2015. Web. 01 Aug. 2015.
147. "Bitcoin/bips." GitHub. N.p., n.d. Web. 01 Aug. 2015.
148. Buterin, Vitalik. "Deterministic Wallets, Their Advantages and Their Understated Flaws - Bitcoin Magazine." Bitcoin Magazine. N.p., 25 Nov. 2013. Web. 10 Apr. 2015.
149. "Bitcoin/bips." GitHub. N.p., n.d. Web. 10 Apr. 2015.
150. "Bitcoinpaperwallet.com." Understanding BIP-38 Password Encrypted Paper Wallets. N.p., n.d. Web. 10 Apr. 2015.
151. Buterin, Vitalik. "Bitcoin Wallet Reviews - Ease Of Use And Security." Bitcoin Magazine. N.p., 04 Mar. 2012. Web. 11 Apr. 2015.
152. "Interview with Rassah of Mycelium." Personal interview. 24 June 2014.
153. "Interview with Lawrence Nahum, Greenaddress.it Founder." Telephone

interview. 11 Sept. 2014.

154. Levine, Adam. "Let's Talk Bitcoin! #215 Innovation On and Around the Blockchain." Let's Talk Bitcoin. N.p., 23 May 2015. Web. 01 Aug. 2015.

155. "Interview with Andy Ofiesh, Armory Lead Developer,." Telephone interview. 3 Mar. 2015.

156. "Interview with Alan Reiner, Armory CTO." Personal interview. 13 Apr. 2015.

157. "Interview with Jassim Latif, Business Development, BitGo." Telephone interview. 22 Jan. 2015.

158. Interview with Canton Becker." Telephone interview with creator of bitcoinpaperwallet.com. 17 June 2014.

159. Murashchik, Dmitry. "Mycelium Demonstration." Proc. of Bitcoins in the Beltway, Washington, DC. N.p.: n.p., 2014. N. pag. Print.

160. Apodaca, Rich. "Five Ways to Lose Money with Bitcoin Change Addresses." Bitzuma. N.p., 20 Mar. 2014. Web. 11 Apr. 2015.

161. "Interview with Bitkee Founders Jason and Christian Gaviria." Personal interview. 19 June 2015.

162. "Brainwallet." Bitcoin. N.p., n.d. Web. 25 Apr. 2015. <http://en.bitcoin.it/wiki/brainwallet>.

163. "Getting Started User Manual." Kryptokit.com. N.p., n.d. Web. 25 Apr. 2015.

164. "Interview with Adam Stradling, Founder Comprabitcoin.com & Tradehill.com." Telephone interview. 24 June 2014

165. "What Maker-Taker Fees Mean To You (NSDQ,CBOE,ICE,RY)." Investopedia. N.p., 24 Apr. 2014. Web. 24 May 2015.

166. "Interview with David Moskowitz, Coin Republic." Telephone interview. 9 June 2014.

167. Rizzo, Pete. "Coinapult Launches LOCKS, Aiming to Eliminate Bitcoin Price Volatility." CoinDesk RSS. N.p., 29 July 2014. Web. 25 Apr. 2015.

168. Demo and Interview with Mary Zigman, Founder of Btc4erp.com." Telephone interview. 13 Jan. 2015.

169. Rizzo, Pete. "Bitcoin Sign-Ups for Intuit QuickBooks 'Higher than Expected'" CoinDesk RSS. N.p., 23 July 2014. Web. 25 Apr. 2015.

170. "Cointracking Founder and CEO Dario Kachel." Telephone interview. 6 Aug. 2015.

171. "Interview with Nucleon.io Founder Brock Wood." Telephone interview. 23 July 2015.

172. ""Interview with Libratax.com Founder Jake Benson." Telephone interview. 12 March 2015.

173. United States. Internal Revenue Service. IRS Virtual Currency Guidance: Virtual Currency Is Treated as Property for U.S. Federal Tax Purposes, General Rules for Property Transactions Apply. Vol. IR-2014-36. N.p.: n.p., 2014. Print.

174. "Price Discovery." Wikipedia. Wikimedia Foundation, n.d. Web. 02 May 2015.

175. "Like-Kind Exchanges Under IRC Code Section 1031." Like-Kind Exchanges Under IRC Code Section 1031. IRS, n.d. Web. 02 Aug. 2015.

176. Internal Revenue Service. Like Kind Exchanges Under IRC Code Section 1031. Vol. FS 2008-18. N.p.: n.p., 2008. Print.

177. "Interview with Marty Yavorcik, Swapper.io Founder." Telephone interview. 4 June 2015.
178. Application of FinCEN's Regulation to Persons Administering, Exchanging or Using Virtual Currencies, § FIN-2013-001 (2013). Print.
179. OCC. N.p., n.d. Web. 16 Aug. 2015.
180. USA PATRIOT Act, Verification of Identification, § 326 (2001). Print.
181. "Canada Implements World's First National Digital Currency Law; Regulates New Financial Technology Transactions." Duhaime Law. N.p., 22 June 2014. Web. 04 Sept. 2015.
182. "Will the World's First National Digital Currency Law in Canada Drive Venture Capital Away?" Duhaime Law. N.p., 22 June 2014. Web. 04 Sept. 2015.
183. Jankelewitz, Eitan. "Bitcoin Regulation in the UK." CoinDesk RSS. N.p., 16 Feb. 2014. Web. 04 Sept. 2015.
184. Lee, Matthew D., and Jeffrey Rosenfeld. McDevitt & Kline CPE Presentation given by Blank Rome. 20 Nov. 2014.
185. "IRS: No Bitcoin Reporting Required This Year for FinCEN Foreign Banking Tax Form." CoinDesk RSS. N.p., 05 June 2014. Web. 02 May 2015.
186. "Florida Man Owes Record 150% IRS Penalty on Swiss Account." Bloomberg. com. Bloomberg, n.d. Web. 02 May 2015.
187. Lee, Matthew D., and Jeffrey Rosenfeld. McDevitt & Kline CPE Presentation given by Blank Rome. 20 Nov. 2014.
188. "The SEC Delay Over Crowdfunding Rules Is Stifling Bitcoin Innovation." CoinDesk RSS. N.p., 13 June 2014. Web. 02 May 2015.
189. Marx, Jared P. "Why a New SEC Ruling Is 'Revolutionary' for Bitcoin Crowdfunding." CoinDesk RSS. N.p., 26 Mar. 2015. Web. 03 May 2015.
190. SEC Adopts Rules to Facilitate Smaller Companies' Access to Capital. SEC. gov. N.p., 25 Mar. 2015. Web.
191. Somensatto, Jason. "Appcoins, Crypto Crowdfunding, and the Potential SEC Regulation Pitfall." CoinTelegraph. N.p., 7 Jan. 2015. Web. 03 May 2015.
192. "Factom Informational Report about the Factoid Software Sale." Message to the author. 30 Mar. 2015. E-mail.
193. Chen, Caleb. "SEC Sends Inquiry Letters to Hundreds of Bitcoin Companies about Unregistered Securities." CryptoCoinsNews. N.p., 28 Oct. 2014. Web. 03 May 2015.
194. Wong, Joon Ian. "CFTC Chairman: We Have Oversight of Bitcoin Derivatives." CoinDesk RSS. N.p., 11 Dec. 2014. Web. 03 May 2015.
195. Bradbury, Danny. "Canada's Finance Minister Prepares to Regulate Bitcoin - CoinDesk." CoinDesk RSS. N.p., 13 Feb. 2014. Web. 03 May 2015.
196. Alexander, Ruben. "The Big Picture Behind the News of China's Bitcoin Bans - Bitcoin Magazine." Bitcoin Magazine. N.p., 06 May 2014. Web. 03 May 2015.
197. Levine, Adam. "51% Solutions and Zhou Tonged!" Audio blog post. Let's Talk Bitcoin! #125. N.p., 8 July 2014. Web.
198. Antonopoulos, Andreas. "Bitcoin and Regulation." Bitcoin in the Beltway. Washington, DC. 21 June 2014. Address.
199. Erman, Michael. "Five Years after Lehman, Americans Still Angry at Wall Street: Reuters/Ipsos Poll." Reuters. Thomson Reuters, 15 Sept. 2013. Web.

03 May 2015.
200. Rakoff, Jed. "The Financial Crisis: Why Have No High-Level Executives Been Prosecuted? by Jed S. Rakoff." N.p., 9 Jan. 2014. Web. 03 May 2015.
201. "Hank Paulson: This Is What It Was Like to Face the Financial Crisis." Bloomberg.com. Bloomberg, 12 Sept. 2013. Web. 02 Aug. 2015.
202. Stigler, George Rand. The Theory of Economic Regulation, Bell Journal of Economics and Management Science. 1971. Whitepaper.
203. Albrecht, Steve, Ph.D. "Iconic Fraud Triangle Endures." Fraud Magazine. N.p., July-Aug. 2014. Web. 09 May 2015.
204. Cressey, Donald R. Other People's Money; a Study in the Social Psychology of Embezzlement. Montclair, NJ: Patterson Smith, 1973. Print.
205. Ibid. "Iconic Fraud Triangle Endures."
206. Ibid. "Iconic Fraud Triangle Endures."
207. 2014 Report to the Nations on Occupational Fraud and Abuse, ACFE, 2014. Rep. N.p.: n.p., n.d. Print.
208. "Invest and Borrow with BTCJam's, the First Global P2P Lending Platform." Btcjam.com. N.p., n.d. Web. 02 Aug. 2015.
209. BTCrow.com - The Bitcoin Escrow Service. N.p., n.d. Web. 02 Aug. 2015.
210. "Identity, Reputation & Trust." Bitrated. N.p., n.d. Web. 02 Aug. 2015.
211. "Interview with Mark Vick, Co-Founder of BillPayForCoins.com." E-mail interview. 19 May 2015.
212. BTCS | Home. N.p., n.d. Web. 02 Aug. 2015.
213. "Interview with Alex Peterson, Vis Nova Ventures CEO and Purse Power User." E-mail interview. 4 Mar. 2015.
214. Levine, Adam, and Shawn Wilkinson. "Let's Talk Bitcoin! 135 Distributed Storj." Audio blog post. N.p., 12 Aug. 2014. Web.
215. "Interview with Storj Founder Shawn Wilkinson." Telephone interview. 31 Oct. 2014.
216. Higgins, Stan. "Factom Partners With Honduras Government on Blockchain Tech Trial." CoinDesk RSS. N.p., 15 May 2015. Web. 02 Aug. 2015.
217. "Interview with Ron Gross, Mastercoin Developer." Personal interview. 15 June 2014.
218. Hill, Kashmir. "The First 'Bitcoin 2.0' Crowd Sale Was A Wildly Successful $7 Million Disaster." Forbes. Forbes Magazine, 3 June 2014. Web. 10 May 2015.
219. Irvine, David. "Maidsafe Presentation." Proc. of Inside Bitcoins, NYC April 7-8. N.p.: n.p., 2015. N. pag. Print.
220. "Beyond Bitcoin - 17 - Counterpartying With Robby Dermody." Audio blog post. Let's Talk Bitcoin. N.p., 7 Oct. 2014. Web.
221. "Interview with Robby Dermody, Counterparty co-founder." Telephone interview. 12 June 2014.
222. "Adam Krellenstein, Counterparty Co-founder." Personal interview. 19 June 2014.
223. Kumparak, Greg. "A Brief History Of Oculus." TechCrunch. N.p., 26 Mar. 2014. Web. 10 May 2015.
224. "Let's Talk Bitcoin! Episode 121 Genercoin & Swarm." Audio blog post. N.p., 24 June 2014. Web. 10 May 2015.
225. Levine, Adam. "Let's Talk Bitcoin! #153 Medici and the Pretense of Law." Audio blog post. Let's Talk Bitcoin. N.p., 14 Oct. 2014. Web. 2 Aug. 2015.

226. Parker, Luke. "Overstock Announces Cryptosecurity Exchange And World's First Crypto Bond » Brave New Coin." Brave New Coin. N.p., 8 June 2015. Web. 02 Aug. 2015.
227. "Interview with Sergey Nazarov, Founder of Secureae." Personal interview. 19 June 2014. Bitcoins in the Beltway
228. Falls, Arthur S. "Beyond Bitcoin - 5 - Delegates and Forgers." Audio blog post. N.p., 20 June 2014. Web.
229. Levine, Adam. "Let's Talk Bitcoin! #223 Some Other Castle." Let's Talk Bitcoin. N.p., 20 June 2015. Web. 2 Aug. 2015.
230. "Main Page." Open Transactions. N.p., n.d. Web. 17 May 2015.
231. Torpey, Kyle. "Chris Odem Explains How Open Transactions Makes Altcoins Irrelevant at Inside Bitcoins Conference." N.p., 21 Sept. 2014. Web. 17 May 2015.
232. Falls, Arthur S. "Beyond Bitcoin - 16 - The Future Is Not Mad Max." Audio blog post. N.p., 29 Sept. 2014. Web. 17 May 2015.
233. Brokaw, Alex. "Crypto 2.0: Counterparty Debuts Multisig & Ethereum's Crowdsale." CoinDesk RSS. N.p., 24 Aug. 2014. Web. 17 May 2015.
234. "Chris Larson Presentation, Founder Ripple Labs." Proc. of Digital Currencies NYC. N.p.: n.p., 2014. N. pag. Print.
235. "Interview with Tradle Founder, Gene Vayngrib." Telephone interview. 1 Aug. 2015.
236. "Interview with Serica Founder, Taariq Lewis." Telephone interview. 7 Nov. 2014.
237. "Interview with Xavier Hawk, Permacredits Founder." Personal interview. 19 June 2014.
238. Visit to Independence Hall, Philadelphia, PA. 25 Sept. 2014.
239. Bartleby.com, No. 323. N.d. Benjamin Franklin Collection.
240. Covey, Stephen R. The 7 Habits of Highly Effective People: Powerful Lessons in Personal Change. N.p.: n.p., 1989. Print.

Made in the USA
Coppell, TX
24 August 2021

61066020R00194